THE
Other Italy

ITALY IN 1939

THE
Other Italy

ITALIAN RESISTANCE IN
WORLD WAR II

———

Maria de Blasio Wilhelm

DRAWINGS BY ENZO MARINO

W · W · NORTON & COMPANY

NEW YORK · LONDON

FIRST EDITION

THE TEXT OF THIS BOOK *is composed in Times Roman, with display type set in Garamond Old Style and Vendome. Composition and manufacturing by the Maple-Vail Book Manufacturing Group. Frontispiece map by Jacques Chazaud. Book design by Marjorie J. Flock.*

Library of Congress Cataloging in Publication Data
Wilhelm, Maria.
    The other Italy.

    1. World War, 1939–1945—Underground movements—
Italy. I. Title.
D802.I8W55   1988   940.53′45   87–31362
        ISBN 0-393-02568-3

W. W. Norton & Company Inc., 500 Fifth Avenue, New York, N.Y. 10110
W. W. Norton & Company Ltd, 37 Great Russell Street, London WC1B 3NU

1 2 3 4 5 6 7 8 9 0

To my mother and father,
Anna Briganti de Blasio
and John de Blasio

Contents

Illustrations

Drawings by Enzo Marino

Foreword

THIS IS not a scholarly history of the Italian Resistance during World War II. It is, rather, an attempt to recreate a period in Italian life through both anecdote and fact.

Although eventually the Resistance became unified, it began as a series of spontaneous actions. Its story is episodic in nature and involves a cast of many characters. As one Italian historian of those times observed, when central coordination is lacking, history must renounce its tendency to tell a unified tale and must depend on chronicles, on little accounts of single groups or even of isolated individuals reacting on impulse, from their convictions, to circumstances. For this reason, each chapter focuses on a theme and varies in historical scope.

But these disparate actions were connected by one strong motive: to gain freedom from oppression, whether by a foreign invader or a homegrown dictator. The strength of this driving force was recognized in a May 1945 editorial in the U.S. Army newspaper *Stars and Stripes,* written just before the European war ended: "Our advance guards and armored troops entered cities full of Italian patriots. They were there in an extraordinary number. The Allied soldiers have finally felt that they were fighting to liberate people who really wanted to be free. After long months in the mud and the rain and the ruins, finally the Allied soldiers have seen another Italy."

Professor Charles Delzell, a leading authority on the Resistance Movement, added this comment in his book, *Mussolini's Enemies:* "It was largely because of this 'other Italy' . . . that a people which had been dazed and demoralized in 1943 could regain by 1945 much of their political and military self-respect. It was because of this 'other Italy' that the nation could become a party to a peace treaty in 1947 that was far more generous than Italians could reasonably have expected on September 8, 1943.''

Most of the information in my book comes from Italian sources. Former members of the Resistance have kindly spent many hours with me reliving their experiences. The libraries of the Resistance Research Centers in Italy provided invaluable resources: on their shelves are thousands of books, memoirs and other documents about both the war and anti-fascism during Mussolini's twenty-year rule. In some cases there are conflicting versions of an event, sometimes trivial, sometimes serious. At times it has been necessary to make a Solomon's choice with which everyone might not agree. I have told the stories of certain people and events, but there were others equally compelling and valid, enough to fill many books.

The list of individuals who have contributed their time and thoughts to the writing of this book would be very long indeed. The names that follow—in alphabetical order—certainly do not include everyone who helped. But I would like to express my special gratitude to Monsignore Redento Bello; Luciano Boccalatte; Claudio Capello; Max Corvo; Raimondo Craveri; Don Ascanio DeLuca; David E. Ellwood; Silvia Facca; Enzo Forcella; Giovanni Garofoli; Sandro Gerbi; Maria Luiga Guaita-Vallechi; Carla and Paolo Gobetti; Luigi Jacchia; Gilda Larocca; Danilo and Giuseppe Missio; Andreina Morandi-Michelozzi; Carlo Mussa; Giulio Nicoletta; the late Aurelio Peccei; Enzo Ronconi; Laura Rossomando; Adriano and Riccardo Vanzetti; and Renzo Zorzi. I would also like to thank Frank Gervasi, correspondent in Italy during World War II, and Edward Malefakis, Professor of Modern History at Columbia University, for their comments and suggestions.

And finally I want to thank my son, Bill deBlasio-Wilhelm, for his constant interest and editorial support in this project, without which it might never have been undertaken much less completed.

THE
Other Italy

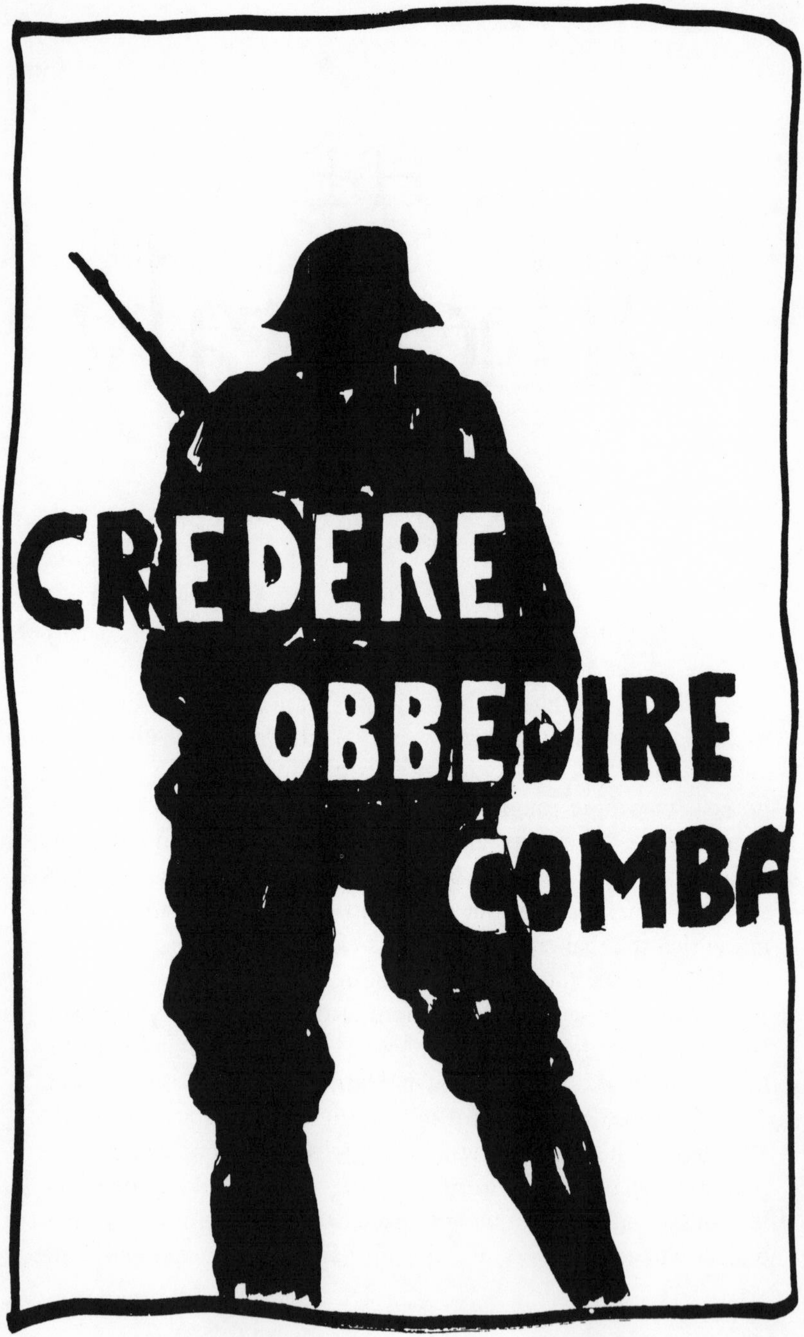
CREDERE
OBBEDIRE
COMBA

=1=
"Even the stones would cry out"

Caesar died, and tyranny lived on. For the seat of tyranny was not in the heart of Caesar: it was in the heart of the Romans. Not from others will the Italians receive freedom, but from themselves.

—G. A. BORGESE, 1937

THE ITALIAN RESISTANCE in World War II was a people's war. It began as a spontaneous rebellion against Nazi oppression in the days following Italy's unconditional surrender to the Allies on September 8, 1943. There was no great leader in the beginning, no organization to weld individuals into a fighting force. Yet people fought with unexpected fury in Naples, Florence, Udine, in towns and remote villages, and in hills and mountains up and down the land. It was a desperate, uneven attack on the German invader but it was also a civil war, a final recognition that the real enemy, fascism, was within.

The story of the Resistance begins with Mussolini and with those who opposed him from the first days of his rise to power. But in a larger historical perspective, the story begins with the birth of Italy as a nation in 1861. Until then the different regions of the peninsula had their own strong and separate identities. "Standard" Italian was the first language of a mere two or three percent of the population. Most of the people spoke a local dialect and to many Italian would have been as unintelligible as their dialect was to outsiders. Centuries of foreign invasion and dom-

ination had intensified strong regional loyalties. The first leader
of the Risorgimento, as the movement for unification and national
independence was called, was Giuseppe Mazzini, who was born
in Genoa in 1805. His dream did not become a reality until 1861,
when the Northern Italian Kingdom of Piedmont succeeded, with
the help of the nationalist military leader Giuseppe Garibaldi, in
defeating the armies of the Bourbon Kingdom of the Two Sicilies
(which comprised all of Southern Italy).

The new Italian regime, under King Victor Emmanuel II of
the house of Savoy, was regarded with suspicion by many people, especially in the South. As Prof. Norman Kogan has remarked,
"The heroes of the Risorgimento achieved legal but not psychological and cultural unification. Italy was created, but not Italians." Lack of political support was not all that would plague the
new nation in the following fifty years. Economically, Italy lagged
far behind most of the rapidly industrializing Western nations.
The demands of colonial expansionism and of an ever-increasing
population severely strained the government coffers. About seventy percent of the labor force was in agriculture, with most of
the peasants living under an essentially feudal system of land
tenure. Agrarian reform was of much greater interest to them than
political unity. In the North this sentiment eventually took an
active form when, in the late nineteenth century, peasants began
to band together, threatening the stranglehold of the landlords in
the Reggio Emilia region by striking for more pay.

A parallel unrest was rapidly emerging among the workers in
the budding industries, especially after the pace of economic
development finally increased in the 1890s. The Socialist party
(Partito Socialista Italiano—PSI), which had been organized in
1892, began to attract both discontented workers and large numbers of peasants. By 1910 it had become a very sizeable force. A
young revolutionary, Benito Mussolini, became a leader of the
PSI's radical faction, which opposed the reformist tendencies of
the party's mainstream. By 1912 Mussolini was the very successful editor of the official Socialist newspaper *Avanti!* Yet he broke
with the Socialists when they opted for neutralism at the begin-

ning of World War I. In 1914 Mussolini formed a new organization, Fasci di azione rivoluzionaria (Bands for revolutionary action) whose slogan was "War Today, Revolution Tomorrow." The first fascio was leftist, anti-capitalist and anti-religious.

Italy's involvement in the First World War further weakened an already precarious economy, with the result that the immediate postwar years were a period of continuous unrest. An epidemic of strikes swept the country and workers even occupied a large number of factories for a brief time in September 1920.

Mussolini quickly took advantage of the situation. He was an excellent journalist of the rabble-rousing variety and had managed to find backers for a new newspaper of his own, which he called *Il Popolo d'Italia*. Mussolini used the paper to rally people to his cause, which was stated vaguely but in fiery language. The gist of his position was to offer something to everyone. By March 1919 he had converted his original fascio into a new movement, calling it the Fascio di Combattimento (Combat Band) and promising to restore law and order. He made good on his promise, using black-shirted *squadristi* (bands of armed thugs) to repress any alleged disturbers of the peace.

Initially, Mussolini had the broad support of conservative Italians, including not only industrialists and landowners, but also the monarchy, the Catholic Church hierarchy, army leadership and much of the middle class. Industrialists and landowners feared the growing power of trade unions and so were very generous in their contributions to the Fascists. The Church, worried by the founding of the Italian Communist party in 1921, saw in fascism an effective bulwark against the perceived new menace of bolshevism, which had revolutionized Russia only a few years earlier. As for King Victor Emmanuel III, he welcomed any force which could end the riots and confusion. Against his own Cabinet's advice the king appointed Mussolini head of government immediately following the so-called "March on Rome" of October 28, 1922. On that day hundreds of Mussolini's followers had travelled to the capital in a show of Fascist party strength with the objective of forcing the king to form a new government. Mussolini prudently remained in Milan until the next day, waiting to learn the outcome of his maneuver.

Alberto Moravia, a leading Italian writer, gave this realistic account of the March on Rome, later to become one of the myths of fascism: "I was 15 years old. I went to the Piazza del Popolo and I sat down under the fountain. The Fascists were just entering through the Porta del Popolo. I had the impression that a crowd of provincial hunters was approaching, men from the country, with shotguns. Some wore black shirts and long pants. Others did not wear black shirts. In the middle of the crowd, I remember, there was someone on a white horse, who was one of the leaders. There were quite a few of them. I was on my way to school and I had to get on the other side of the Piazza, but I didn't dare cross through their ranks. There wasn't much of a crowd on the streets, just an ordinary citizenry. They watched, a few applauded, others did not. It wasn't a very enthusiastic audience."

With Mussolini established as undisputed leader, his *squadristi* set out to make short order of any opposition. Beatings and even killings failed to silence a slowly growing number of anti-Fascists. Some went underground, some went into exile, and many went to prison.

The experience of one man is a microcosm of the anti-Fascist movement of that period. Sandro Pertini, who would be president of Italy from 1978 to 1985, spent 15 years in prison during the Mussolini regime. He had joined the Socialist party in 1919 when he was 23, soon after he returned from the battlefields of World War I. For the next few years he tried to mobilize public opinion against the activities of the Fascist *squadristi*.

The *squadristi* retaliated by beating him up several times, but he was not actually arrested until 1925, when he was charged with being a "dangerous subversive" for writing and distributing anti-Fascist leaflets. He was given a suspended sentence but in October of the next year a particularly vicious *squadristi* attack left him with a broken arm. He was also threatened with death if he appeared again on the streets of Savona, the city in which he had established a law practice. So he went to Milan, where in 1926 he became involved in planning the escape to France of Filippo Turati, the elderly Socialist leader, whom he accompanied to Paris. Pertini returned to Italy in 1929, using false ID papers stating that he was a Swiss citizen. He was soon recognized by a man from Savona who denounced him to the police. On November 30, 1929 he was sentenced to ten years and nine months in prison, and was forever forbidden to hold public office.

Pertini began his sentence in solitary confinement in a damp, dark cell in the prison of San Stefano, near Naples. An old jail originally used by the Bourbon Kings, it was considered the worst prison in Italy. At dawn prisoners were given a cup of watery coffee and at ten a plate of pasta and beans, the only food for twenty-four hours. After two years of this existence Pertini's health had deteriorated badly. In Paris, Turati learned about Pertini's condition through the underground grapevine. He initiated a vigorous letter-writing campaign from influential people, protesting Pertini's treatment. Finally the Fascist authorities transferred Pertini to the relative freedom of exile on the island of Ponza, and from there to a similar facility at Ventotene. He should have been freed in September 1940 but Mussolini intervened personally to extend his sentence another five years on the grounds that Pertini was dangerous to the national security because of "his absolute dedication to the Socialist cause."

While there was slowly growing covert opposition to Fascism during the twenties and thirties, Mussolini's undeniable charisma and his promise of peace and prosperity had mesmerized most Italians. They were not alone in this. In the United States some Americans—including Americans of Italian descent—applauded Mussolini. Dr. Nicholas Murray Butler, president of Columbia University, declared: "The Italian national vigor is being reborn with the advent of Fascism. . . . It is safe to predict that just as

Cromwell made modern England, so Mussolini will make modern Italy.'' The English, too, had words of praise, especially Winston Churchill.

But the climate of adulation began to change in the mid-thirties. Since 1935, when Il Duce invaded Ethiopia, Italy had been mobilized for war and not for the "peace and order" Mussolini had promised. In the name of imperialism, Mussolini had bequeathed growing hardship on the average Italian. Even worse, in 1939 he led the nation into an alliance with a traditional enemy—Germany—against the English and French whom many Italians admired and respected. And though there had been dutiful registration in the Fascist party, many a card-carrying member was totally cynical about his loyalty to the regime: it was a pragmatic choice, not devotion to a principle.

An example of the atmosphere of this period comes from Val Sangone, a center of Resistance in the Piedmont region near Turin, which recently published a survey of the years from 1939 to 1945. Val Sangone comprises six villages; in 1943 they had a population of 20,328. The people who lived there were a cross-section of different living styles: peasant-farmers, factory workers, middle-class white collar employees, and a sprinkling of professionals. Answers to questions about fascism put to all these groups were based on hindsight, but there is no reason to doubt their essential sincerity.

The attitude of the peasants was generally that they minded their own business until the forced collection of grains and other foodstuffs began when Mussolini embarked on his foreign wars. Several farmers said fascism was good in the beginning "because it brought order"; others voiced the common perception that the Fascist membership card was the price one paid to get ahead. Most expressed the opinion that everyone was a Fascist but nobody was. An old joke was repeated by one farmer: "Agnelli (the president of Fiat) looks at his workers and says, 'Half are Socialists and half are Communists.' And which are Fascists? 'All of them!' " Some distinction was also made between "good" and "bad" Fascists. The peasants were reluctant to name names, saying that if they knew friends were anti-Fascists they usually looked the other way. There was little informing on one's neighbor, in spite of large rewards.

The blue-collar workers said they had not been able to be indifferent to fascism because there was no work to be had without a party membership card. Several admitted they had felt like sheep, especially when it was obligatory to attend meetings. They told of workers at local plants being carried by bus to form part of a welcoming crowd when Mussolini once made a quick visit to the area. Quite a few in their group thought that the indoctrination of children in Fascist dogma, though started at an early age, was ineffective. Even children three to six years old were included: they were called "the sons of the wolf." At school the children wore uniforms and male instructors were supposed to wear black shirts, though some did not. And though textbooks stressed Fascist ideals, in subtle ways many teachers tried to encourage independent thinking.

As for the middle class, on the whole they agreed that they had felt that early on fascism had brought order out of the post-World War I chaos. This group also pointed out that the Fascist ID card had been essential for those in government-related work and in banks and many industries. Even shopkeepers had to have the card or their licenses would be taken away. A few explained they had never been involved in the party because where they worked a card was not required. The middle class was aware of the anti-Fascist movement which many believed was led by the Communist party. The interviewees recalled discussing politics in the home, but never in public and always only among family or trusted friends. They knew public discussion could result in beatings and the infamous castor oil treatment (one of the favorite Fascist punishments was to force the recalcitrant to drink large doses of this purgative).

The ambivalence of the general public was one side of the coin; the other was the clear and unrelenting opposition of thousands of anti-Fascists to the equally unrelenting loyalty of true Fascists. The anti-Fascists were the nucleus of what was to become, in 1943, the armed Resistance against both the Nazis and the Fascists. The following chronology gives a few highlights of developments from 1922 to 1943.

Fascist events are in roman type.
Anti-Fascist events are distinguished by italic type.

1922

FEBRUARY *Piero Gobetti starts first anti-Fascist weekly,* Rivoluzione Liberale, *in Turin. Gobetti hopes to consolidate an alliance of liberals and Marxists to oppose Mussolini.*

OCTOBER "March on Rome." Benito Mussolini appointed head of government and president of the Council of Ministers by King Victor Emmanuel III.

NOVEMBER *Some anarchists and socialists begin to emigrate to nearby France and Switzerland.*

DECEMBER Fascists bomb headquarters of Confederation of Local Trade Unions in Turin, kill some 20 workers at random "to inflict a terrible lesson on the revolutionaries of Turin."

1923

FEBRUARY *Courts release 2000 Communists and Socialists arrested by Fascist police. Gobetti jailed briefly. Mussolini comments: "The bench acquits, I shoot."*

APRIL *Fascism condemned at Turin Congress of Catholic-oriented Partito Popolare Italiano (PPI) founded in 1919 by Don Luigi Sturzo.*

AUGUST *Squadristi kill Don Giovanni Minzoni, the priest-organizer of rural cooperatives.*

NOVEMBER *Squadristi beat Giovanni Amendola, Neapolitan deputy in Parliament and leader of Constitutional Democrats.*

1924

APRIL Mussolini wins control of Chamber of Deputies by altering electoral system.

Milan newspapers criticize new electoral law. New anti-Fascist weekly appears, Il Caffe, *co-edited by Ferruccio Parri and Riccardo Bauer.*

MAY *Giacomo Matteoti, secretary of Socialist party, denounces election tactics in two-hour speech in Chamber of Deputies.*

JUNE *Squadristi* kidnap and kill Matteoti, increase physical attacks on opposition leaders.

OCTOBER *Don Luigi Sturzo, forced into exile, seeks refuge in London.*

1925.

JANUARY Mussolini in speech to Parliament takes full responsibility for past violence and promises more action against opposition.

JUNE *New Florentine anti-Fascist daily* Non Mollare! (Don't Give In!) *gains quick and wide circulation.*

JULY *Squadristi* again badly beat Amendola, who dies a year later at age 44.

Opposition parties publish document attributing long list of crimes against anti-Fascists to General De Bono, a leader of the March on Rome.

1926

JANUARY Mussolini assumes more power, now responsible only to the king. Parliament forbidden to discuss legislation without Il Duce's permission.

FEBRUARY *Gobetti dies in exile in Paris as result of Fascist beatings. Exiles increase flow of publications to be distributed in Italy by anti-Fascist underground.*

OCTOBER *Third attempt in year on Mussolini's life.*

NOVEMBER New laws in name of national security abolish all trade unions and political parties and organizations, establish press censorship, cancel passports.

DECEMBER *Socialist leaders escape abroad, other party leaders and many members arrested.*

1927–1935

The next eight years were a period of consolidation for Musso-lini, and of passive resistance for those anti-Fascists who were not in exile or in jail. OVRA, the Fascist secret police, was estab-lished in 1927 to ferret out the opposition. A new and important underground movement Giustizia e Libertà (Justice and Liberty) was founded in 1929 by Carlo Rosselli, a protégé of Gobetti. In Parliament Senator Benedetto Croce continued to make a stand against fascism. Croce, an internationally acclaimed philosopher, was both feared and respected by Mussolini, who left him alone after one aborted attempt by the Fascist militia to destroy Croce's library.

Among the intellectuals many university and secondary school teachers paid lip service to fascism, but continued to teach dem-ocratic principles while using Fascist textbooks. The heavily cen-sored press was less successful, though periodic attempts were made to publish rather thinly veiled criticism.

One of the most significant events of this period was the sign-ing in 1929 of the Lateran Accords with the Vatican. The treaty made Catholicism the religion of state and gave territorial inde-pendence to the Holy See. The quid pro quo was that the clergy would use its influence to spread Fascist thought. Pope Pius XI saw in Mussolini an ally to combat bolshevism, which he equated with liberal ideas. The Fascists, well aware of the strong anti-Fascist feelings among many Catholics, did not waste time in eliminating possible sources of opposition. Even the Catholic youth clubs in the nation were shut down on May 30, 1931.

As this period of consolidation drew to a close, events on the international front began to impinge on Mussolini's power. The worldwide economic depression had a negative effect on Italy, which had been declining economically since 1926. Of much greater importance was the appearance on the scene of Adolph Hitler, who became chancellor of Germany in 1933. Hitler admired Mussolini and the following year travelled to Italy to meet the Duce. (The latter was not at all impressed by the Führer at that time.) Mussolini was then working on the imperial phase of his plan for Italy, which he saw as the crowning touch to make Italy a respected world leader. In 1935 Il Duce declared war on Ethiopia: the League of Nations responded by imposing economic sanctions on Italy.

1936

FEBRUARY *Carlo Rosselli, leader of Justice and Liberty group, meets with Luigi Longo, Communist leader, to discuss joining forces to stir up dissension in Italy. Longo sends men to infiltrate Italian Army.*

MAY Ethiopia defeated, King Emmanuel assumes title of Emperor of Ethiopia.

JULY Italy sends bombers to Spain to aid General Franco's attack on the legitimate Republican government.

OCTOBER Formation of Rome–Berlin Axis by treaty.

Italian exile groups join International Brigade to fight with Loyalists in Spain against Franco. In Italy, college students oppose Franco and increasing numbers join anti-Fascist underground.

1937

JANUARY Some 50,000 Italian troops sent to Spain.

JAN.-MAY *Sporadic demonstrations on behalf of Spanish Loyalists, especially in Milan and Turin, lead to arrest of students, workers and professionals.*

JUNE *Carlo Rosselli and his brother Nello murdered in France by Fascist-paid French agents.*

JULY *Students organize against Fascists at universities of Bologna, Naples and Pisa.*

SEPTEMBER Mussolini makes first visit to Germany.

NOVEMBER Italy joins Germany and Japan in pact against Communist International.

DECEMBER Italy withdraws from League of Nations.

1938

JULY   *Exodus of Jews begins, some join underground. Anyone aiding Jews threatened with arrest: threats generally ignored.*

OCTOBER   Anti-Semitic decrees announced following publication of manifesto on racial purity in July.

1939

MAY   Pact of Steel signed by Mussolini and Hitler.

AUGUST   Nazi–Soviet pact announced.

SEPTEMBER Germany invades Poland. (France and Great Britain declare war on Germany.)

                France takes action against Italian exiles. Foreign communists arrested, including Togliatti and Longo. Italian language anti-Fascist publications banned, activities of Justice and Liberty group greatly curtailed.

1940

JUNE   Italy declares war on France and England June 10, France surrenders to Germany June 22.

                Anti-Fascist exiles in France extradited to Italy. More than 1,000 Communists, including Longo, are sent to island prison of Ventotene, off Naples. Some exiles escape to Switzerland and North and South America.

OCTOBER   Italy attacks Greece with disastrous results and without Hitler's knowledge.

1941

JUNE   Germany invades USSR.

OCTOBER   *Anti-Fascist Italian exiles in America and England plot for separate peace with Allies. Communication with Italian underground almost completely cut off.*

DECEMBER   Italy declares war on U.S., following Pearl Harbor. Food and clothing shortages increase. Average Italian income $400 yearly: shoes cost $35, an egg 18 cents.

1942

JULY   *Former members of Justice and Liberty, now in Italy, form new Party of Action (Partito d'Azione) with financial back-*

ing of bankers and industrialists, now totally disillusioned by Mussolini. Party's seven-point program advocates abdication of King Emmanuel and establishment of a republic.

OCTOBER   Italian army in USSR given no support by German troops. Badly equipped Italians begin bitter retreat.

NOVEMBER   Fascist government struggles to cope with stepped-up Allied bombing of Italy.

DECEMBER   *Workers and farmers increase strikes for better wages as economy further deteriorates under stress of war. Strike slogan: "For bread, peace and freedom."*

1943

FEBRUARY   Fascist Grand Council members opposing war lose Cabinet posts.

MARCH   *General strikes in Turin and Milan severe blow to Mussolini's prestige as entire city joins workers.*

Mussolini takes over foreign and military affairs.

In March 1943 workers went on strike in many industrial cities, signalling the beginning of the end for Mussolini.

JULY   Allies land in Sicily.

Populace of Naples and Rome openly demonstrate for peace.
Increasing numbers of people listen avidly to Radio London
though absolutely forbidden.

On 19th, 1,000 tons of bombs dropped on Rome in first all-
out Allied bombing of that city. On 25th Grand Council
overthrows Mussolini. General Badoglio becomes new head
of government. King approves a military dictatorship.

**Romans destroy symbols of Fascism immediately after the radio announcement of
Mussolini's dismissal by King Victor Emmanuel.**

JULY-AUG. Fascist party officially dissolved but many Fascists retain government positions, including former chief of military intelligence (now assigned to break up mass meetings).

Most anti-Fascists released from prison. Political parties begin to regroup although officially still outlawed. All Fascist slogans and insignias disappear.

SEPTEMBER Italy surrenders unconditionally to Allies.

The bare bones of the chronology from 1936 to 1943 only hint at the catastrophic slide in Mussolini's fortunes after his victory in Ethiopia. Although Galeazzo Ciano, Foreign Minister and Mussolini's son-in-law, had at first urged the alliance with Germany, by 1939 he was having second thoughts. The sorcerer's apprentice had taken over, and his teacher had become the toadying assistant. Ciano's *Diaries* give firsthand and eloquent behind-the-scenes descriptions of the ineptness and confusion of the Fascist government. Few in the hierarchy were willing to challenge the Duce. One was Italo Balbo, who in March 1939 had the audacity to say to his chief at a Grand Council meeting, "You are shining Germany's boots."

Ciano noted a few days later, "The Duce . . . agrees that it is now impossible to present to the Italian people the idea of an alliance with Germany. Even the stones would cry out against it. . . . The events of the last few days have reversed my opinion of the Führer and of Germany." He added that the king, too, was more than ever anti-German, alluding to "Germanic insolence and duplicity" and praising the "straightforwardness of the British." Nevertheless, two months later, in May, Ciano went to Berlin to sign the Pact of Steel.

Mussolini's increasing vacillation in his enthusiasm for Hitler did not prevent him from going along obediently with the Führer's decisions. However, Ciano wrote that by this time most of the Fascist leaders were well aware of the anti-German sentiments of the Italian people. Nevertheless, in August 1939, Mussolini, who knew of the impending invasion of Poland, did nothing to interfere. Ciano commented, "It would be a mad venture, carried out against the unanimous will of the Italian people who as yet do not know how things stand but who, having had a sniff of the truth, have had a sudden fit of rage against the Germans. . . . A policy of neutrality will, on the other hand, be more popular, and if it were necessary later, war against Germany would be every bit as popular."

A few days later, Ciano said, he himself told Mussolini that he believed the Germans were betraying the terms of the Alliance (to maintain peace for several years) in which, said Ciano, "we were to have been partners and not servants." Ciano claimed he advised the Duce to tear up the pact and throw it in Hitler's face—advice which Il Duce ignored. Hitler's disdain for the opinions of his "partner" were never more clearly evident than in Ribbentrop brushing aside Ciano's request for a meeting on August 21 with the brusque response that he was "waiting for an important message from Moscow." The message was the announcement of the Nazi-Soviet pact, which rocked the world on August 22.

As events pointed towards an impending clash with Great Britain, Ciano disclosed in no uncertain terms that Italy was not ready for war. "The officers of the Italian Army are not qualified for the job, and our equipment is old and obsolete. To this must be added the state of mind of the Italians, which is distinctly anti-German. The peasants go into the Army cursing 'those damn Germans'."

In spite of all this, Mussolini embarked on a series of military disasters in a vain attempt to show he was still the great leader. The attack on Greece in October 1940, which failed miserably, was made without Hitler's knowledge. Later, according to Ciano, Mussolini sent Italian troops to the Soviet Union against the Führer's wishes. For this Il Duce was rewarded with no support from his ally, and Italian troops were forced to make a long, sad retreat from the Russian front, losing many men along the way.

By mid-1941 Ciano's apprehensions were shared by many in the Facist hierarchy. He noted in his diary that anti-fascism was taking root everywhere, "threateningly, implacably and silently."

Buffarini, the Minister of the Interior, had prepared a well-documented report backing up this apprehension, a report so damning that he was afraid to show it to Mussolini. According to Ciano, Il Duce was not really convinced of the growing discontent until 1942, when riots caused by food shortages extended from Venice to Matera, in the deep South. Mussolini tried to shrug off the riots, saying "there is really nothing to be feared, at least until some new and serious incident develops."

A few months later, in November, Allied bombs began to fall on Italy in large numbers and the Fascists at last accepted that the game was over. Mussolini's obtuseness is well-described in Sumner Welles's introduction to the Ciano diaries: "The Dictator's obsession that Germany's armed might could overcome every other force in the world, his black rancor, his ruthless cruelty, his dense ignorance of the world at large, his gross failure to comprehend the power which men's passion for freedom represents, and, above all else, his utter contempt for the Italian people themselves, stand out unforgettably in the passage of this Diary."

The announcement of unconditional surrender on September 8 ended 45 days of limbo. The euphoria after Mussolini's dismissal on July 25 had vanished almost overnight, to be replaced by confusion and apprehension. The 74-year-old king's appointment of the also aging Marshal Pietro Badoglio, a career officer, to replace Mussolini was hardly a revolutionary change. Badoglio had led the victorious Italian war effort in Ethiopia, and at one time he had been chief of General Staff and president of the Army Council. But he had failed miserably in Greece in 1940 and had been unceremoniously retired by Il Duce. Badoglio was totally loyal to the king, and represented the same conservative values held by the monarchy.

Badoglio's new Cabinet was made up mostly of former Fascists, although they were bureaucrats rather than dedicated politicians. To further confound the situation, in Badoglio's first radio address announcing Mussolini's dismissal, he had made the ambiguous statement "the war goes on." This hardly reassured the Italian people, most of whom had hoped peace was now at hand. The Allied landing in Sicily on July 10 had confirmed the fears of most Italians that their country was soon to become a battleground. Unconditional surrender, distasteful as it was to national honor, clarified the situation. The enemy was again Germany, the traditional enemy, and in short order the enemy would also be Mussolini and the remnants of fascism. Well before the Armistice, Hitler had ordered the systematic German occupation of Italy. Then, on September 27 the Führer, having rescued the imprisoned Mussolini shortly after the Armistice was announced, established Il Duce as the head of a new regime called the Italian Social Republic (Repubblica Sociale Italiana—RSI) with headquarters in the northern city of Salò, on Lake Garda. Mussolini's new followers were still regarded as, and called, Fascists by the Italians.

Meanwhile, the king and Badoglio had ignominiously escaped from Rome on September 9, after Badoglio had broadcast this

In July 1943 Mussolini was rescued by Hitler's paratroopers.

radio message: "Hostilities against the British and American forces will now cease on all fronts. The Italian Army will, however, resist any attacks from other sources." With the collapse of the government the whole administrative system disintegrated, including the military. It was every city, village and person for themselves. Italian soldiers were trapped in the North between the Allies stalled below Rome and Germans pouring in through the Brenner Pass. The disbanded soldiers hastily discarded their uniforms, replacing them with whatever clothing was offered by sympathetic civilians. Thousands were given shelter by peasants, who had to hide their own sons because the Nazis were daily rounding up able-bodied men to serve in labor battalions in Italy or to be deported to factories in Germany. The mountains of the Apennines and the Alps became a haven not only for Italian ex-soldiers but also for anti-Fascists and escaped Allied prisoners. Many of the latter were trying to reach Switzerland or to rejoin the American and British armies in the South.

In the first weeks after the armistice many young Italians were literally just hiding, almost camping out. Paolo Gobetti, the son of anti-Fascist Piero Gobetti, described how he and his friends reacted as they banded together in the mountains above Turin: "We felt completely free and secure. We were armed and we knew who the enemy was. This was a moment of absolute liberty because the State had vanished, both the Fascist State and the State of the king and Badoglio—there was no more State. The State was the Germans, who were oppressors and invaders and who had no legitimacy, nor did the Fascists who worked with them. So as we walked among the trees and the mountains we had a feeling, almost a sensation, that we could reach out and touch utopia, the possibility that we could build something entirely new."

The reality of their situation became clear in short order, as supplies and food began to dwindle and the weather changed. The "camping out" was soon to become not only guerrilla warfare against the invader, but also civil war as the Resistance confronted Mussolini's new Fascist state.

=2=
The Four Days of Naples

IT WAS a little past three PM on Sunday, September 12, 1943. Four days earlier Italy had signed an armistice with the Allies. Some 7,000 men, women, and children, surrounded by German soldiers pointing machine guns at them, had been herded into the huge square facing the University of Naples. Most of them lived in the neighborhood and had just finished a meager Sunday dinner when they had been forced from their homes into the streets. Seconds later, German soldiers raced through their apartments, setting fire to some of the buildings.

As the Neapolitans stood, silent and terrorized, a Nazi appeared at the front of the crowd dragging by one hand a young Italian sailor. The boy was screaming his innocence. In the other hand the soldier held a small, battered suitcase. A German officer ordered the crowd to kneel. Suddenly there was a volley from a small cannon facing the university and the main building caught fire. As the fire spread rapidly, the sailor was dragged to the steps leading into the burning building. A Nazi officer shouted in Italian that the boy had thrown hand grenades at German soldiers, and that the little suitcase was full of grenades. The sailor's punishment: he must enter the flaming doorway. The crowd, which could feel the heat of the fire even where they knelt, watched in horror as the boy, crying for his mother, started to walk into the building. Before he could enter he was shot in the back.

The people were then ordered to stand and cheer for Hitler and Mussolini. The able-bodied men among them, about 4,000, were separated from the women, children and old people, who were told to return home. For hours the men were made to march away from Naples, until at midnight they were allowed to stop and rest. Along the way, stragglers and anyone attempting to escape were shot and left by the wayside. After a night sleeping in the open, the march resumed. At no time, survivors said, were they given food and water or told where they were headed. Finally, around noon they were stopped again and told that those with proper identification would be freed. As each showed his documents he was stripped of his wristwatch, money and any other valuables. Forty unfortunates could not produce IDs but eventually they, too, were released. (After the war, Nazi reports captured by the Allies disclosed that the men were supposed to have been sent to Germany for forced labor but there were no vehicles available to transport them.) So began the terror leading to the days of rebellion known throughout Italy as the "Four Days of Naples."

To call the Four Days an insurrection suggests a well-organized, planned revolt of the type seen later in the cities of the North. This was not the case in Naples. Leaders of the six political parties had formed, on September 24, a Committee of National Liberation. But the group was not strong enough to provide real leadership for the city, where the population in any event was largely apolitical. (The Naples Committee was, however, the prototype of a great number of Committees of National Liberation which would multiply throughout occupied Italy to become the core of the unified Resistance.)

The spontaneity of the rebellion in a city of over a million is the phenomenon that makes the Four Days so special. That, and the fact that a modern armed force, part of a seemingly invincible war machine, was attacked and routed by civilians who even resorted to stones, brooms and shovels for weapons. It was David and Goliath in the twentieth century. Granted that the Neapolitans knew the Allies were close at hand, they still did not wait, supine, to be liberated. They fought back. For the first time in the European war, German officers capitulated to a band of civilians.

The brutal behavior of the German soldiers had been something of a turnabout for the Neapolitans. Wehrmacht uniforms had been a familiar sight in Naples since early 1940. The city was a convenient midpoint between Berlin and the African campaign sites. The Germans complained Naples was too dirty but they liked the climate, and it was an excellent place for recreation and rehabilitation of the Afrika Korps. Members of the Reich hierarchy enjoyed outings to Pompeii, Sorrento and Capri. They even built a Lutheran Chapel in which to hold their own services. Neapolitans became accustomed to the presence of German soldiers, who behaved themselves on the whole and fraternized quite willingly with the local girls. At Christmas the Reich Navy band paraded through the city playing Italian songs, and in the spring and summer the German musicians gave frequent outdoor concerts. Even Hitler once visited Naples.

But there was a dark side of the picture. Hitler, in return for supplying armaments to the Italian armed forces, demanded men to work for his own war machine. Trainloads of conscripts from Naples left frequently, with much ceremony and promises of a fine life and good pay. Once in Germany they were trapped in misery, housed in crude barracks, fed poorly and ostracized by the local population. Worst of all, they were forbidden to return home.

Although Naples had fared badly during the early years of Fascism, the really severe deprivations began with the bombings of the city, first by the French in June 1940 and then by the Allies. Bombardment was especially heavy from July 1943 to September, following the landing of the Allies in Sicily. In all, by the time the Armistice was signed on September 8, Naples had undergone 120 air raids leaving 22,000 dead and thousands more injured. The city itself suffered incredible damage. Food

The Reich Marine Band entertains Neapolitans in the early 1940s.

had become very scarce, transportation was almost at a standstill and the anger and resentment of the inhabitants had reached a boiling point.

After the fall of Mussolini and during the 45 days of the Badoglio government, there had been sporadic demonstrations for peace. In August a group of students tried to organize a peace march to take place September 1 at the Piazza Plebescito. They printed flyers announcing the event and plastered them all over the city. But according to Badoglio's equivocal statement on July 25, when he took over after Mussolini's dismissal, the Germans and the Italians were still allies. The student movement was quickly repressed. On September 1 German Tiger tanks appeared for the first time on the city streets, patrolling the Piazza. Using tear gas, Nazi troops soon dispersed the crowd but not before many students as well as bystanders were arrested.

For a week the protesters remained in jail. Finally, late in the afternoon of September 8, Major Malfitano, head of the local military tribunal, went to the prison to interrogate the young people responsible for the demonstration. His questioning was interrupted by a great commotion outside. Crowds had gathered in the street, screaming with joy. The radio had just announced the Armistice had been signed with the Allies. Now the bombing would end. Malfitano released the young people and soon vanished himself, together with many other officers of the Italian armed forces, leaving the soldiers and sailors stationed in Naples to fend for themselves.

The Nazi commander in Naples, Colonel Scholl, was caught completely by surprise by the announcement of the Armistice. His first reaction was to pack up and leave the city. Lights at the Hotel Parco, German headquarters, burned long into the night while documents were being destroyed. On the ninth the few Germans who ventured into the streets wore white armbands as a precaution. They were afraid of an attack by the considerable number of Italian soldiers who were wandering about the city. The civilians were also a concern. That day women and children had thrown garbage at passing German vehicles. Shots had been

fired at them from windows and a group of young men had captured a few German soldiers and held them prisoner. Actually,
the Germans had little to fear from the Naples military command.
General Deltetto, commander of the 19th Armed Corps, had no
intention of defending the city. He gave orders for his men to
disband and on September 11 he himself changed into civilian
clothes and took refuge in a convent.

Some people believed that if the Italian Army and Navy officers in Naples had ordered their men to round up the German
troops on September 9, Allied ships would then have been able
to enter Naples harbor unopposed and the city would have been
spared the ordeal to come. This appraisal of the failure to take
advantage of a military situation was to be echoed several times
during the Italian campaign, a failure attributed to the Allies, the
king and Badoglio, and in no small part to the Italian officer
corps, with a few exceptions.

If Colonel Scholl at first had considered a quick retreat, Hitler
had no such intentions. He reacted in fury at the "treachery" of
his former allies, and personally ordered that Naples be reduced
to "mud and ashes." On the twelfth, Scholl assumed "absolute
command" of Naples. He declared a state of siege, established a
curfew from eight PM to six AM, and ordered that all weapons
possessed by Italians be immediately confiscated. In no uncertain
terms Scholl proclaimed: "I will protect citizens who behave in
a calm and disciplined manner. However, whoever acts openly
or surrepticiously against the German armed forces will be executed. In addition, the place in which the incident took place and
its surroundings will be destroyed. Each German soldier wounded
or killed will be avenged 100 times. . . . Citizens, be calm and
reasonable. These orders and the reprisal already taken [reference
to the burning of the University and killing of the sailor and oth-
ers] are necessary because a large number of innocent German
officers and soldiers, simply doing their duty, have been vilely
assassinated or seriously wounded."

The people were given twenty-four hours to give up their
weapons. During the following days hardly any were turned in

ON THE FACING PAGE
Women and children drawing water at one of the few fountains which continued to function during the German occupation of Naples. *Reprinted with permission from* Napoli 1940–1945, *by Lambiase and Nazzaro, Milan: Longanesi & Co.*

A grain warehouse in Naples harbor, destroyed by the Germans before they were forced out of the city by Neapolitan patriots at the end of September 1943.

except old hunting guns, historic swords and a few souvenirs from the African campaigns. Good weapons were well hidden. For the next two weeks the Neapolitans were subjected to ruthless looting and pillaging. Food stocks, already badly depleted, were appropriated. Innocent people were shot, often without any provocation, simply to intimidate. In the Torretta zone three people in a breadline were casually shot in the back. Homes and businesses were systematically destroyed, block by block, by commandos equipped with containers of liquid incendiary materials. To prevent fire trucks from extinguishing the flames, mines were placed around the buildings after the commandos left.

Neapolitan *scugnizzi* pose for Allied soldiers after the liberation of Naples in October 1943.

Port facilities were also destroyed, as well as whatever transportation and communication facilities had not been already bombed. These actions were accompanied by a flood of manifestos designed to further frighten the populace, by now reduced to fighting a daily battle for self-preservation in an elemental search for food and water. Bread, severely rationed, could be bought only at certain stores and at certain times, and the hours were changed arbitrarily to make it even more difficult for a housewife to buy a loaf. Pasta, the real staple for the Neapolitans, was often unavailable and some neighborhoods had not yet received their August ration. Long walks into the countryside to forage for greens sometimes netted a few eggs as well, but the peasants had also been subjected to frequent Nazi raids and they had little for themselves. For a short time a black market flourished, often operated by German soldiers, but soon there was no money left to buy back the goods stolen from the Neapolitans.

The water situation was also a disaster. Several aqueducts had been blown up by the Germans, so that some parts of the city were completely without water. Elsewhere the flow had been reduced to a trickle. Women swarmed by the thousands to the few fountains that worked, and water sold by the flask on the black market cost even more than bread. To add to the misery, trash piled up in the streets, and the smell of rotting garbage under collapsed buildings was nauseating. Flies and mosquitos swarmed over the ruins and rats crawled in and out of gaping holes. The danger of an epidemic was obvious, and to protect their own health the Nazis were finally forced to allocate a few of the still operative trolleys to haul away some of the garbage.

Nazi strategy was now concentrated on blowing up the remaining aqueducts and electrical plants before they departed. Day and night, mines exploded constantly and some sections of the city were always in flames. Due to the lack of fire trucks and water, Hitler's edict was quickly being carried out. Meanwhile the search intensified for able-bodied workers to send to Germany. The disbanded soldiers and sailors were especially vulnerable. On September 22 the prefect of Naples, who was collaborating with the Nazis, announced that all males between the ages of 18 and 33, representing some 30,000 of the population, had to report for obligatory labor by September 25. The men responded by disappearing from the main streets. It was not so difficult to find a hiding place in the alleys that honeycombed the poorer sections of the city. German soldiers stayed away from these little, dark streets because it was all too easy to be ambushed there, and the roads were much too narrow for armored vehicles.

The hunted men were helped by a vigilante corps of women. They would watch from windows and doorways, quickly passing the word if Nazi troops approached. Renato Sansone remembers one day when he was walking along Via San Giuseppe Dei Nudi. The street was silent and empty except for a woman standing in her doorway. As he passed she exclaimed, "Where do you think you're going? They're taking men at Salvator Rosa!" and she pushed him into her house. Renato was shoved into a huge wooden wardrobe which already hid two boys. Then the woman returned to her post. After about an hour the all clear was given over the grapevine, and when Sansone emerged he saw at least fifty men of all ages coming out of the nearby houses. If the women had been caught, they would have been shot on the spot together with the men.

On Saturday, September 25, the deadline for reporting, only 150 men showed up of the eligible 30,000. That morning another disastrous edict was announced. Everyone living within 300 meters of the harbor and shoreline would have to move to the inner city by the 8 PM curfew that day. More than 200,000 people were affected by the order. Hastily gathering together the little they could carry in their arms and on their backs (including babies, the sick, and infirm old people) they trudged away from their homes, prodded by German troops with their ever-present machine guns. Some lucky families crowded in with relatives, but many had to camp out in the streets or in the few bomb shelters.

Scholl dealt with the failed roundup of 18 to 33 year olds by threatening that all those defying his order would be found and shot. Armored trucks appeared on all the main roads. Soldiers advanced door to door, forcing them open with the butt of their guns, sometimes shooting out a lock. Some of the inhabitants tried to bribe them with a last bit of gold, but the soldiers typically took the gold and continued to search for men to take away. Even those who showed a Fascist ID card were taken away, ID and all.

If the Italian men had no weapons on them, they were pushed into the street and onto a waiting truck. If anyone was caught armed, he was shot on the spot. Courageous women tried to intercept the advance of the soldiers, going to the doorway as the Germans arrived, explaining apartments above were empty. "No one lives there. They're refugees—they left town," or "They're away, in the country because of the air raids," or "It's empty. He's dead, air raid. The Americans." Sometimes the Germans were satisfied with the explanation; other times they sprayed the house with machine-gun fire and threw in a hand grenade for good measure.

A few desperate bystanders tried to interfere with the roundups. As men were being loaded onto a truck in the Piazzetta Giardinetto, shouts suddenly filled the air. A hundred screaming women and old men armed only with brooms and sticks hurled themselves at the German soldiers with such ferocity that the startled soldiers jumped into the truck and took off, leaving most of their quarry behind.

Passive resistance was coming to an end, but a few Neapolitans still obeyed orders. Piero Gasparri had initially ignored the ultimatums, until he began to fear for the safety of his family if he remained in hiding, so he gave himself up. It was raining heavily the day he reported for compulsory labor. He joined other men in an open truck for the hour-long drive to Caserta, where they would stay overnight before leaving for Germany. At Caserta they were put in an empty barracks: 150 men had to share three blankets. The next day they were given some bread, their entire food ration for the day, and a little water. Doctors, medical students and engineers were separated from the group, to be flown to Germany.

At four PM the others began a long march to an unknown destination. A boy who tried to escape was shot. Women who offered them water along the way were beaten. After eleven hours of walking they were permitted to rest at a deserted gas station. Some of the men managed to build a fire. A young German soldier, joining them to keep warm, told them the group was to be sent to the Russian front as soon as transportation could be arranged. Gasparri and three others decided to make a break for it. While the guards slept they quickly hid in a huge, empty septic tank lying near the gas station. If any of their companions noticed their absence, none gave them away. Later in the day the four found refuge in a peasant's barn, where they remained until October 4, when the Allies advanced into that area.

By September 27, after almost three weeks of ruthless oppression, the people of Naples had reached the limits of endurance. Isolated as they were from each other, the different sections of the city burst into action almost simultaneously. The spontaneous outburst was supported by a complete cross-section of the population: young and old, rich and poor, intellectuals and the *popolani*. Hunger, outrage and desperation drove them against the "invincible Wehrmacht." There were no generals or politicians to lead the Neapolitans, no plan of attack, just the feeling that they could stand no more.

The night of the 27th and into the 28th was spent hunting for weapons. Guns were found in the arsenals of the disbanded Italian armed forces, left unguarded by the Germans who thought the populace would never have the temerity to raid the stockpiles. Most of the weapons retrieved there were old guns, including the 91s of World War I vintage, but they worked. As word spread that an attack was to be made on the invader, other hidden caches were revealed: 100 bombs in a basement on Via Foggia; pistols and ammunition in an old palace in Poggioreale; the guns of the Italian 107th anti-aircraft battery concealed for a long time in the Villa Rotonda, on the Via di Cappella dei Congiani. Even in the Hospital for Incurables the "patients," some of them former political prisoners hiding there, had been able to arm themselves.

Neapolitans joined disbanded soldiers, still wearing their uniforms, to chase out the Germans during the Four Days of Naples.

For some time, patients and staff had been filling caskets in the mortuary with rifles of all kinds, hundreds of hand grenades, boxes of bullets, bayonets and even three machine guns.

Disbanded soldiers who had buried their guns dug them up and put them in working order. The *scugnizzi,* the famous street urchins of Naples, had been especially adept at raiding the arsenals and even occasionally the unguarded vehicles of German soldiers. The latter regarded the *scugnizzi* as something of a harmless nuisance and no one bothered to search their ragged pants. The children were also expert at stealing gasoline from German cars and trucks, which was used to create homemade bottle bombs, nicknamed the ''Molotov cocktail.'' One of the biggest arms caches was located in Castel Sant'Elmo, an old fort and a Naples landmark. But the best hoard—including submachine guns—was found in the deserted Vasto barracks, enough to supply the masses of people living near the railway yards. A few Italian police showed up at one point, but they were easily persuaded to look the other way. During the night, with the help of the ever-present *scugnizzi*, house-by-house distribution of weapons was underway.

Open combat began on the afternoon of September 28. The day before a rumor had circulated that an Allied landing was

Gennaro Capuozzo, the boy on the right pointing toward a sniper, was killed shortly after this photograph was taken during the Four Days of Naples.

imminent, and indeed from the harbor warships could be seen on the horizon. The attack began in the old Vomero section, where a group of men demolished a German armored car, killing the driver. Similar attacks rapidly took place in the Vasto and near Porta Grande in Capodimonte, where many German soldiers were stationed. The Neapolitans quickly adopted the tactics of guerrilla warfare, striking and then disappearing into the familiar alleys and side streets which were a confusing maze for the Germans. The Nazis, aware of the Allied advance and now concerned about the outpouring of armed people on the streets, abandoned their original scheme to destroy the city block by block and began to make plans for a quick escape. But German troops trying to move out in trucks soon ran into road blocks the Neapolitans had made by piling rubble or overturned trolleys in the middle of the streets.

The *scugnizzi* were especially helpful at this juncture, even though a few fathers tried to send the boys home. Gennaro Capuozzo, a 12 year old, crawled on all fours to carry ammunition to a group of barricaded rebels. At one point he joined a machine gunner stationed on a first floor terrace of a building, overlooking the street. A man ran by, yelling that Germans in armored cars and trucks were heading their way. Gennaro stretched himself out beside the machine gunner to hand him belts of cartridges. When the trucks arrived, the gunner opened fire. The lead truck spotted the machine gun and headed towards the terrace, its small cannon swivelling to get a better aim. Gennaro jumped up and threw one, then another, grenade to stop the advance. As he prepared to throw a third, he was shot dead.

The role of the *scugnizzi* has been romanticized to the point of implying that gangs of young boys forced the Germans out of Naples. Robert Capa's remarkable photos for *Life* magazine probably helped create this legend. But there is no doubt that the fearless children contributed a great deal to the Four Days. One of the heroes of that time, still remembered today, was a 15 year old named Giacomo Lettieri. Giacomo was a blacksmith's apprentice, working in a shop on Piazza Umberto in the main shopping area. Much of his time in September 1943 was spent shoeing horses of the Nazi guards. One day as a German patrol was rounding up men in the Piazza they spied two unarmed Italian soldiers. Without a word of warning, the Nazis raised their guns and fired. One soldier fell to the ground, his arm blown open, the other managed to stumble away. The Nazis had left some guns stacked against a wall near the blacksmith's shop. Giacomo grabbed one and aimed a volley at the patrol, killing the man who had shot the unarmed soldiers. The Germans, thinking it was an ambush, ran off leaving Giacomo alone in the Piazza. "Bravo," screamed a woman from the window, "now go home quick, they'll be back."

For days Giacomo stayed home, but his family desperately needed the few lire he earned and he was sure that the Germans had not seen who shot at them or they would have arrested the blacksmith. He returned to work and for a few days all went well. Then Giacomo was approached by a young man on a motorcycle who said he knew about Giacomo's exploit and invited him to join a group arming themselves to ambush Germans. Giacomo accepted the invitation and after work climbed onto the back of the motorcycle. And rode right into a trap. The young man was a spy who drove him to a German barracks on the outskirts of the city. There Giacomo was herded into a truck together with other prisoners. They were taken to the countryside, forced to dig a mass grave and then all were murdered. The next day the newspaper *Roma* reported that a group of looters, among them one Giacomo Lettieri, had been apprehended and shot. (Lettieri was later awarded the silver medal of honor posthumously.)

As the 28th drew to a close the German retreat was also hampered by problems of their own creation. Communication facilities had been almost totally destroyed so that they could not coordinate their own movements. There was no electricity, making every street a site for a potential ambush. Tanks and armored trucks were too cumbersome to get around road blocks hastily constructed by the Neapolitans. By the 29th intense battles had been fought in all sections of the city. In each neighborhood the spontaneous outbursts were becoming more organized, as natural leaders appeared from the ranks. Sometimes it was a former officer of the Italian Army, sometimes a longtime anti-Fascist, but often just an ordinary man or woman. In the Vincenzo Cuomo neighborhood a young priest, Father Matteo Lisa, led the fight. Elsewhere a local doctor took charge, or a shopkeeper, or a young man who had been a waiter in a nearby trattoria and who knew everyone in the neighborhood. Their names are still remembered today: Stefano Fadda in Chiaia, Ezio Murolo in Piazza Dante, Aurelio Spoto in Capodimonte, Antonio Tarsia in the Vomero.

Although the basic objective of the Neapolitans was to kill, capture or at least harass the departing Germans, the citizens also tried to save what was left of the city and its facilities. One of the major arteries connecting the lower, central part of Naples with the hilly Capodimonte area was the bridge over the Via Sanita. The bridge literally skims the rooftops of the densely populated Via Sanita. (Some of the buildings are six stories high.) The Germans had cleared the bridge of traffic and had made a big indentation in the center, in which they placed sticks of dynamite to blow up the structure. As the Germans worked to connect detonators, a group of armed men and women slowly approached from one end of the long span. Among them were a few Sicilian sailors and a butcher, a huge man still wearing his dirty apron, a pistol in each hand. They were joined by Maddalena Cerasuolo, a 20 year old *popolana* of Santa Teresa, who had already distinguished herself in street fighting at the side of her recently wounded father.

When the Germans realized they were about to be attacked they retreated to the end of the bridge abutting the road to Capodimonte. Hiding behind a small truck, they opened fire on the advancing crowd which promptly returned a volley of their own. For a few minutes it looked like a stand-off. Then two of the sailors disappeared. They scrambled along the side of the bridge to a small road which enabled them to creep up behind the Germans. A few shots killed the officer in charge of the dynamiters and wounded his aide. The others jumped into the truck and drove off. The bridge was saved and more important, so were thousands of people living on the streets below, who would have been crushed by the falling debris.

By afternoon of the 29th the Nazis realized that they had lost control. There was no more time to reduce Naples to the mud and ashes demanded by Hitler, but a good deal more could be destroyed. Scholl ordered a long line of Tiger tanks to head down from Capodimonte towards the heart of the city. However, he had not reckoned with Lieutenant Droette, a partisan leader in the area, who was equipped with a long-range cannon unearthed from its hiding place. As the tanks rolled down the hill, Droette and his men opened fire, destroying several tanks and immobilizing the rest. Five tanks coming from another direction were blown up by mines placed by the partisans, who also managed to save the huge, remaining reservoir and its water supply. The Germans had ruined the aqueduct leading to the reservoir, leaving six men to guard their handiwork. The Italians succeeded in capturing all six and took them away as prisoners, but not before forcing them to dismantle the explosives planted at the reservoir.

In the Vomero, where Scholl was located, activity was especially intense. An elderly former Italian Army officer, Col. Antonino Tarsia, had taken charge of the patriots in the area and was quickly accepted as their commander. Tarsia's men were well-armed and tightly coordinated. The Vomero's Campo Sportivo was also the base of operations for a large German squadron under a Major Sakau. Patriots had killed one of Sakau's men and in reprisal Sakau sent twenty soldiers armed with machine guns to arrest any citizen found on the streets and to shoot anyone who resisted. Forty-seven men, women, and children were quickly taken hostage.

Regardless of the danger, residents of the Vomero could not stay indoors indefinitely: they had to go out for food and water. On the 29th Tarsia and one of his chief aides, former Army Captain Ezio Stimolo, decided it was time to counterattack. By afternoon Sakau's patrols had been chased back to the Campo, which was now besieged by armed partisans. Towards evening Sakau suddenly appeared in the main doorway of one of the buildings adjoining the Campo. He was accompanied by an officer carrying a white flag. Sakau's request to meet with the patriots' representative was quickly relayed to Stimolo and Tarsia at their headquarters in the Sannizzaro high school. Stimolo and an interpreter rode to the Campo, where Sakau told them "stop firing on us and let us leave freely in our cars and trucks: if you do not agree to this you will regret it." Stimolo answered: "You will leave only if you succeed in annihilating us. Until then, you'll have to fight and we have enough men and weapons to hold out." The major turned and started to walk away, then he added angrily, "Remember, we have 47 hostages."

Stimolo was well aware of this, and that both his men and his firepower were limited. He did not have the cannon and heavy equipment needed for a definitive assault on the Nazis. But Sakau was at a serious disadvantage too. Thanks to their destruction of most of the aqueducts, the Germans quartered in the Campo had run out of water. An hour after the meeting between Sakau and Stimolo the main gate of the Campo opened again and through it came a small armored car driven by Sakau, accompanied by his aide bearing a white flag. "Hold your fire!" Sakau demanded. The partisans were suspicious, but they allowed the car to move towards the high school. Stimolo, unarmed, went out to meet Sakau, first requiring that the major drop his gun to the ground.

Sakau explained that he had no authority to make important decisions and suggested that they both go to talk with Scholl. Stimolo agreed, but insisted that they use his Fiat so that they would not be fired on by the partisans. By then it was dark and a large crowd, including friends and relatives of the 47 hostages, had gathered outside the Campo. At the Hotel Parco candles illuminated all the windows (there was no electricity) and people could be seen hurrying back and forth. Sakau and Stimolo were quickly led into Scholl's office where the colonel sat, rigidly upright, smoking a cigaret. Sakau began to explain his request for safe passage but Stimolo interrupted, "Before we come to any such arrangement you must agree to free the 47 hostages. If you do, we will give you safe conduct as far as the crossroads at

An Italian submarine surrenders to an Allied warship in Salerno Bay, near Naples, on
September 29, 1943.

Cappella Dei Congiani but your soldiers must go unarmed. If you
don't agree, we shall resume fighting.'' Scholl was silent for a
few moments, then he uttered a terse *"Jawohl."*

Sakau and Stimolo returned to the Campo, where the hostages were immediately released to the cheering crowd. Sakau's
car then led a procession of trucks out of the encampment and by
10:30 PM the Campo was empty. For the first time in weeks people walked unafraid on the streets of the Vomero.

The retreating Germans fired a last salvo from the hills of
Capodimonte hours before the Allies entered the city on October
1. In a final act of senseless savagery, as their troops passed through
Nola they destroyed the Historical Archives of Naples kept there,
a priceless record of the city since medieval days. Colonel Scholl,
humiliated at having to capitulate, lost no time in making his own
departure. He was gone before dawn, flying the white flag of
defeat as he left the city he was to have reduced to ''a sea of mud
and ashes.''

The partisans had provided the margin of difference that saved
the city. How close Naples came to destruction has been starkly

described in the following report by Col. E. E. Hume, Chief of Military Government, United States Army.

---

20 October 1943

Hon. Henry Morgenthau,
Secretary of the Treasury,
Care of Lieut. General Mark W. Clark, U.S.A.,
Headquarters, Fifth Army,
NAPLES.

My dear Mr. Secretary:

In compliance with your request I give you herewith a brief report of acts of German cruelty and wanton destruction committed in Naples, chiefly during the three weeks before our capture of the city. This period is called the "Reign of Terror" by Neapolitans. I am, of course, not giving any instances of damage to the city or to individuals which took place as a result of acts of war (bombings, etc.). The things that I list were unnecessary from any military point of view.

OFFENSES AGAINST THE CITY
AS A WHOLE

Water Supply: When the Fifth Army reached Naples we found that there was an almost total failure of the water supply. People were carrying water in pails, jugs, bottles and every type of container. There was a small trickle of water from some of the hydrants but many persons standing in line were unable to receive enough to quench thirst. Naples had been famous for an abundant supply of pure water. The Germans had blown up the main aqueduct in seven places and all of the reservoirs save one had been drained. . . . The Germans were well aware that there was ample facility for our bringing in water for the troops, as was done in the desert campaign, so that this destruction of the city supply was an act of cruelty against civilians, young and old. The enemy likewise destroyed the pumping plants, thereby making it impossible to raise the water, had any been available, to the higher parts of the city. The water mains in many parts of Naples were deliberately cut.

Sewage System: The pumping facilities of the sewage disposal system of Naples were destroyed. Thus, even had there been enough water to enable sewers to function, they would have been unable to do so because much of the Neapolitan sewage disposal depends not on gravity but on a series of pumps. The city is built on volcanic rock so that, even had there been space available for them, it was all but impracticable to dig latrines. The danger of epidemics of intestinal diseases, such as typhoid fever and dysentery, was obviously very great particularly at this season of the year.

Electric Light and Power Systems: Naples was in darkness when we took over. The Germans had destroyed both the generators of the current and likewise the transformers. The Italian metropolis depends largely on hydro-electric power not only for lighting, but for the water and sewage pumps, the mills for grinding wheat, the newspaper presses, the heating of buildings, cooking, and indeed practically all power machines.

Transportation System: The street car system was wholly out of commission both because the electric current had been cut off (see above) and because the Germans carried away or destroyed the greater part of the rolling stock. Buses also were taken away. A large number of them were found to the north of the city where the enemy, unable to carry them further, had burned them. There are of course no taxicabs other than a few old wrecks, and only a few horse-drawn vehicles in the city. People who are not physically strong enough to walk from one locality to another are practically prisoners. This has seriously affected the earning capacity of many. The Germans carried away every automobile, both passenger and truck, that they could find. In some instances they took only the tires and destroyed or abandoned the bodies of the cars. Ambulances and fire-fighting vehicles were not spared.

Communication Systems: The telegraph lines were put out of commission. The main telephone exchange was blown up.

Demolition of Hotels: The group of magnificent hotels along the Via Partenope, facing Vesuvius, used to be one of the outstanding groups of such institutions in the world. Such names as the Excelsior, Vesuvio, Santa Lucia, Royal, etc., are known to travelers everywhere. These buildings, without exception, were blown up and fire set to what remained. They cannot be repaired. The only first-class hotel left was the Park Hotel, which was mined.

Blocking of Tunnels: There are a number of tunnels in Naples built to give ready access from one quarter to another at a saving of much hill climbing. These were blown up.

Demolition of Flour Mills: Naples, like most Italian cities, grinds its wheat a little at a time, rather than converting a whole crop to flour at once. Thus flour mills are an essential feature of the city's economic and welfare system. All of the large mills were wrecked by the Germans.

Destruction of the University of Naples and of its Famous Libraries: The University of Naples is one of the oldest and most famous in existence. The library of the Royal Society of Naples, one of the great learned societies of the world, was housed therein. It was put to the torch on 12 September, a little more than a fortnight before we took the city. Several witnesses agree that the notorious Col. Scholl, Commander of German troops garrisoned in Naples, arrived in person when the work was finished and read a proclamation in German and Italian announcing that the university had been wrecked as a punishment to Naples. When I first visited the ruined buildings the ashes of the Library of the Royal Society were still warm and the pool of blood on the front steps, where the shooting of the Carabinieri was reported to have occurred, was still evident.

I wish that there were time to give you more details and to complete the report of the first two weeks of the work of the Allied Military Government of this great city . . . we have been able to keep the city running in something like a normal fashion, despite the handicaps imposed by war and by the German studied policy of destruction.

May I wish you a safe journey home and once more thank you for your interest in what we are doing.

Respectfully yours,

EDGAR ERSKINE HUME,
Colonel, General Staff Corps,
United States Army,
Chief of Military Government.

=3=
The Mountain Partisans of Piedmont

THE ROYAL AIR FORCE Halifax droned northward over the Tyrrhenian Sea. Its three passengers were silent, watching the Italian Riviera disappear as the plane headed northwest, towards the snow-covered Alps. "No clouds tonight," commented the pilot, a Free Poland Air Force lieutenant, "I told you we'd make it this time." The day before Riccardo Vanzetti and his team-mates had flown the same route. They had left the southern Italian city of Bari expecting to be parachuted into Val Pellice, an Italian war zone near Turin occupied by German troops. A storm and dense clouds had prevented the drop.

The group was flying to join the mountain partisans of the Piedmont region, to help them establish radio contact with Allied forces in the South. Desperately needed weapons and other supplies could not reach the partisans until an effective communication system had been established between the North and South. Now it was two AM on March 17, 1944 and Vanzetti's Neapolitan radio operator had begun to fall asleep. The flight engineer joined the three men and started to unscrew wing nuts holding down the plywood cover of the drophole. As he lifted the cover a rush of cold air filled the cabin. The men sat on the edge of the round, seven-foot opening, facing the nose of the plane. Vanzetti, who had often skied in the Turin mountains, stared hard trying to identify familiar peaks. He shifted the packs behind him. Besides the

---

radio equipment, each man would be supplied with skis, enough food for two weeks, spare clothing, and a blanket. They were dressed in the white suits of civilian skiers, who might be on a brief vacation away from frequently bombed Turin.

The pilot called over the loudspeaker: "Action Station," and a few seconds later "Ready—Go!" One by one the men slid off their perch. At an airspeed of 180 kilometers per hour the plane travels 50 meters every second, so no time must be wasted between jumps or the men would be hopelessly separated from each other. Vanzetti, a veteran of only four practice jumps, could hear the air whistling softly through the top hole of his parachute. He could see the other men drifting nearby, clearly visible in the star-lit, moonless night. The snow-covered peaks surged up much more quickly than he expected, and suddenly he found himself resting comfortably on soft, deep snow.

First Vanzetti unhooked the parachute, to avoid being blown away by the wind. Next he pointed his flashlight towards the sky, signalling the circling plane to drop the skis and other equipment, then, with tail lights flashing in Morse Code "OK—Goodbye—OK," the plane disappeared. Vanzetti looked about him. The pilot had studied a detailed map of the Val Pellice area and it was up to him to select a suitable pinpoint. The first priority now was to locate the packs, which took several hours of hunting in the knee-deep snow. By the time they found the skis and had buried the tell-tale parachutes, dawn was lighting up the mountains and the green valley below. The sleepless night made them all the more appreciative of the peaceful quiet when suddenly a bugle wake-up call filled the air. They had spotted a ski hut just above them, and now as the sun rose they could also make out a large, square building taking shape below. It was surrounded by a fenced yard, and as they watched, German soldiers lined up for morning call. This was obviously a well-established military barracks.

Without waiting to see any more, the men beat a retreat to the ski hut, hoping their camouflage would protect them from the curiosity of a sleepy soldier who might have spotted them. Previous visitors had scribbled their names on the walls of the hut:

most of them seemed to be French. On the lintel over the door there was a carving of a trumpet on a bed of laurel branches, the symbol of the French Alpine Troops. It quickly became evident that the plane had dropped the men on the French side of the Alps. They had no French money, no suitable identification, only Vanzetti spoke French, and worse of all, they did not have a map of the area. One thing was clear; they would have to cross to the Italian side. Crossing the Alps on skis is difficult in any season but in March it is especially hazardous because the melting snow causes avalanches. To further complicate matters, Giorgio, the radio operator, had lied about his skiing ability in his eagerness to join the expedition.

For three days and most of two nights (except for a few hours sleep) the men slowly pushed on. Towards the end Giorgio vanished in an avalanche, and though his companions were able to dig him out, he had lost his skis, the poles, gloves and cap. But by now they were in Italian territory and relatively safe. Marcello, the third member of the group, left the other two huddled

Vanzetti's shortwave radio operator in one of his mountain hideouts.

in a make-shift shelter and set off to find help. Within a few hours he reached a small village, established his credentials and returned with a rescue party to haul Giorgio and the radio equipment into the valley. On April 4, two weeks after they had left Bari, Vanzetti was able to radio his first message. He estimated that over the next year the same transmitter sent some 900 messages, and received at least 400.

Vanzetti went on to organize sabotage of railroads in Turin, essential to German troop movements. He had been an Italian Air Force engineer and after the Armistice had managed to reach the Allied-held South. There he had been selected by the local head of the American OSS (Office of Strategic Services) unit to be trained. Vanzetti was awarded the American Bronze Star for his bravery for underground work in the North.

During the twenty months of the Italian campaign, OSS had established similar teams in northern Italy, as well as clandestine radios. The teams were trained for sabotage but they also were expected to collect military, economic and political intelligence, working closely with the partisans. Radios set up by OSS regularly transmitted information about German strategic and tactical planning, and pinpointed military targets for Allied air raids.

The political relationship between the Allies and wartime Italy is a long and complicated story, even a controversial one. But in spite of the complex issues sometimes unjustly hampering aid to the Resistance, the missions of men like Vanzetti exemplified the efforts made to supply the patriots with whatever they needed. The Allies had only a sketchy knowledge of the situation within Italy, which fascism had essentially isolated from the rest of the world. Information provided by refugees was regarded with considerable skepticism. When England went to war with Italy, one of the early moves was to send units of its Special Force (SF) into the country, to act as intermediaries with whatever local elements could be of assistance to Britain.

Unlike the American OSS, SF was not an intelligence gathering operation, except for information about the legitimate needs of cooperative Italians. SF's function was to help, and sometimes to stimulate, the patriots opposing Nazi and Fascist forces. Members of the SF were recruited from the military, but acted independently of the army, navy and air force units from which they were selected. As soon as it was ascertained that a partisan movement existed in a particular region, an SF mission was sent in to establish contact. The "mission" might be a single man who spoke fluent Italian and who was able to operate a shortwave radio, or it might be a head of mission plus a radio operator and one or two others, sometimes a volunteer not necessarily British.

The SF mission might be parachuted into an area, or its members might reach the partisans by boat or submarine. If necessary, the journey would be made on foot, slipping through enemy lines. As soon as contact was made with the Resistance, the assignment was threefold: to establish communication with the British base; to inform the partisans of Allied objectives and to tell the Allies what the partisans required; and to supervise when and where supplies would be dropped and how they would be distributed.

The OSS operated somewhat differently, since it was also an intelligence-gathering service. Many of its operatives were not Americans, and in Italy much of its personnel had been recruited from a Resistance organization called the Organization for the Italian Resistance (ORI), a group of volunteers established in 1943 by Raimondo Craveri, Sen. Benedetto Croce's son-in-law.

The life of OSS and SF men and women was precarious and difficult, quite unlike the romantic adventures described in cloak-and-dagger spy novels. They were isolated for months from their countrymen. Most of the time they had to rely solely on their own judgment, unable to get information or advice from a colleague or a supervisor. Sometimes they were torn between conflicting objectives and demands of the partisans and of Allied headquarters. Since many of these people knew little about Italian history and about fascism, it was difficult for them to understand the political orientation of the Resistance and its major political parties.

Both SF and OSS began operations in Italy shortly after the Armistice was signed, but it took months to establish regular and reliable contacts with the Resistance and months more before adequate supplies began arriving. The Resistance often protested at both the quality and quantity of weapons and other supplies, especially at the lack of heavy artillery. Because the Allies wanted the Resistance to restrict its operations largely to sabotage, much of the supplies were intended to help such operations rather than equip the partisans for warfare. Also, not infrequently, parachute drops either missed their target due to bad weather, poor map information (one valley looked much like another) or diversion by the enemy. Apart from debatable political considerations in Italy, the Allies also had to cope with the demands of other areas of the Western Front.

An important directive given to both the SF and OSS was to help whichever partisans—regardless of party affiliation—were effectively fighting the enemy. The ins-and-outs of the five political parties and their internal disputes were not supposed to concern these Allied forces, although at times and certain places, especially in the Friuli region, these disputes became impossible to ignore. With the consolidation of the Resistance and the formation of a unified command after June 1944, coordination of Allied/Resistance activities was greatly improved.

The Turin mountains, where Vanzetti operated, sheltered some of the earliest bands of partisans to become organized into guerrilla fighting forces. Among the young men who struck out for the Piedmont hills was a disbanded second lieutenant in the Italian army, Giulio Nicoletta. He had been born and brought up in Calabria, the southernmost part of the Italian peninsula. Nicoletta, a slim, dark-haired 22 year old, was to become Commander of the autonomous 43rd Division ''Sergio de Vitis,'' which operated in Val Sangone, not far from Val Pellice. He had attended Fascist schools but like so many Italian children, at home he had heard another story. He remembered how his old anti-Fascist uncle, Zio Salvatore, gleefully predicted that Mussolini would one day discover he was a fool to train young people to fight: ''Eventually they'll turn against him, you'll see, Giulio.''

On September 8, the day Armistice with the Allies was announced, Nicoletta was in Turin, where he had been sent to help the Alpine troops maintain order after the fall of Mussolini on July 25. Turin had been a center of anti-fascism since the early twenties when Piero Gobetti began publishing his weekly, *Revoluzione Liberale*. The city was the home of Carlo Levi, Leone Ginzburg, the late Primo Levi and of many other dedicated anti-Fascists. Turin was also the home of Fiat and other large industries, and so was of great importance to both the Germans and the Allies. On September 9 Giulio Nicoletta was joined by his older brother, Franco, who had arrived the day before in Trieste from Yugoslavia, where he had been stationed in the Italian Army. Franco originally planned to try to get home to Calabria. The Trieste–Turin leg of that journey, normally a trip of just a few hours, disabused him of that notion. The train was full of German soldiers. Friendly Italians in Franco's compartment quickly dug out spare clothing to replace his uniform, so that he could leave the train as a civilian.

During the afternoon of September 10 the first line of cars carrying German officers entered Turin, followed by a long convoy of armored trucks filled with German soldiers. That morning Giulio Nicoletta had reported to his unit's headquarters on Corso Matteoti. He had asked his captain for orders and the answer had been brief: "Do what you want—save yourself." Armed only with a pistol, Giulio jumped on his motorcycle and drove out of the city in a driving rain. As he rode past the gates of the Fiat Mirafiori plant he could see tanks and trucks approaching in the distance. The Alpine Troops officers' quarters were located just beyond the Fiat plant. Near the officers' quarters there was a cluster of small, peasant-owned farms, some half-dozen stone houses with red-tiled roofs, each surrounded by a few acres under cultivation. Giulio and Franco quickly changed into borrowed peasant clothes. A friendly farmer agreed to drive them to the Val Sangone in his truck. By then the rain had stopped and they were able to hide a dozen rifles, ammunition and food under a load of hay. Giulio knew of a sturdy *baita* (a mountain hut), well-sheltered by the trees, which would make a safe haven for quite a few people.

At first the flight to the mountains seemed an adventure to many of the young men hiding there from the Germans. September was a beautiful month. It was easy to descend at night to the plains to buy food from the peasants and money was still available from family and friends. The leaders among them, some of them veterans of the Spanish Civil War, had not yet begun to organize the refugees for combat, so their days were relatively carefree. In those early months the Germans, with a few exceptions, did not take seriously what was going on in the mountains, as they concentrated on roundups of available manpower in the towns and villages.

Reprisals for hiding wanted men became increasingly severe as call-up demands went unheeded. Peasant farmers especially were targeted for revenge because their barns and fields could conceal runaways. The punishment for this was devastating: homes, crops and livestock were destroyed, and not even the churches were safe. So the men increasingly took to the hills and mountains, forming isolated bands with little communication among them. Soldiers from Nicoletta's unit soon caught up with him as did local refugees. Among the young men joining Nicoletta was a university student called Guido Quazza.

Quazza had not been actively political in his student days. He was morally against fascism and contributed essays to a clandestine newspaper in 1942. But he did not get involved in an ideological sense, on the whole choosing to watch from the sidelines as he continued his historical studies. He was called up for active army service early in September 1943, just days before Italy surrendered to the Allies. For several months Quazza hid in the mountains with friends, finally joining Nicoletta's unit in February 1944. Quazza kept a diary at that time, one of the few day-by-day accounts of partisan life as it took place rather than as a memoir.

Right, **Guido Quazza.**
Below, **his official identification card inscribed with his pseudonym, "Guido Berti."**

September 3, 1943, Friday. Card arrives requesting me to present myself at [Army] headquarters in Vercelli. Go to see aunt and Lino. The British have landed in Calabria.

September 6, Monday. 25-hour trip in troop train [from Turin] continually interrupted by alarms and delays. We arrive in Rome. . . . Frightening ruins [from Allied bombings] in cities along the way, Livorno, Pisa, Grossetto, Civitavecchia and Rome.

September 8, Wednesday. Work-out with the regulars. Frascati bombed. Spent evening in barracks. Great news at 10:15 PM: Italy has asked for an armistice! Officers and men indescribably happy and waiting to start fighting the Germans. Many concerned as news sinks in.

September 9, Thursday. At 3 AM my unit leaves to defend Centocello [airport] against Germans, until 9 AM. We encounter a Tiger Tank. I return on foot, a mess, for a brief rest. . . . Alarms in the evening, fear of attack by Germans. Always at the ready. Much shooting nearby.

September 10, Friday. They tell us a cease-fire has been signed between Italians and Germans. We hope to return home soon. In the afternoon alarming rumors circulate. Much confusion in the battalion: officers try to undermine the general desire to leave. Some run off. Atmosphere of organizing uncertainty. I am one of the few calm ones.

September 11, Saturday. At 11 AM 30 Germans led by a colonel arrive at the barracks, disarm the guards and order us to bring all weapons to Monte Soere. At noon I leave and walk 9 km. to Tor Sapienza where, at 2:40, I catch the train to Pescara.

September 12, Sunday. 17-hour trip in converted box-car to Pescara, change trains. During trip people very friendly towards us soldiers, as were railroad workers. Trains from north bring news of danger of inspection by Germans, who are sending people to Germany. We get off at noon at Civitanovo Marche to try to find civilian clothes. . . . At 9 PM we continue north. It is a disheartening spectacle to see an entire army in disarray.

September 14, Tuesday. At 1:40 PM home again [Borgata Quazza, near Turin] after 61 hours of travel.

September 15, Wednesday. Rome Radio announces German order for all Italian soldiers to turn themselves in.

September 16, Thursday. The situation keeps getting worse. . . . Turn oneself in, escape to Switzerland, or hide in the mountains? I'm tending towards the last and am trying to convince my reluctant friends.

September 18, Saturday. Getting ready to leave. Razor, mirror, hairbrush, binoculars, medicines, scissors, shoe polish, geographical maps and Piedmont map, combs, card, shoelaces, pencil, knife, fountain pen, books, flashlight, diary, briefcase, wallet, three towels, two undershirts, candles, two batteries, two brown sweaters, a heavy black sweater, a hat, ten handkerchiefs, paper, black socks. Alfonso came to discuss food supplies.

September 20, Monday. At 8 PM Giorgio, Renato and I left with 60-lb. sacks on our backs. At 1 AM we met Lino, Dario, Dante, Alfonso, Carlo and Uncle Gildo. After nine hours of an exhausting walk, part of it in the dark, in fog and in rain and in the sun, we reached the *baita* (at about 1500 meters) at 10 AM. We decided to camp there for a while: Giorgio, Carlo and Uncle Gildo went home.

The next few months were spent in comparative isolation. Quazza read a great deal and continued to prepare for his exams. Different members of the group took turns going for food, cooking, chopping wood. Occasionally one of them would go home for a few days and come back with news heard from Radio London, the only outside source of news they would trust. No move was made to join any of the militant partisan groups, and when winter set in the men decided to take a chance and return to their families until spring.

Quazza stayed home until late February, when he was jolted into action by the news that he had been denounced as a partisan to the local Fascists and that they were looking for him. If he was found at home not only would he be taken away, but the house would be burned down and his parents arrested, perhaps even killed. Having been denounced as a partisan, Quazza decided it was time to join them and he chose a unit (Nicoletta's) in the Val Sangone area, which he knew well. As the diary entries show, this time it was no longer a "camping out" adventure, but a commitment based on principle and necessity.

February 25, 1944, Friday. I am very enthusiastic about my new companions with whom I share a desire to fight the Fascists and a new sense of patriotism, a new spirit of sacrifice. We have joined together in a warm and passionate atmosphere.

Above, **Quazza (right, wearing dark glasses) and members of his brigade in Val Sangone in 1945.**
Right, **a patriot's body hangs in a town square. The Germans often forbade anyone to cut down the victim until several days had passed.**

By April, Quazza was a full-fledged guerrilla.

April 1, Saturday. At Cumiano, Nino and five men attacked 300 Fascists and there was a massacre. They were joined by Nicoletta who completed the job: 40 dead Fascists and 35 prisoners, among them two Germans and one officer. One dead on our side. The people of Giaveno cheer our men as we descend to Pontepietra to block the road.

April 4, Tuesday. In retaliation, the Germans shot 57 civilians in Cumiano [men ranging in age from 16 to 70] even after the parish priest got from the partisans the concessions the Nazis wanted.

As the partisans attacked more vigorously, the Nazis increased their pressure on the local citizenry. Anyone caught helping the partisans was tortured and frequently killed, the body hung in a marketplace where it was displayed for days. Relatives were forbidden to take it down for burial. In spite of the brutal persecution, the small hamlets of Val Sangone almost totally supported the partisans. The communication network devised by these villagers was almost as important to the Resistance forces as the food supplied by the peasants. The partisans had very few shortwave radios and telephones were out of the question. To coordinate their activities they relied mostly on women and children taking messages back and forth. A small boy trudging up a hillside with a basket of potatoes might be relaying a verbal instruction, or even carrying a letter hidden in his shoe. The basket of laundry on a woman's head could include a handkerchief with a coded message scribbled on it.

Nicoletta's men had established excellent rapport with the six villages of Val Sangone. When there were lulls in military action the partisans would help with farm chores, chop wood, make repairs and in many ways substitute for the men who were no longer around. The partisans were also able, sometimes, to defuse the wrath of the Nazis by means of prisoner exchange. Although it was difficult for the partisans to guard and feed prisoners in their makeshift camps, bartering lives was one way to save them and the original "shoot to kill" order was modified, especially in the case of Nazi officers. Quazza notes in his diary:

June 27, Tuesday. I spent the day in bed. In the evening, we received orders to be ready to go down to Trana. Giulio Nicoletta was able to exchange Germans for Fassino and civilians.

Nicoletta remembers that day. (The week before he had been made commander of all the forces in the valley.) The Nazis had agreed to meet with him to negotiate a prisoner exchange involving civilians. Nicoletta and the parish priest of Trana drove to the rendezvous, a road near Trana just beyond the bridge over the Sangone river. It was a hot day and Nicoletta was wearing cut-off shorts and sneakers. He did not carry a gun and a white flag fluttered above the windshield of his battered Fiat.

The road to Trana was lined (and still is) with locust trees and huge bushes of Queen Anne's lace. Ten Germans awaited them at the appointed spot, in full dress uniform and led by a major who clicked his heels in greeting, Nicoletta said, "Just like a Siegfried." The proposal was to exchange 25 Germans for three partisans and 50 civilian hostages from Trana held by the Nazis. Nicoletta refused to make final arrangements until the priest had made sure the civilians were released. The Cumiano massacre in April was too vivid a memory. While Nicoletta waited, trying to make small talk with the Germans, the priest drove to Trana. On his return, Germans were exchanged for partisans, and Nicoletta rejoined Quazza and his men who had been hidden nearby in case of a surprise attack by the Germans.

As commander of the 43rd Sergio de Vitis Division, Nicoletta had to coordinate the activities of the seven units which made up the division. He also had to establish both military and political rapport with the central Piedmont Committee of National Liberation (CLN), with other partisan forces in the area and above all, with the local population. By the summer of 1944 the Resistance was becoming a unified force in which all sections of the population participated. Local CLNs had become firmly established: even a small town like Giaveno (one of the communities in Val Sangone) had a CLN which could relay information and instructions from the Central Turin CLN (and through it to the Committee of National Liberation for Northern Italy—CLNAI—

headquartered in Milan) to partisan commanders. Men like Van-zetti, who worked closely with the American OSS, since Spring had also been able to put the partisans in direct radio communication with the liberated South. The resulting increase in parachute drops of weapons and supplies had boosted the effectiveness and the morale of the embattled North.

Parachute drops were generally made at night, although if an area was securely in partisan hands sometimes a daytime drop was viable. Imaginative code phrases were used to indicate that the coast was clear: "Albert's chocolate," "the world is round," "the marmot sleeps," "Lauretta is pretty"—and even "fried potatoes." A great deal of careful planning, much of it by short-wave radio, went into each air drop. A target date and precise location had to be established. Contingency codes were necessary in case either end had to cancel the operation. On the receiving end frequently two and sometimes three listening posts were involved, to allow for possible transmission failure or for an operator suddenly having to abandon his equipment. (Giorgio, the Neapolitan radio operator, had hit upon the novel idea of hiding his equipment in a row of beehives. Except for a few stings, he operated there undisturbed until the end of the war.)

The reception area had to be secured. If it was a night drop a hollow in the hills was safest, so that flashlights and signal fires could not be spotted by the Germans. (Smokeless materials were used in building the fires.) Men had to be posted at strategic spots around the pinpoint to rapidly hunt down the parachutes. Road-blocks had to be set up and manned, in case German soldiers accidentally approached the pinpoint area, or if they had inter-cepted a decoded message. Advance planning was kept as secret as possible and was revealed only at the last moment to those who would participate, because of the ever-prevalent danger that spies might have infiltrated the partisans.

As soon as the radio operator received the message that a plane was on its way, he had to relay the information to the division commander, who would then alert those who were to be present at the pinpoint. A single plane could haul a ton and a half

Partisans guard the signal fire as an Allied plane approaches to drop supplies by parachute.

Partisans examine small motorcycles dropped by parachute from Allied planes.

Vanzetti inspects shortwave radio equipment hidden in beehives.

of machine guns and other supplies. (American planes flew 70 percent of the completed sorties in Italy and dropped 68 percent of the tonnage.) The multicolored parachutes would drift down, as one partisan described them, ". . . like many huge flowers. Many would get caught in the tall pines. A red, but very vivid red, electric, like the backdrops in a theatre; an electric color, not a dead one. They were red, blue and yellow but a yellow yellow: it was beautiful to see those enormous flowers." The color of the parachute indicated what it was carrying. Most desirable was a black and white parachute, from which a big mattress dangled. Inside the mattress would be complete radio transmitting equipment. Huge cans were attached to the others, containing cigarets, coffee, cocoa, sugar and clothing or dismantled machine guns, with instructions sometimes very difficult to follow.

Once the parachutes were on the ground the men and women assigned to retrieve them moved quickly to unload the contents. The parachutes themselves and the empty containers were usually given to the local people in payment for the use of their horses and wagons loaned by them to carry away the contents of the drop. The material then had to be divided and delivered to various partisan units. The drops were crucial to partisan warfare, supplementing the weapons they were able to capture from the Germans and the Fascists. Sometimes there were bitter disputes among the partisan units, each accusing the other of taking an unwarranted share of a drop. Fair distribution of the goods was the responsibility of each unit commander. At times the British seemed to favor the autonomous (non-political) units at the expense of the Garibaldi (Communist) Brigades. In spite of the in-fighting, most of the material reached the partisans needing it with the exception of some intercepts by the Germans or by civilians involved in the black market.

Essential as the weapons were, the little luxuries like cigarets and coffee also filled a desperate need. As the mountain bands grew into large military units, feeding and clothing them became a serious problem and luxuries became nonexistent. The CLNAI, through the regional CLNs, provided most of the funds required by the partisans but sometimes money was slow in arriving, or insufficient. Quazza noted in his diary that he received his first pay three months after joining the unit in Val Sangone. Many of the men were the sole support of their families, to whom they gave whatever pay they received. The local populace had to be reimbursed for the food and whatever else they supplied, though when money ran short they had to be satisfied with receipts promising postwar payment. Barter arrangements also thrived. In quiet times partisans would cut down trees and exchange the wood for food. The black market was another source of financing. Thanks to friendly workers and guards in the main Fiat Mirafiori plant, there was no interference with well-planned raids on the factory. The partisans would drive off with more cars and trucks than they needed, which they would then sell on the black market, often to the Germans.

Although the partisans now functioned as military units, unlike a regular army, bureaucratic procedures were kept to a minimum. Each commander had full authority over his unit. Officers were elected or appointed on the basis of leadership and ability, not because of previous military experience. A youth like Quazza could (and did) quickly become an officer. Duties, even cooking, were assigned in rotation, the only exception being the chores assigned to foreigners among them. In the Sergio de Vitis units there were 28 Russians and 35 Czechs, which created a considerable language problem though they were very able fighters. Guard duty was most important to the safety of a unit, so that it would never be caught by surprise. Weapons and quarters were inspected regularly and breaches of discipline were promptly punished. Punishments varied from a cut in tobacco ration to expulsion from the unit and on rare occasions, the death sentence, usually given for collaborating with the enemy. If a death sentence was involved there would be a jury trial.

Many units required that a new recruit sign an oath of loyalty and obedience. In the case of more politicized units associated with specific parties, a vow was also taken to fight both the Germans and the Fascists, and to restore in Italy a social and political order worthy of a free nation. As the Resistance movement grew stronger and more unified, its aims began to broaden beyond the initial objective of fighting the invader. By mid-1944 even members of the autonomous units (like Nicoletta's) were holding political discussions. The Communist Garibaldi Brigades had from the beginning included "commissars" in their organizational make-up, who would explain the party line to its members. Quazza's diary entries for mid-1944 reflect how the units were maturing politically and militarily:

July 25, Sunday. The organization of the platoon is getting better. Today the cooks prepared excellent gnocchi. We beat the Reano platoon 16 to 7 at soccer. In the evening I talked with Franco C. about the problems of the unit: attacks, organization, political questions. . . . We learned new details about the burning of 33 houses in Orbassano and the hanging of two partisans, two civilians and two others in Cumiano. Frico is in Grandubbione: the squadron of Giaveno, guilty of embezzlement, has been disarmed by Giulio Nicoletta.

September 21, Thursday. I buy drinks all around to celebrate a year with the partisans. Our Campana unit has won a citation for accomplishing 31 attacks in a few days.

September 22, Friday. I organized an evening attack on the Fiat Mirafiori plant, 20 of us surprising the guards and after being in there three hours we left with two Fiats 626 and eight Fiats 1100—and the guards' guns! We could have taken more if we had more drivers. At my order, we approached a road block rapidly with our headlights blazing, and the Germans thought we were some of theirs! We passed through and later we sold some of the cars.

September 23, Saturday. Pio carried out a beautiful raid on a German command pack in Turin: he brought back two officers, a suitcase full of documents and 2 1/2 million lire.

But though the mountain units were scoring many victories, their problems were increasing too. As new recruits swelled their ranks, not infrequently bitter disagreements developed between them and the early partisans. It was also getting more difficult to screen the newcomers properly, and spies too often were slipping in. To further complicate matters snow had begun to fall early in November, making camp life very difficult.

Then came a severe blow. On November 13, Gen. Harold R. Alexander, commander of the Allied Forces in Italy, advised the Resistance to sharply reduce activities and prepare for a difficult winter which would hamper the Allied offensive. The message signalled to the Nazis that attacks on the partisans should intensify because they were now in a weakened position. Regardless of Alexander's advice, the partisans knew they had to leave the mountains for the winter. But now the withdrawal had been made even more difficult.

Nicoletta's division had continued to make forays on German forces in spite of the Alexander proclamation. In December a disastrously uncoordinated airdrop convinced Nicoletta that it was time for him, too, to join the migration to the *pianura* (the plains). The daylight airdrop, unprecedented in size to that date (300 to 400 parachutes) was apparently to have supplied all partisan units in the Piedmont zone, and had been made in spite of Alexander's warning that help would be curtailed. Owing to a slip-up on the part of an Allied officer operating in the region, the planes arrived without advance notice. The partisans, taken by surprise (Nicoletta was away at the time) thought a paratrooper action was taking place because of the huge number of parachutes. They rushed to the site, only to be confronted and greatly outnumbered by German troops that happened to be near the drop area. The Germans not only seized all the parachute supplies, but they forced the partisans to scatter and take refuge in any mountain crevice that would hide them. In the bargain, they discovered most of the campsites used by the partisans, removing their weapons and supplies and burning the huts.

By the time Nicoletta returned, many of his partisans had been captured. Essentially it was the end of the 43rd Division as a mountain unit. Nicoletta was forced to leave Russian and Czech ex-prisoners in a safe mountain hideout. It would have been too difficult to disguise them as Italians, especially since they did not speak the language. They could still function to a limited degree, attacking the few German Alpine guards braving the mountain winter. The remaining partisans were furnished with suitable identification and, disguised as civilians, they turned their attention to sabotage on the plains.

In early December the CLN's military command had given its official answer to General Alexander:

We must make it absolutely clear that the partisan war is not, on the part of the Italian people and the patriots who have taken up arms, a mere whim, an idle caprice to be refrained from at will. It arose from the vital necessity of defending our material, moral and social heritage; this is the supreme cause for which we have been fighting and must continue to fight day after day. It was and is the duty of every patriot to participate in this war in order that he may retain his individual freedom, his right to live.

The war must go on. There must be no relaxation, no weakening. On the contrary, the struggle must be intensified, the armed forces engaged in it greatly increased. We cannot, indeed, we must not, consider any suggestion calculated to deflect us from our purpose: that of widening the sphere of our activities, bringing still larger numbers into the field, and fighting on with an ever-growing resolution and will to win.

The effect of this statement was electrifying. Both patriots and civilians had been dismayed by the Alexander proclamation, which was viewed as a betrayal at a time when help was most needed. Heartened by the CLN statement and by the progress of the war in Europe, the Resistance movement forged ahead. Also, Allied policy reversed itself to some degree as airdrops continued, though on a much reduced scale, owing to bad weather and to the diversion of many planes to the European theatre.

Nicoletta's men, now operating in the plains, were concentrating on destroying German supply lines. Armored trucks travelling through the *pianura* were at a tactical disadvantage, because the winding roads were lined with tall hedgerows which provided perfect cover for sneak attacks. The partisans, thoroughly familiar with the region, could disappear instantly up a lane, leading the pursuing Germans into a neat trap. The local railway line was easily sabotaged; tracks and railway bridges were the main targets. As fast as tracks were repaired, they were again blown up as was the rolling stock using the lines. Although the former mountain partisans were badly outnumbered and totally lacking in heavy armaments such as cannon and tanks, they were able to cripple Nazi troop movements either through their own efforts or by radio messages to Allied headquarters, which would guide Allied air attacks.

In February 1945 Nicoletta decided, with the agreement of the men, to make Quazza joint commander of the Ruggero Vitrani Brigade, replacing a man who had been severely wounded. Though no longer a mountain division, on the *pianura* the 43rd had again become a formidable adversary for the Nazis. The division, which had been politically neutral from its earliest days, was now being seriously pressured by the Action Party to join its ranks. For a year the division had also been approached by the Garibaldi Brigades (Communist) and the Matteoti units (Socialist). Quite a few partisans in the 43rd Division favored the Action Party, whose members were sometimes called GL or Giellisti because they had belonged to the defunct Guistizia Liberta movement. Others were partial to the Garibaldini. Nicoletta recalls a night-long conversation with Duccio Galimberti, a GL leader later killed by the Nazis. The upshot of all the pressuring was an amicable agreement to live and let live. Although in 1945 half of one Sergio de Vitis unit did join the GL, essentially the 43rd remained autonomous, though totally loyal to the CLN and its objectives.

Quazza was concerned about the attempts to politicize the division. He himself was deeply involved in local affairs, especially in helping the civilians cope with Fascist administrative orders.

March 21, 1945, Wednesday. I go to Giaveno. . . . Discuss with Paolo C. the roundup (ordered by the Fascists) of livestock in Giaveno and how to prevent it.

March 22, Thursday. Spoke with Rodolfo, Commissar of the Party of Action for Val Sangone. Pressure to get my Brigade into the Guistizia e Liberta (GL). Complete failure of the Giaveno roundup: not one of the 270 beasts were carried off.

March 23, Friday. Relentless discussion about Division joining GL. The Campana Brigade agrees to. I, Falzone, Franco N. [Guilio Nicoletta's brother] and Cecco are opposed because we don't think the men are politically mature enough to make a choice. . . . Guilio gives us orders for counter-sabotage of the bridges.

Partisan involvement in local politics became inevitable, especially as the CLNs took over increasing responsibility for governing occupied territories, even to running schools and hospitals, as Fascists began to disappear from their posts. The teamwork between partisans and civilians now went far beyond supplying the partisans with food and a hiding place. In Valle Stura the partisans organized and participated in the establishment of an efficient air raid warning system complete with a squadron trained to extinguish fires and help the wounded. In Valle Gesso civilians helped partisans set up a massive barbed wire blockade: the war of liberation was now clearly a common cause.

Daily living in the villages was very different from the close companionship of the mountain *baita*. In their new life on the plains the partisans had to use false names and false IDs (Nicoletta called himself Giulio Piperis). They mingled as inconspicuously as possible among farmers and townspeople. Some found legitimate work but many were listed as having fictitious jobs as well as false names. The local people usually saw through the covers but there was little danger of being denounced, in spite of substantial rewards offered for information about partisan activities. This is not to say that there weren't complaints about the partisans. They were criticized for taking supplies from stores and not making good on reimbursement; for arbitrarily requisitioning the livestock of a peasant and even for selling foodstuffs needed by the villagers to the city black market, in order to get lire for dynamite and weapons—also on the black market. But the consensus seems to be that as the war dragged on, the partisans were generally accepted as an essential civic as well as a military force.

In the spring of 1945 Nicoletta regrouped his units to make a final all-out attack on the Germans. By mid-April the war in Europe was almost over. In Italy, the Allies had moved rapidly up the peninsula and were now approaching the major northern cities of Genoa, Milan and Turin. The Resistance leaders were determined to liberate those cities before the Allies arrived, to prove to themselves and the world that Italy had earned its way back among free nations. In Turin, where the Nazis had a large-scale headquarters, a general strike on April 18 set the stage for the planned uprising which would get rid of the Germans. When the Piedmont CLN learned on April 24 that the Allies had crossed the Po River near Mantua, the signal was given for the Turin uprising to begin on April 26–27.

Partisan units, with Nicoletta's men in the vanguard, quickly headed towards the city to join the patriots in the long-awaited uprising. Quazza noted in his diary:

April 27, Friday. At 1 PM we began to march from Beinasco towards Turin. My Brigade was in the center of the column, together with Nino's. We occupy the Fiat Mirafiori plant and the Hippodrome. There were scenes of delirious enthusiasm as we passed through towns and into the city. We seemed to be dreaming.

April 28, Saturday. Parades of partisans, enormous amount of traffic, incredible enthusiasm, newspapers are already being published, the local CLN is in control. Meanwhile the Allies are still far from us.

The rejoicing was at its peak when the first Allied troops arrived on May 2. On May 6 the partisans paraded triumphantly through the center of the city, and then paid farewell visits to the villages. Most of Nicoletta's men were from the Piedmont region, but a fair number were from the South. Besides the Czechs and Russians, foreigners to be repatriated included 13 Frenchmen, several Argentinians and Mexicans, a South African, two Germans and two Americans. Giulio Nicoletta (who received a silver medal for valor) did not return to Calabria but instead remained in Turin. Vanzetti, now an American citizen, is president of his own company in Massachusetts. And Quazza, a history professor at Turin University, is also president of the National Resistance Research Center in Milan.

The partisan dead of the Val Sangone units are buried on a hill near one of the *baitas* that was home for some during the war. A small gray stone building nearby contains an altar and six pews where people sometimes come to sit in the quiet and remember. The altar is flanked by two terra-cotta statues of Saint George and the dragon and of Saint Sebastian. Behind them are draped the flags of the Allies. On the walls are 3 by 5 plastic cards with the names of the dead and their photographs. Pine trees surround the building, and only the birds and a mountain stream break the silence.

Giulio Nicoletta leads his men in a triumphant procession through the streets of Turin, after the city's liberation.

=4=
Words and Music: The Voice of the Resistance

THERE IS a popular myth that Italians are born singers, and that they burst into song at the slightest provocation. Although neither behavior is a reality, the songs of the Resistance were perhaps the most sincere expressions of the feelings as well as the thoughts of the patriots and their supporters. Together with the newspapers and bulletins circulated by the political parties and by almost every partisan unit, the words and the music communicated to the rest of Italy both the progress and the spirit of the war against naziism and fascism.

Unlike the press, whose role was chiefly to inform, the songs of the Resistance reflected the hopes and fears, and often humor, of men and women patriots. In most cases the melodies were not original. Some were popular tunes, others were adaptations of Italian Army Alpine Corps favorites or of battle songs from other wars.

Many of the words of these songs were composed around a campfire in the evening, when the partisans were relaxing after a typically harrowing day. One of the favorites was set to the tune of a traditional peasant song of the Romagna called ''E Canta la Sighela'' (''The Cicada Sings''):

> The cicada is singing: Taia, Taia
> The corn is for the master, the straw for the peasant

The cicada is singing: Tula, Tula
The corn is for the master, the chaff for the peasant
The cicada is singing and it gives a laugh
The corn is for the master, the peasant gets the chaff.
But the Germans, the Fascists and the master
Will fight about the sheaf they have made
And all will go to hell.

(The word sheaf is "fascio" in Italian and refers to the Fascist emblem.)

The dirge-like "Julia" of the first World War became the melody for the mournful "Pity for the Dead."

Up there on the mountains a black flag flies
A partisan has died fighting the war.
Another Italian dies under other skies,
Under other skies you'll find an Alpine soldier
Fallen in Russia.
But before dying he prayed
That God would put a curse on the ally who betrayed him
Leaving him to die beside the Don, as he fled.
German traitors, the Alpine soldier is dead
But another fighter has arisen
The partisan fights his battle now.
Germans and Fascists—get out of Italy.
We cry out, in pity for the dead.

Not all the songs were sad. One of the most popular was a very long, sarcastic and rather bawdy ballad about Badoglio and King Victor Emmanuel, set to music from an operetta called "Il Boccaccio." A sampling of the verses reflects the contempt felt for both Badoglio and the king.

Badoglio, oh Pietro Badoglio
Fattened well by the *fascio*,
With your worthy partner Vittorio
You have really busted our balls!

You called back the *squadristi*
You threw anti-Fascists in jail,
The shirt wasn't black anymore
But Fascism was still master.

While you were busily blowing
The horn for Petacci's lover,
Bombs were falling on Italy
And Vittorio's pants were falling!

One song became as popular in Italy as "Lily Marlene" was for the Allies (especially the British), and like "Lily Marlene" the tune was imported. "Fischia il Vento" ("The Wind Whistles") was set to the melody of a Red Army song, "Katyusha." It ends with these defiant words:

The wind dies, the storm calms down,
The proud partisan returns home,
Waving his beautiful flag,
Victorious and free.

The songs did not die with the war. Some of them, among them two written for Alpine Corps melodies by Riccardo Vanzetti, are still popular in Italy today and have been recorded on cassettes.

The press was more prosaic in its style. Clandestine journals ranged from a few roughly mimeographed sheets to well printed city newspapers (usually fortnightlies) with a large circulation, as many as 20,000 a printing. Pamphlets explaining ideological positions were also produced by the parties, some of them as long as 200 pages. The city newspapers emphasized information rather than opinion, reporting spot news of battles and other partisan activities. They also provided bulletins on daily events of interest to civilians, such as warnings about Nazi or Fascist activities and tips on where to find food or other supplies. The most prolific publishers were the Communist (PCI) and Action (Pd'A) parties, whose papers were called, respectively, *L'Unita* (Unity) and *L'Italia Libera (Free Italy)*.

Each of the parties also tailored publications for specific audiences. The PCI covered the concerns of the industrial workers in its paper titled *La Fabbrica (The Factory)*. The same group was addressed by the Socialist party's *L'Operaio (The Worker)*. Peasant issues were the subject of *L'Azione Contadino (Peasant Action)* circulated by the Pd'A. The functional nature of these publications did not preclude a certain amount of political rhetoric, but on the whole they were practical and informative.

In the process of reporting the war news, the newspapers also made readers aware of changes taking place in the structure of Italian society. Liberated towns and villages administered by local CLNs were experiencing a radical change from Fascist dictatorship and manipulation. The CLNs asked civilians to participate in decisions, and to take part in managing affairs which affected their daily lives. The CLNs also had their own newspapers: In Milan, *La Liberazione,* in Turin, *La Riscossa Italiana (The Italian Revolt)* and in the Veneto, *I Fratelli d'Italia (The Brothers of Italy)*.

By the summer of 1944 almost every partisan outfit in the North had its own publication. (In central Italy the press was less organized and the issues appeared sporadically.) The partisan papers differed greatly from the "Trench journals" of World War I, which were usually inspired and edited by the Italian Army hierarchy and rarely reflected opinions of the ordinary soldier. Partisan journals emphasized news of their own battles and of fallen comrades, but they also supplied information about the entire war, received from Radio London and other clandestine sources. An effort was made to include the accomplishments of widely scattered partisan units in other regions.

Although party leadership sometimes complained about the relatively apolitical nature of many partisan papers, they recognized that polemics might detract from unification of the Resistance movement. A paper that succeeded quite well in bridging the gap between party proselytizing and objectivity was *Il Partigiano,* the journal of a Garibaldi Brigade in Liguria. Although the Garibaldi units were largely PCI-oriented, the four-page newspaper was essentially objective and factual. The first page featured an editorial signed ''Il Partigiano,'' which generally covered whatever was the most important news of the day. The second page was devoted to feature items and obituaries of fallen comrades. The third page contained bulletins on military action by the partisans under the heading ''Danger Zone: Infested by Rebels'' (a take-off on the warning commonly posted by the Nazis in partisan regions). The last page concentrated on news from liberated areas, telling how administrative, economic and social problems were being solved.

Il Partigiano, like most of the partisan papers, was written in a simple, straightforward style, forceful but unemotional, avoiding a dogmatic stance that might turn off some readers. An example is this appeal addressed to veterans of the former Fascist armed forces who had been sent back from Germany to serve with Mussolini's new Republican army: ''In every village you return to, the population flees from you and your Fascist officers (those men who even in Germany treated you worse than the Germans did) who order you to burn their homes. You have come back,

A cartoon making light of the daily life of the partisans.

but to fight on enemy territory? Every evening, in every section, 20, 30 refuse to answer your call: they have escaped with their weapons to zones liberated by the partisans. Leave these Fascists alone, before it is too late. Come with us: then you will really feel that you have come back to Italy.''

Women also launched a substantial clandestine press designed both to print news about their participation in the Resistance and to air the debate on womens' future role in a democratic society. The names of their newspapers reflected these interests: *Defense of the Female Worker, Woman's Voice, The Rebirth of Women, Women at War* and *The New Reality.*

The essence of the emotion conveyed by these songs and newspapers is captured by the late Italo Calvino. In the preface of his own book about the Resistance, *The Path to the Nest of Spiders,* he describes the feelings of those who had been part of the Resistance: ''We . . . did not feel crushed, defeated, beat! On the contrary, we were victors, driven by the propulsive charge of the just-ended battle, the exclusive possessors of its heritage. Ours was not easy optimism, however, or gratuitous euphoria. Quite the opposite. What we felt we possessed was a sense of life as something that can begin again from scratch.''

=5=
The Patriots of the City and the Countryside

THERE WERE approximately 224,000 militant partisans at war's end. Of these, some 63,000 were killed and over 33,000 badly wounded. To these figures must be added the many men and women who participated in the Resistance in other guises. Additionally, an estimated 15,000 to 20,000 civilians were murdered and some 5,000 were wounded.

Viewed against a population of 42 million, these figures may seem relatively small. However, the success of the partisans was possible only because they were supported by millions of factory and office workers, peasants, middle-class professionals and wealthy bankers and industrialists. Such mass participation was new in Italian history. Most of these people had not been political activists, certainly not in the preceding 20 years.

THE PATRIOTS OF THE CITY

In the cities, the first well-organized rebels were the men and women of a movement called "GAP" (*Gruppi de Azione Patriotica*—Groups for Patriotic Action). GAP was originally a Communist party movement, but in time membership cut across party lines. Organized into units of three or four people, the Gappists struck day and night in guerrilla-like attacks. These efforts were aimed at terrorizing an enemy who, until then, held in contempt the people they intended to control. The Milan GAP was already well-organized within a month of the Armistice. Early in October 1943 Gappists in that city captured Aldo Resega, the local secretary of Mussolini's new Republican Fascist party. Resega was tried and executed.

Just as the mountain partisans were harrassing German troop movements, the Gappist objective was to make the enemy in the city feel insecure everywhere: on the streets, in their armored cars, in restaurants and even within the four walls of their headquarters. A Gappist could be a man standing on a street corner, a woman on a bicycle or even a student (carrying a grenade in his book bag). Usually the target was a person of some importance, both because it was useful to eliminate him and because it helped destroy the image of German invincibility.

Although the hit and run tactics created the impression of a large network, GAP membership was limited. The units were entirely separate from each other, and in fact were unaware of each other's existence, so that if members of a unit were captured and tortured, they truthfully could not give away the identity of other members. Each GAP unit had a leader who reported to an overall commander. The rank-and-file Gappists were usually young people from all walks of life. The commanders were frequently longtime anti-Fascists, some of them veterans of the Spanish Civil War who brought the methodology of guerrilla warfare to city streets. Weapons were supplied from secret depositories.

Tactics were pretty much left up to unit leaders, but overall strategy was the province of the GAP commander, who in turn received orders from the local Committee of National Liberation and eventually also from the Allies, after communication was established. Once the target was agreed upon, the unit leader had to devise a plan of action. He would observe the daily habits of the intended quarry, where he went at what hour, who accompanied him, what route he took, etc. Then the leader had to decide which of his men (or women) was best suited to the task and discuss with him how to proceed. Service in GAP was voluntary and so was each action: if a person felt he could not undertake an assignment it was his responsibility to the group and to Italy, as much as to himself, to refuse. Nor was a refusal looked upon as dishonorable. Discipline in GAP in no way resembled traditional armed forces which relied on unquestioned obedience to rules and regulations. Discussion and argument were the order of the day, but once a plan was determined and accepted, loyalty and results were expected.

A Gappist's chief weapons were pistols and hand grenades. He had to be an expert marksman, because he would rarely have a second chance. Mishandled, a grenade could kill him as well as innocent bystanders. He had to have very steady nerves and a quick wit—courage goes without saying. Gappists liked to tell the story of a woman member carrying a load of grenades in her bicycle basket, covered with vegetables she had found in the country. When she was stopped by a German soldier who asked what she was carrying, she laughed and answered, "Bombs." He laughed too, and waved her on. Fear was a Gappist's worst enemy. Even when he carried out his mission successfully, he was haunted constantly by the possibility that the enemy might have seen him as he got away and would recognize him at some other time. The Gappists had one rule that was especially difficult to obey. If someone was wounded in a venture it was his companion's duty to rescue him. But if this was impossible, he was obligated to kill the fallen man rather than to let him fall into enemy hands to face torture, possibly inadvertently betraying his companions.

Two episodes are most often recalled in the annals of Gappist history. The first took place in Florence at the popular Café Paskowski in Piazza della Repubblica, then called Piazza Vittorio Emanuele. The Café had long been a favorite meeting place for Florentine society: now they were joined by the Nazi/Fascist hierarchy. Among those who frequented the Café was the much hated and feared Mario Carità, head of the Fascist secret police in Florence. The Gappist leadership decided it was time to get rid of Carità, and cocktail hour at the Café seemed the best time and place. A young couple was selected to carry out the assignment:

Tosca Buccarelli, the 18-year-old daughter of a longtime anti-Fascist and Antonio Ignesti, a 25-year-old with a serious lung disease but a great deal of courage. The two were to act like an engaged couple. For weeks ahead of the designated date—February 8—they met at the Café frequently, exchanging loving looks and noticing where people habitually sat. The plot was to plant a bomb underneath a table near Carità's preferred location. A waiter, who was also a GAP collaborator, would screw a hook under the tabletop on which to hang a bomb. Once the explosive was set to go off, the couple would make their departure.

There was a good crowd at the Café on the 8th. The tall, blond Tosca—better known to her friends as Toschina—attracted a certain amount of attention but by now the habitués were used to her and her attentive escort. The couple ordered vermouth and began to chat. After a bit, Toschina drew a small, tissue-wrapped object from her purse. Simultaneously, Ignesti lit a cigaret and using the same match he ignited the wick of the bomb hidden in Toschina's package. She quickly slipped it under the table, groping for the hook. The latch on the bomb was too narrow and the bomb fell to the floor, the wick still burning. Toschina leaned down, quickly picked up the smoldering device, extinguished the flame with her fingers and dropped the bomb in her bag. However, an officer at the next table had noticed what she was doing and demanded to see what was in her purse. She said it was nothing of any interest and the two began to leave, but the officer followed them outside. Toschina managed to break away before he could grab her, but looking back as she ran she saw several men were now holding Ignesti. Tosca realized because of his poor health he might break down under torture. She went back and in the general confusion at her return, Ignesti somehow managed to slip off.

Toschina was taken to secret police headquarters where she was questioned by Carità himself, and then by Nazi agents. The questioning was followed by days of torture, sometimes watched by Carità and his mistress. Finally one of the interrogators, real-

izing the semiconscious girl would never talk in that state, had
her transferred to Santa Verdiana, the womens' prison run by
nuns. Mother Superior Ermelinda was instructed to nurse Toschina back to health and notify Carità when she was well enough
to be questioned again. Toschina was barely recognizable when
she was carried into the prison and for months she could hardly
move. Luckily Carità seemed to forget about her, but not so the
Gappists.

At dawn on July 9 several men in Nazi uniforms arrived at
the prison doors. They showed the guard a release document and
demanded that Tosca be produced immediately. As the guard went
to the telephone to confirm the order with the SS, the "Nazi
officer" drew his pistol and forced the guard to drop the phone.
The Mother Superior, hearing the commotion, came to investi-
gate. When she realized what the men were up to, she insisted
that all the political prisoners be freed (the prison also held ordinary criminals). She was afraid if Carità learned of Tosca's escape,
he would kill the others in reprisal. So though Toschina failed in
her original mission, she succeeded in saving many lives.

The other incident, which ended in one of the grimmest episodes of the Resistance, took place in Rome. Three hundred and
thirty-five men and boys paid with their lives for a Gappist attack
which caused the death of thirty-three German soldiers. Although
there are differing versions of what happened, the following account
is substantiated in interviews with Giorgio Amendola, a prominent member of the Resistance who had been an active anti-Fascist since 1926.

Amendola described how the plan evolved. As he sat at a café
in the Piazza di Spagna, he had observed that with Teutonic reg-
ularity a column of German guards passed by every day at the
same time, singing as they marched towards Via Rasella, as if to
prove how secure they felt in the streets of occupied Rome.
Amendola, then commander of the Garibaldi Brigades in the area,
gave the order to the Rome GAP commander to attack the column. As was customary, he left the details up to the commander.

At 3 PM on March 23, 1944 a road-sweeper was at work on
Via Rasella. The industrious man was actually a Gappist and a
good-sized bomb was concealed in his cleaning cart. Because Via
Rasella is a narrow street in a heavily populated area, several
Gappists hovered nearby, ready to keep passersby from walking
into the path of the road-sweeper. The blast was tremendous.
Thirty-two Germans were killed outright and one died shortly
after in a hospital. Lt. Colonel Kappler, chief of the SS in Rome,
immediately ordered that Italian political prisoners should pay for
the deaths on a ten-to-one ratio, though one account says that
Hitler himself wanted the ratio to be thirty-to-one. Only 280
political prisoners were in Roman jails at that time and some were
there only because they were Jews. To make up the deficit, the
Fascist chief of police simply rounded up at random men and
boys on the street. In their haste, the police miscounted and brought
the total to 335.

A Rome taxi driver, who found out later his uncle was among
the innocent victims, remembers seeing a line of trucks escorted
by armored cars heading out the Appian Way the next day. Their
destination was the Ardeatine Caves located just outside Rome,
near the ancient Christian catacombs of San Calisto. The prisoners were herded into the caves and sprayed for hours with
machine guns, until all were dead. Grenades were then thrown
into the entrance of the cave, blocking access to the bodies for
days. On the day of the massacre the German High Command
announced:

On the afternoon of March 23, 1944, certain criminal elements in
Rome attacked one of our military police columns as it was marching
along the Via Rasella. Caught by surprise, 32 of the men were killed
and a large number wounded. This outrage was the work of Badoglian
Communists, incited, it is believed, by the British and Americans. The
matter is being investigated. In order to prevent any more crimes of this
nature from being perpetrated, and in order to make it clear, once and
for all, that Germany and Italy, whose solidarity has again been reaffirmed, will not tolerate any further attempts at sabotage, the German
Command, after consultation at the highest level, decided that for every

German killed in this ambush, the lives of 10 Badoglian communists should be exacted. The execution of these criminals has already been carried out.

The Resistance lost many fine members in the massacre. The intention was to intimidate and there is no doubt the people of Rome were terrorized, but the Ardeatine murders became a symbol for the rest of Italy both of the cruelty of the Nazis and of the need to fight them. Some Italians criticized the Gappists for their attack, contending it was an unnecessarily provocative action which caused too many deaths of innocent people. Others said if the Gappist leaders had immediately surrendered themselves, perhaps the hostages would not have been taken. But as Amendola pointed out, the Nazis never asked for the leaders to give themselves up, nor did they lose any time in rounding up and killing the hostages. Sandro Pertini was not involved in the planning, but he said that in retrospect he totally agreed with the concept because it was the mandate of the Resistance to strike the enemy wherever and whenever possible. In any event, the Gappist policy was declared correct by a Rome Court of Appeals which in 1954 gave its verdict unanimously, saying ''Whoever, when the country is in a state of war, acts in the interests of the country, carries out his highest duty as a citizen.''

THE PATRIOTS OF THE COUNTRYSIDE

The mass participation of peasants in the Resistance was a new phenomenon in Italian history. Immediately after the September 8 Armistice, it was the peasants who harbored most of the hundreds of thousands of stranded Italian Army ex-soldiers and Allied ex-prisoners of war. The peasants' warm hospitality became legendary, and without their cooperation the first bands of mountain partisans could not have survived. Although most of the peasant class had been fairly apolitical to this point, in the North they had been exposed to socialist ideology. It is important to remember that Italy was a thoroughly agricultural society in the nineteenth century. Industrialization came late in the century, and was concentrated in the North. Trade unions did develop, and new political movements gained a foothold among factory workers. However, the principles of the Italian Socialist party, founded in 1892, appealed not only to workers but also to farmers, who had gained little as a result of the unification of Italy. In fact, as Prof. Norman Kogan has pointed out, "Italy was exceptional among continental countries in the support given to a socialist party by the countryside."

Mussolini, a native of northern Italy, was well aware of growing peasant-class unrest. In the early 1920s, Il Duce's *squadristi* had swept into the more troublesome regions, such as Emilia Romagna, to put a stop to upstart rebellions against landowners and to squash embryonic cooperative movements, echoes of the post-World War I strikes taking place in all the major cities. As Mussolini expanded his role of imperial conqueror in the 1930s, he stepped up his demands on the peasants, increasing forced requisition of agricultural output and taking their sons for his military adventures. These actions eventually became counterproductive to the Fascist cause, because it forced the peasants to begin to think politically.

The Germans had much the same objectives as the Fascist *squadristi*. When they took control of central and northern Italy after the Armistice, they regarded the peasantry as essential to the Nazi war effort for two reasons: as a source of foodstocks for Germany and German soldiers stationed in Italy, and as a reservoir of manpower for the German war machine. If farmers resisted, their homes and farms would be looted and burned. By terrorizing the peasants the Germans expected they would quickly subjugate them: the result was to be exactly the opposite, as they would soon find out.

Wherever Germans were bivouaced they were subjected to sabotage difficult to track down. Three-pronged nails on main roads ruined the tires of passing convoys; telephone lines were cut; and nighttime raids on parked vehicles caused them to be stripped of weaponry and gas, and sometimes to disappear alto-gether. The explanation was simple: hardly a farm household existed that was not hiding a vulnerable son or husband, or a disbanded soldier. When barns became unsafe, the ingenious peasants had created well-disguised underground hideaways in the fields. At night the men hidden there would emerge to exer-cise, do chores, and do what damage they could to the invader.

Farm women played an important role in this dangerous game. They had to be on constant alert for sudden appearances of Ger-mans trying to surprise the hidden men. The women developed many tricks for signalling each other that Germans were ap-proaching: special cries, a certain song, hanging a sheet from a window in a particular way. Sometimes a child would run from house to house to carry the warning. When the Germans arrived they would find only women and children and perhaps an old man. Where were the other men? ''In the woods, cutting fire-wood''; ''at the market delivering today's requisition''; ''at the mill, grinding wheat,'' were the stock answers.

At night, when the men came out of their holes they would learn from the women what might be the best targets for that night. The Germans usually remained in their quarters after dark, well aware that ambushes were easy for those familiar with every inch of the territory. This made it possible to hide explosives under a bridge a convoy would cross the next day, or to layer a road with mines carefully covered with dirt. But in spite of the inventive hiding places and other precautions, peasant casualties were heavy. A tragic example is the story of the Cervi brothers, which has become one of the legends of the Resistance.

In September 1943 the extended Cervi family—23 people in all—lived on a prosperous farm in Praticello, near Reggio Emi-lia. Reggio lies between the Appenines and the Po River, in the province of Emilia. Four of the sons of Alcide and Genoveffa were married and among them they had ten children, with one more on the way. The Cervis had come to Praticello in 1934 as tenant farmers on a dilapidated farm completely neglected by the absentee landowner. In ten years they had transformed the acreage, and the four cattle the Cervis brought with them were now a herd of fifty.

Alcide Cervi had great respect for knowledge. His neighbors marvelled at the boys who worked long hours in the hot sun, and then studied at night how to improve the crops. Most of the tenant farmers near the Cervis clung to traditional methods of cultivation and they regarded the Cervis as slightly mad. Of what use to poor peasants were books on mechanical harrows, irrigation, vine cultivation and mechanized cow stalls? Each of the Cervis concentrated on some aspect of farming, but they pooled their information and always planned their work together with their father.

Aldo, the third eldest, had the most education and was more familiar than the others with life beyond the farm and the village. He had done his compulsory stint in the Army to which had been added three years in prison, essentially for carrying out orders. On sentinal duty one night he had shot at a shadowy figure who refused to answer to the obligatory "Who goes there?" The person turned out to be a lieutenant colonel whose injured finger was enough to send Aldo to jail in Gaeta, a coastal town some seventy miles south of Rome. There Aldo was thrown in with some political prisoners, and there began his political education. His brothers and their father were to spend many long winter nights discussing what Aldo had learned.

When the family had finally saved enough money to buy a tractor, it was Aldo who went to Reggio to collect the machine. People for years later recalled the tractor trundling by on the main road, a huge map of the world draped over it like a flag. The map was kept in the house of a neighbor who had a radio, and Aldo showed his brothers how to follow world events on the map as the shadows of war deepened. It was not surprising that the boys should begin to question fascism. They resented the increasing demands made by the government on their prosperous farm, and their openly voiced opinions brought several visitations from Fascist officials, warning them to comply silently or face the consequences.

When the September 8 Armistice was announced the Cervis did not hesitate. Entirely on their own, they prepared to defend their home. Aldo, with his military experience, led a surprise attack on a nearby Fascist garrison where they found a good supply of guns. As disbanded soldiers began to roam the countryside, the Cervis provided a refuge. For a few months all went well, until one wet and foggy November morning. Six foreign soldiers and one Italian anti-Fascist were hidden in the hayloft of the Cervi barn and in the cow shed. Just as the family was gathering for breakfast, they heard the roar of several automobiles outside, followed by a sudden silence; and then a voice shouted "Cervis, surrender!" Under cover of the fog, preventing even early rising neighbors from giving a warning, a patrol of Fascist soldiers had surrounded the farm. There was no answer from the farmhouse, and keeping a prudent distance the soldiers opened fire. The Cervis grabbed their rifles and fired back, hiding behind the window blinds. The women and children quickly hid in the halls and inside rooms, where the bullets could not reach them. After two hours of stalemate the Fascists, not daring a direct attack on the house, set fire to the barn which formed one wing of the building.

The brothers instinctively turned to Aldo as their leader. With the house on fire,the obvious answer was to surrender or all of them as well as the refugees would perish in the flames. Aldo quickly decided on a course of action. Realizing that if they surrendered they might be tortured and give out information on the refugees, Aldo said he would take full responsibility for anything the Fascists might accuse them of. The others were to pretend not to know about Aldo's involvement with refugees or with the newly formed partisan groups. If absolutely necessary, Gelindo as the oldest could admit he suspected something but the others were to profess complete ignorance. Aldo hoped that by this maneuver at least Alcide and five sons would survive. So, led by their father, the eight men went into the courtyard, arms raised. They were immediately loaded into the cars and taken to Reggio, together with the refugees. The Fascist soldiers left behind put out the fire with the women's help, and then at gunpoint escorted the women and children to a neighboring farm, before returning to loot the empty Cervi compound.

Following is the report of the raid as it appeared in *Il Solco Fascista,* the Fascist daily newspaper of Reggio Emilia: "For some time the military police were aware that there were ex-prisoners of war in the province and that they moved frequently from one hiding place to another, so as not to be traced. For several days the police had observed that a principal hiding place seemed to be at the farm rented by the Cervi family. The refugees, with the consent of the Cervis, were hiding in the barn and there we found a Russian, two South Africans, a French De Gaullist, an Irishman and a renegade Italian. At dawn on the 25th the police surrounded the house and forced the occupants to surrender."

At that point, the only charge against the Cervis was harboring the refugees, who had been turned over to German authorities. The Cervis were taken to a prison in San Tommaso to await trial. While they were waiting, the secretary of a local Fascist party unit was assassinated near the railway station of Bagnolo-in-Piano at about 6 PM on December 27. Regional officials hastily convened at Fascist headquarters in Reggio and decided, a few hours later, on a reprisal which was announced the next day in *Il Solco Fascista:* "The Party secretary of Bagnolo-in-Piano has been villainously killed. The Tribunal has condemned to death eight individuals and the sentence has been carried out." The Cervi brothers and a refugee were the scapegoats. The article went on to say that the eight had confessed to conniving with Communists and to armed violence against the State, and also to have plotted to overthrow the government.

Alcide, inexplicably, was not included in the execution. When he protested at being separated from his sons at dawn of the 28th, the prison guards told him "You're an old man. Go back to sleep." Alcide thought the brothers were being taken away for the trial, and for days he waited for the verdict. An Allied air attack on January 8 destroyed the prison, enabling Alcide to escape. When

The Cervi family, seven sons and two daughters. All sons were killed by the Germans and their home virtually destroyed.

The memorial to the seven Cervi brothers, executed by the Germans on false charges.

he finally arrived at his half-burned home he learned the truth.

The Cervis, like so many peasant families in the first months of the German occupation, had fought the enemy almost alone. They were not part of a partisan group because the Resistance had not yet become a unified force in the countryside. As the Resistance movement became more cohesive, peasant participation increased rapidly. In the Romagna, eventually 70 percent of the partisans were peasants. The famous Florentine Brigata Sinigaglia had a 40 percent peasant membership. The memoirs of a member of that brigade record a revealing conversation between Gigi, the political leader of the group, and Pino, the oldest son of a peasant family and a recent recruit. As they rested in the shade of a chestnut tree, Pino expressed his resentment of the conventional view of the "apolitical peasant." "Why, Gigi," he asked, "do city workers insist on thinking of us as reactionary? Believe me, their remarks offend me. I realize we're behind the times because of our isolated country life with no one to keep us up-to-date. But you can see for yourself that when the time comes to protect our rights, we're inferior to no one."

During the Spring of 1944 the Committees of National Liberation, originally a city development, had become strong regional organizations with well-established lines of communication between city and rural areas. Meanwhile peasants and farmers had begun to form local committees to try to protect themselves more efficiently. With the organizational help of the CLN, there evolved in the countryside the counterpart of the more politically oriented GAP. The new organization was called SAP (Squadre di Azione Patriottica—Squads for Patriotic Action).

The squads first appeared in the Emilia region as groups of four or five armed men and women, civilians prepared to go on the offensive rather than merely defend their homes and families. To ensure the security of the farms it was necessary first to disrupt enemy operations. Sappists attacked enemy barracks, waiting until only a few guards were left, overpowering them, and leaving with a good supply of weapons. Sometimes they set fire to the barracks as they left (taking a leaf out of the Nazi book), or they crept up at night, hurling grenades in the windows as the soldiers slept. Of major importance was the harassment of troop movements and the severance of communications between Nazi headquarters in different towns. On another level, SAP hampered requisition of foodstuffs, assaulting or even bribing the Fascist agents who supervised collections. SAP spread to towns and cities, operating on a level quite separate from GAP but equally effective.

All this activity, often in concert with the strategy of the mountain partisans, began to intimidate the enemy, who finally realized they faced an increasingly rebellious Italy. Now many sections of the North were under control of the partisans. As the peasants in the Resistance-controlled areas became less fearful of reprisals they were able to work more closely with the Sappists and to provide more help to the saboteurs. SAP units were also being formed among plant and office workers in towns and among students and teachers. This network could provide valuable information about the enemy. Most importantly, a new feeling of unity was being created which would make possible coordinated, strategic action.

The Nazi reaction to this ferment was terrorism. One of the communities to bear the full brunt of their fury was Marzabotto, a small town a few miles from Bologna. The Sappist movement had found especially rich soil for growth in Marzabotto. A farming community with a long history of independent behavior and rebellion, Marzabotto (like Bologna) had elected a Socialist mayor in the 1920s. To the dismay of the landowners, this situation was compounded by the appointment of peasants and workers to administrative positions in the town government, rather than the conservative farm managers the owners could depend on to protect their interests. Shortly after the elections Fascist *squadristi,* supported by the landowners, made their appearance, administering their customary beatings and threats. But anti-Fascist sentiment, supported by the local priests, simmered throughout the years of the Fascist regime.

Immediately after the September 8 Armistice, the community began not only to hide *sbandati* (disbanded soldiers) but to organize groups for action long before SAP existed. Quite a few of Marzabotto's own *sbandati* had managed to make their way back to the village, and these men formed the nucleus of the Resistance there. Chief among them was Mario Musolesi, who had adopted the nickname "Il Lupo"—the wolf. Many partisans used pseudonyms, largely to protect their real identity, and peasants were especially fond of animal names. *Lupo* was a favorite, but there were also *volpe* (fox), *corvo* (crow), *pecora* (sheep) and names derived from natural phenomena like *terremoto* (earthquake), *tempesta* (tempest) or *fulmine* (lightning).

Musolesi had fought in Ethiopia. He had been an excellent soldier and had won two medals and a promotion to sergeant major. However, on his return to civilian life he had been denied permission to study mechanics because he was the son of a Socialist and had publicly made known his own anti-Fascist sentiments. On reenlisting, he was given a demotion because of his opinions. Musolesi happened to be stationed in Rome on September 8, 1943. He was among those who fought desperately at Porta S. Paolo, one of the gateways to Rome, to halt the columns of advancing Germans. While Musolesi was trying to return home, Marzabotto was briefly rejoicing in the end of the war against the Allies. The euphoria was short-lived. German troops arriving in the area quickly made clear that requisition of crops would continue and even worse, that all returned soldiers would have to report for duty with the Germans.

There were some Fascists among the citizens of Marzabotto and these joined forces with the Germans. When Musolesi arrived back home, he was quickly denounced as a troublemaker by the Fascists and held in the barracks of the local police. Fortunately his brother Guido had managed to get possession of some weapons. At an opportune moment he appeared at the barracks with a pistol and hand grenades, threatening to blow the place up if Mario was not released. The officer in charge gave in, and Mario left to hide in the nearby woods. He was soon joined by some 40 men from Marzabotto and neighboring villages and by English, South African and Russian ex-prisoners. This group was the nucleus of a band to become one of the most renowned of the Resistance, the Stella Rossa (Red Star). Most of the villagers were aware of Stella Rossa's existence and did what they could to supply it with food and even with a few guns.

In the beginning Stella Rossa concentrated on sabotaging German use of the main railroad line between Bologna and Florence, which went on to Rome. The first attempts did not amount to much, but on November 13 Lupo's men succeeded in blowing up a Nazi supply train, destroying six tank cars full of gas and four freight cars loaded with trucks. By spring Guido had managed to establish radio contact with the British Special Forces, a breakthrough which finally assured regular supplies of weapons and explosives. Between March and September 1944 the British made four successful airdrops, each with 36 parachutes. Elaborate precautions were necessary for each drop, because now the Fascists were determined to rout out the partisans.

As Stella Rossa's membership grew, more food was required from the peasants. They, in turn, were more reluctant than ever to submit to Fascist requisitions. Unlike the Fascists, Stella Rossa was selective in its demands, knowing well which families could afford to give and which required the little they had for themselves. Also, the support of most of the local priests was an important element in maintaining Stella Rossa's close ties with the peasants.

During the summer months the now well-armed partisans made almost daily attacks on the enemy and the local Fascists began to disappear, afraid for their lives if and when the Germans should leave. The news in August of the liberation of nearby Florence by the partisans, just before the Allies arrived, had made the people of Marzabotto certain they, too, would soon be rid of the Nazis. An Allied offensive was expected against the Gothic Line, the German fortification extending from Massa Carrara on the west to Pesaro on the east coast. Many were convinced, Allies included, that by November the whole of northern Italy would be liberated. On September 8, 1944, the first anniversary of the Armistice, Marzabotto even dared to celebrate openly. On September 10 the Allies broke through a barrier which brought them in sight of the plains stretching below Monte Sole, the mountainous region near Marzabotto which was a partisan stronghold. They were so close that some of the Germans even wanted to negotiate with the partisans to ensure a safe retreat, much as had been done in Naples.

Il Lupo, seeing the Allies so near, contacted an OSS agent to ask how Stella Rossa could help out. He was told the best strategy was to remain in the mountains until the arrival of the Allies. The decision to remain on Monte Sole turned out to be a bad one, compounded by the fact that meanwhile one of Lupo's most trusted men, Cacao, had turned double agent. Cacao had been with Stella Rossa for many months and had won the respect of his companions. But he had one weakness, a love of money. Somehow the Germans had discovered this. When he disappeared in mid-September it was presumed he had been killed in action. Lupo did not suspect treachery until late September, when the partisans captured a Fascist who admitted that the Germans knew the location of the Monte Sole stronghold and were planning an attack. This news seemed to be confirmed by the arrival of several peasants late one night with the information that they had observed mysterious German troop movements in the area. They also reported the arrival of a large contingent wearing storm trooper helmets and jackets decorated with a large skull and crossbones on the chest. This was a crack unit of the German Army, used in special maneuvers. Some of Lupo's men opted for a quick strike against the SS troop but others—Lupo included—thought it best to coordinate with Allied strategy. One of the survivors of Stella Rossa, Gianni Rossi, said he could see through his binoculars that the Allies were only about a mile away, as the crow flies, and the firing of Allied artillery was clearly audible.

Members of Stella Rossa had good reason, from these observations, to trust in the success of the Allied offensive. But as David Ellwood writes in his excellent book, *Italy: 1943–1945* (an analysis of international politics as they affected Italy): ''The longed-for final advance had been stopped in the mud, rain and gales of the battle for the Gothic Line, and the military campaign practically shut down for the winter at some points only 15 miles from Bologna and the Po Valley plains. The Resistance movement had been keyed up to its highest pitch during September waiting for the final signal to release the great insurrection. When the signal never came, bitter disillusionment set in, adding to the physical and psychological difficulties of clandestine survival in alpine winter conditions.''

Lupo's decision to wait for the Allies to get closer before launching a full attack on the Germans in hindsight was a bad one. But luck, always an important element, was also against him. The Nazis planned to encircle Monte Sole on September 28, thus trapping Stella Rossa. Thanks to Cacao's information, they knew exactly which approaches to take. Unluckily, on the 27th Lupo, his vice-commander Gianni Rossi and ten others had gone to the nearby village of Cadotto, where they were to spend a few nights. The SS troops, commanded by Major Walter Reder, had to pass through Cadotto on their way to Monte Sole. Under cover of convenient heavy rain and fog, they advanced almost without detection. As soon as Lupo and Rossi were aware of what was happening, they tried desperately to rejoin their men. In the ensuing shoot-out Rossi was seriously wounded. Lupo was never seen again alive. A year later his bullet-ridden body was found in a field outside Cadotto. It was the end, too, for the Stella Rossa brigade, effectively ambushed and soon out of ammunition.

For Marzabotto itself the worst was yet to come. There was no military reason to attack people living around Monte Sole now that Stella Rossa had been liquidated, but Major Reder's SS troops immediately started on a three-day rampage which threatened to massacre every man, woman and child. At Marzabotto the storm troopers surrounded all the houses and set them on fire. The inhabitants had two choices: to die in the flames or to be shot as they ran out of their burning homes. Some 1800 people perished that day.

There were survivors. Ten Stella Rossa partisans tried, unsuccessfully, to organize a new unit of Stella Rossa. Several joined the Allies and the rest returned to their homes, but not before ferreting out and executing Cacao, who was hiding under an assumed name. The few remaining civilians found refuge in neighboring villages.

In 1951 the Bologna military court sentenced Major Reder to lifetime imprisonment at Castello Angiono prison in Gaeta. At the trial Reder gave the usual excuses, chiefly that he was simply following orders. In his testimony he declared: "It is true that I gave orders to burn all the houses in which my men found weapons or partisans, and especially the home of Commander Musolesi. But I did not give orders to kill civilians." Reder's sentence was "commuted" to 34 years in 1980, in accordance with Italian laws that limit jail terms to 34 years. In 1985 he was returned to Austria over the protests of most Italians. At a meeting of the survivors of the Marzabotto massacre on December 30, 1984, they had voted 171 to 4 against clemency. One woman who lost her husband in the massacre exclaimed, "God may be able to forgive him. I can't." Before Reder left, he sent a long plea for forgiveness to the people of Marzabotto, repudiating his wartime behavior.

The Allies did not break through the Gothic Line until mid-April 1945. The massacre at Marzabotto would be followed by a long, cruel winter but the fate of the village became a symbol of defiance as the Resistance gathered momentum.

=6=
Women of the Resistance

AN OLD Italian proverb says "When women take up a cause, you can assume it has been won." Their participation in the Resistance was so ubiquitous that statistics are useless to describe their contribution. Women in all walks of life hid, clothed and fed disbanded Italian soldiers, Jews, and refugees from prisoners-of-war camps. Farm women cooked food and walked miles, past Nazi / Fascist blockades, to reach partisans in the hills and mountains. Women employed in factories sabotaged products destined for Germany. Office and bank clerks perfected the slow-down to an art. Perhaps the greatest contribution was that of the *staffettas,* the messengers who became the vital link fusing all aspects of the Resistance movement.

There were also many women who fought alongside the partisans. Of these 35,000 women, some 5,000 were imprisoned, 650 were executed or died in combat, about 3,000 were deported to Germany, and 17 were awarded the gold medal for valor. For the first time in Italian history large numbers of women were partners with men, fighting together as equals for a common cause.

Until the end of the nineteenth century, Italian women had traditionally deferred to men, especially in politics and the workplace. During the nineteenth century a few women took part in political activities, but they were exceptional albeit effective participants. In 1848 several women joined revolutionary movements in Sicily, and fought alongside men in Milan and Rome to protect their cities from foreign armies. The first coordinated women's actions grew out of their demands for better working conditions in the 1870s and 1880s. Italy was then primarily an agricultural nation, and women predominated in the cultivation of rice, hemp and silkworms. Industrialization was slow to take place in Italy, except for the textile industry, and there, too, women were in the majority. During the 1880s women began to band together in associations, even striking for better hours and more pay.

The formation of the Italian Socialist party in 1892 gave some impetus to the women's movement. They began to be recognized as a force in the trade unions, and in the revolts against landowners organized by the Socialists. Many women joined the Socialists in peace demonstrations opposing Italy's entry into World War I. Once the nation went to war, women became a crucial part of the workforce, replacing the conscripted men even in heavy industry. Their efforts did not win them the vote, but in 1919 legislation was passed to permit them to enter all occupations except those connected with the law or politics.

Fascism put a stop to the budding emancipation of women. Mussolini declared that women's main function was to procreate, "for the invigoration and growth of the race." Women were permitted to work, but only in certain occupations and at a lower rate of pay than men. Teaching and nursing were the favored occupations. Not all women were intimidated by the new regime, nor did the *squadristi* spare female activists. Like the men, anti-Fascist women were forced to go underground or into exile, and quite a few joined the newly formed (1921) Italian Communist party in the 1920s. The laws of 1926 establishing Special Tribunals to try "Enemies of the State" sentenced hundreds of women to prison. In 1938 the government imposed even more severe restrictions on the kind of work women were permitted to do.

With the start of World War II in 1939 came bombings of Italian cities, new deprivations and an increasingly open discontent with Mussolini and the Fascist government. Women were now in the forefront of peace demonstrations, and they were an important element in the general strikes of March 1943 which signalled the beginning of the end for Il Duce. During the 45 days of the Badoglio government, between the fall of Mussolini on July 25 and the signing of the Armistice with the Allies on September 8, 1943, women were especially active in the regrouping of anti-Fascist organizations, especially in the cities of the North.

When, after September 8, the people of Italy began to fight both the German invaders and the remnants of fascism in what amounted to civil war, a subtle change came over the position of women. Many continued in their traditional, subordinate occupations but with a difference: they were recognized as essential to the defeat of the enemy no matter how small their contribution. The *staffetta* perhaps symbolizes their transition more than any other wartime category. For one thing it was the patriot role most played by women. More important, the *staffetta* was clearly recognized not just as a messenger but as the indispensable link in a chain of command. She was as valuable as the leader of a brigade, or the shortwave radio she carried from one place to another. To define the word *"staffetta"* is almost as difficult as defining the parameters of her work. "Messenger" is hardly accurate, although a principal function of the *staffetta* was to serve as a substitute for the nonexistent or unsafe-to-use telephone and mail service.

Besides having courage and stamina, a *staffetta* had to be ingenious in dealing with the unexpected. She carried ammunition, or parts of a printing press in an old shopping bag that appeared to be filled with wornout clothing. She would casually push a baby carriage, its occupant reclining on hand grenades and bags of flour. "Pregnant" women concealed leaflets and contraband ID cards in skirts covering what appeared to be swollen bellies. A "Red Cross nurse" hurried along a country road, not to take care of a sick peasant but to take medical supplies to the partisans.

The life of a *staffetta* had its humorous moments, albeit of a somewhat black nature. Maria Luigia Guaita, coordinator of the

Fascist police inspected womens' handbags, searching for clandestine newspapers, pistols, and other contraband.

staffettas who worked for the Florentine Party of Action, recalls their early base of operations in the headquarters of the Society for the Cremation of Cadavers. Their meetings were held in a gloomy room decorated with samples of urns meant to hold ashes. A large coffin in the center of the room contained a collection of small guns and ammunition.

Andreina Morandi-Michelozzi was a student at the University of Florence when she began her life as a *staffetta*. The Morandi family was middle class: the parents had owned and operated a radio store since 1924. In 1943 their son, Luigi, was serving his stint in the army and Andreina was a relatively carefree college sophomore, a pretty girl with shoulder-length auburn hair. She had joined the outlawed Party of Action in her freshman year, but was not seriously involved in politics. During the 45 summer days of the Badoglio government, Andreina and her friends spent most of the time hiking and camping in the nearby Tuscan hills.

September 8 happened to be the silver wedding anniversary of the Morandis. Luigi, who had been in Lucca on maneuvers, was expected home for the celebration, but with the announcement of the Armistice that day the party ended before it began.

In the days that followed, Florence quickly became an armed camp as German troops poured in and the first ominous official warnings appeared on the walls. The University had not yet reopened for the fall term but the Party of Action lost no time in organizing its student members. Andreina spoke English so her first assignment was to help British prisoners-of-war known to be hiding in a village outside Florence. Andreina and two of her friends caught an early morning train. They carried suitcases full of men's clothing and each had a revolver well hidden in her handbag. The problem would be to find safe lodgings for the British soldiers until, when and if escape routes to Switzerland could be established. Since the soldiers did not speak Italian, it would have been foolhardy to risk being stopped by Fascist or German police, even if the men had convincing identification papers. Visits to farm households resulted in finding refuge for most of the Englishmen.

Only once, Andreina recalls, did she really feel afraid as a *staffetta*. A successful Allied airdrop of desperately needed weapons turned into a disaster when a spy infiltrated the group assigned to recover the parachutes. All the partisans were seized and thrown into jail. Andreina was assigned to take food packages to the prisoners and she remembers to this day her feeling of being trapped as she crossed the jail's threshold, though she completed her mission successfully.

Staffettas were also a main distribution channel for clandestine newspapers. The papers kept civilians informed about both the Resistance and enemy maneuvers. For the partisans the papers were a major source of news about each other's activities. The journals also provided a sense of solidarity, especially in the editorials. Sometimes poems and cartoons lightened the news. Andreina and three other women were assigned to distributing *La*

Libertà, the journal of the Tuscan Party of Action. As soon as they were printed, bundles of papers were delivered to a tiny apartment on Via Paganini. The next few days would be spent dropping them off at preestablished destinations, a long process because the carefully disguised papers (sometimes folded into an official Fascist publication) could only be handled a few at a time. Occasionally Andreina still had some papers left over at curfew and she would take them home, hiding them among the books in the library. A mistake, as it turned out.

On June 4, 1944, the Morandis learned from Radio London that Rome had been liberated. Every night they, like many others, carefully shut windows and doors and huddled over the radio, pulled out from its hiding place. On June 5 the Party of Action, convinced that the Allies would now move quickly towards Florence, proposed to the Tuscan Committee of National Liberation that leaflets be distributed urging everyone to be ready for a general uprising. On the morning of June 7, as Andreina carried her bicycle down the stairs to help with the leaflets, she bumped into Luigi, rushing briefly into the house. He had not been home for several days and after a hurried embrace, Andreina left. She would never see her brother again. That afternoon he, and all those involved in the underground Radio Cora, were seized by the Gestapo (see p. 132).

Until June 7 the older Morandis did not know how or with whom Luigi was involved in the Resistance, although Andreina was aware of his work. At 10 PM that night, as they sat in the living room listening to Radio London—Mr. Morandi was also scanning the newspapers—there was a knock on the front door. Andreina opened it a crack to find a young man on the door step, someone she had never seen before. Without wasting words, he told her Luigi had been arrested and that if she had any incriminating things in the house to get rid of them right away. Aware that he could be an impostor and that this might be a trap, Andreina reluctantly let the man in. She led the way to the living room where, she remembered, she had hidden a few leftover copies of *La Libertà.* Just as the young man began repeating his story, there was another knock on the door, this time loud and peremptory.

Telling her mother to delay answering, Andreina grabbed the clandestine newspaper, ran to her room, climbed through a window onto a little terrace and threw the papers into an alley below. Meanwhile the frightened Mrs. Morandi had opened the front door. When Andreina returned to the living room, the house was filled with men, some in Fascist uniform. They searched the house, still saying little. Luckily, they did not notice the papers scattered in the alley. Finally, when Mrs. Morandi protested weakly as they searched her bureau drawers, one of the men told her to be quiet, adding she should have brought up her son better. Luigi had, the man said, killed a German soldier and had himself been badly wounded. Without further explanation the Morandis and the unknown young man were put into a small truck and taken to Gestapo headquarters at Via Bolognese 67, commonly known as "Villa Triste," Sorrowful Villa.

They waited by themselves, in a small room, listening to harsh voices barking orders in German and to an occasional muffled scream. Then a warden led them down a long flight of stairs to a room divided into small cells. Andreina and her mother were put into one and the men in another. Two women were already in Andreina's cell, one of them curled up asleep, moaning softly. The other introduced herself: Orsola Biasutti De Cristoforo. Andreina recognized the name as one of the people who had worked hardest to help Jews and Allied prisoners. Orsola had been arrested a month earlier and sentenced to be sent to a German concentration camp. A few minutes later the cell door opened again to let in Ruth Piccagli, the wife of a member of Radio Cora, who was able to confirm for the Morandis that Luigi had indeed been shot and captured, and that he had been working with the clandestine radio group.

The next day Andreina was questioned at length by a woman. A copy of *La Libertà* had been found in the house, but she accepted Andreina's story that she had been given the paper by a fellow student at the University. No one questioned Mrs. Morandi and both were transferred to the women's prison, Santa Verdiana, after a brief last moment with Mr. Morandi. He was never heard from again, but long investigations after the war ended seem to confirm that he died at Auschwitz in the winter of 1945. Mrs. Morandi was released after a few days: Andreina was among those liberated when the Gappists freed Tosca, the Florentine Gappist whose bomb plot had failed.

Among the women in the Resistance nuns deserve a special place. Nuns were the caretakers at Santa Verdiana and, like Italian nuns in general, were a quiet but invaluable force in the Resistance. Years before Catholic nuns became the political activists some of them are today, Italian nuns (like the parish priests) considered it their Christian duty to save the lives of the persecuted, although the Vatican was officially neutral during World War II. These religious women ran many of the hospitals and prisons and so were in an excellent position to help.

Convents proved to be safe havens because they were usually ancient buildings with many hidden passages and spaces easily overlooked in an occasional raid by Nazi or Fascist police. The refugees were equipped with false identification papers to allow them to leave the convent in search of food, since the nun's supplies were limited. Sometimes the only meal of the day was a plate of wormy rice. The refugee women would try, with their forged ration cards and counterfeit lire, to bring back some bread or a few eggs for the children among them. When they could be spared from their work, the nuns themselves would go on foot into the countryside to bring back chestnuts or a few vegetables. Because the police tended to ignore them, a nun's habit also became a useful disguise for partisans. The mother superior in charge of Santa Verdiana prison was a remarkable woman called Mother Superior Ermelinda (Carducci). A tall, imposing figure with a stern face and a commanding voice, she had in her charge ordinary criminals as well as political prisoners. Some of the inmates had been convicted of serious crimes and could be violent and unruly.

Although she was an intensely religious woman who had

declared her vocation as a small child, Mother Ermelinda never proselytized, respecting the right of each individual to live by her own ideals. She made this clear to the political prisoners, though in indirect ways she expressed her disapproval of Fascist beliefs and methods. The prison was a government operation so that technically she was bound by Fascist regulations. The political prisoners, soon aware that they could trust their warden, were able to establish contacts with the Resistance, which permitted a valuable exchange of information.

The *staffetta* entrusted with this exchange of messages was a young woman called Carmela Mazzarisi. She was the daughter of the director of prisons and since childhood had been a favorite of the Sisters who operated Santa Verdiana. No one would be suspicious of her comings and goings. Her father was well aware of her activities, and had himself joined the Tuscan Committee of National Liberation. Had Mother Ermelinda betrayed them, these two and a great many partisans would have suffered.

The Mother Superior showed her concern in other ways, too. Jewish women enroute to German concentration camps were often left at the prison for a few days. Mother Ermelinda was especially solicitous of these victims, trying in whatever way she could to make them comfortable for a short time. She frequently sent them to see Silvia Facca, a political prisoner who was also a competent nurse. A small, blue-eyed blond, Facca had specialized in surgical nursing and lab analysis. She had been working with the Resistance—as had her husband—since September 12, 1943, first as a *staffetta* and then as a nurse. By wearing a Red Cross band on her sleeve, and because of her "Aryan" appearance, she had been able to move around freely for a time. Eventually she was caught and spent over four months in prison, until a German cousin managed to gain her freedom on the guarantee that she would end her Resistance activities. With her husband she was able to reach the liberated South, where they joined the American OSS.

The Resistance inadvertently was forced upon a colony of cloistered nuns who lived in the town of Fontanigarda, on the Ligurian coast near Genoa. As cloistered nuns they were forbidden to be seen by the outside world, though people came to their door to leave donations and to pray. The only human being allowed in the convent was the local priest, who also provided the only medical help available. One night there was a knock on the convent door. Through the grill a voice begged for help, explaining he was a partisan named Ferruccio and that the Germans had been chasing him for hours. The local priest, also a member of the Resistance, had told Mother Superior that almost a thousand partisans were hidden in the mountains beyond the village. The nun knew if she turned Ferruccio away he would likely die, and perhaps many more would too, if he was caught and tortured. So she let the man in, and hid him from the other nuns until the next visit from the priest.

The priest's solution further complicated life for the nuns. The priest decided that if Ferruccio and a woman, presumably his wife, were to be seen leaving the convent together it would be assumed that they were average townspeople who had gone to make a donation and to ask the nuns to pray for them. The priest told the Mother Superior to send a message to him the next evening, saying one of the nuns was very sick. He would return with his black bag of medicines, only it would contain a skirt and sweater. One of the nuns would have to dress in these clothes and pretend to be Ferruccio's wife. The nuns were appalled at the suggestion but finally a nun named Martha volunteered because she spoke German and could deal with any Nazi questioning. Leaving the cloister was tantamount to breaking her vows, but the priest assured her God would forgive her.

Early the next morning the couple appeared at the grille at the entrance of the convent and remained there, kneeling and praying for some time. Then they rose and went down the road, heads bowed but occasionally greeting a passer-by. Ferruccio timidly took Martha's arm as they walked silently towards the village of Casoni, where he knew he could hide until the Germans moved on. Halfway to Casoni they ran into a truckload of German soldiers. Without warning, one of them took a shot at Ferruccio and hit him in the shoulder. As the blood spurted out, Ferruccio collapsed. Sister Martha threw herself on him, screaming in German "Why have you killed my husband? What did he do to you?" The soldiers, surprised at this tirade in their own language, quickly moved off. (Ferruccio lived to participate in the liberation of Genoa, and Sister Martha returned to the cloister, never to go out in the world again.)

At the opposite pole from the nuns, who operated largely behind the scenes, were the women who had joined the armed Resistance. The first detachment of women partisans was formed in Piedmont, as a unit of the Eugenio Giambone / Garibaldi Division. Ninety-nine women partisans died in Piedmont, among them Maria Agazzi, who was attached to the 42nd Garibaldi Brigade. She took part in many guerrilla attacks on both German and Fascist forces, but was best known for her spy work in the Valle di Susa zone. Without any regard for her own safety, she frequently went to the town of San Giario, the site of a German artillery fortification. The town was off limits, except to the inhabitants.

As Agazzi wandered through the streets one day, a guard stopped her. When he discovered that she was not a native of the town, he threw her into the local prison. Agazzi was an attractive and clever woman, and after a few days she had persuaded the Fascist chief of police that she did not realize San Giario was a restricted area. The chief not only freed her, but took her on a tour of the gun emplacements. He even allowed her to look through a gunsight, which was trained on the mountains across the valley. To her horror, Agazzi could clearly see her partisan comrades, moving about in the distance. As she watched, the officer explained how the gun worked, and told her that in two days time there would be a bombardment of the partisan hideout. Agazzi listened attentively, then pointed out that the partisans could hide behind outcroppings of rock and so save themselves. The officer answered that he appreciated her observations and concern, but that there was nothing to worry about because Fascist units planned to come up from behind the partisan camp, thereby trapping any partisans who tried to hide from the blast. That night Agazzi left the town unobserved, and within a few hours the partisans had been fully warned of the attack. Agazzi fought with the 42nd Division for almost a year, before she was killed in November 1944.

Not all Resistance activity involved danger. When food requisitioning began to fail in Bina, in Romagna, the peasant women were called to a meeting at Fascist headquarters. Everyone, a captain announced, would help cultivate a new field "to provide minestrone for our brave soldiers." The women protested that there was not enough time even to finish their own work let alone start a new field, but the captain abruptly ended the meeting with instructions to report at dawn the next day to plant seedlings. That evening the women met to decide what to do. The next morning they showed up in strangely good spirits and set to work vigorously, but they planted all the seedlings upside down, with their roots in the air.

The citizens of Giovecca, a farm village also in Romagna, had a long history of rebellion dating well before Fascism. Young and old saw the Resistance as part of a continuing fight against oppression. Giovecca was especially proud of a ten-year-old girl who lived there, named Dorina. She became an indefatigable lookout for the partisans meeting in her father's kitchen. No matter how cold or wet the day, Dorina would be at her post at the end of the dirt road about half a mile from her house. The road joined a main highway frequently used by German and Fascist troops. As soon as she spotted them coming down the highway, Dorina would run back to the house, giving the partisans plenty of time to disappear into the root cellar until the coast was clear.

To do justice to the women of the Resistance would require several volumes, but perhaps the odyssey of one woman—Gilda Larocca—can serve as a microcosm of the life of so many who, in spite of capture and torture, managed to survive and even to continue their work. At 21 Gilda had gone to work as a secretary to Enrico Bocci, a distinguished Florentine lawyer, a longtime liberal and a member of the Party of Action. Early in 1944 Bocci was approached by Allied agents in Florence to help set up short-wave communication between the Florence underground and the Allies in southern Italy. The idea was to facilitate transmittal of information about German strategy and movement, and to establish pinpoints for Allied airdrops to the Resistance. Two radio operators and their equipment arrived soon after Bocci accepted the assignment, organizing an operation known as Radio Cora. The problem then became one of logistics, of having to move the radio frequently so that the Germans could not trace the signal. It was one of Gilda's responsibilities to find places for the equipment, which she herself frequently carried from one place to another.

Another problem for Bocci was to set up a network to gather information needed by the Allies. Luigi Morandi (among others) had become part of this network, also occasionally helping with transmissions because of his expertise with shortwave equipment. Soon Radio Cora had become so useful that General Alexander himself praised it in a Radio London broadcast, thereby redoubling German efforts to locate the operation. Bocci, meanwhile, had to make a pretense of continuing his law work and for this purpose Gilda remained in the office when she was not delivering coded messages or the radio.

One day in mid-May 1944 Gilda received a phone call that German tanks were headed South along the Arno River, which flows through the city of Florence. She closed the office and hurried towards the Ponte Vecchio, arriving in time to see the column drive by. For a long time she counted the tanks, and when they disappeared she ran to tell Bocci. The news, quickly transmitted, proved to be invaluable advance information that the famous Herman Goering Division had mobilized for action. An hour later Allied planes swooped down on the column, bombing it heavily.

Keeping Radio Cora one step ahead of the Nazis became increasingly difficult as the supply of hideouts dwindled. Many buildings had been destroyed in Allied raids, and few places had the facilities for the requisite outside antenna. Finally Gilda found a top floor available at Piazza d'Azeglio 12, which had a small room just under the roof perfect for shortwave. To give the impression that this was a rental for a bombed-out couple, Bocci and his wife moved in. On June 2 radio equipment and four operators were parachuted into nearby Prato, with instructions to spread out to other Tuscan towns, to take some of the pressure off Cora in Florence. Then in rapid succession came the liberation of Rome on June 4 and the Normandy landing on June 6. At the same time General Alexander sent a message to Cora, requesting a quick answer to a long list of questions about Nazi fortifications, partisan formations and numbers, viable locations for future airdrops, mined areas south of Florence, and all details available on the German Gothic Line.

Because the General had stressed the urgency of his request, Bocci decided to have a group meeting at Piazza d'Azeglio on the afternoon of June 7. For security reasons they had never met as a group before, Larocca says, but Bocci thought that by pooling their information they could expedite an answer. None of the radio operators happened to be available, so Luigi Morandi offered to help and he went to the upstairs room to prepare the equipment. The others gathered in the living room, spreading out maps and coded messages on a large coffee table. Bocci sat in an armchair near the table, dictating the message to be transmitted to Gilda.

Suddenly the apartment door opened and Focacci, a member of the group who had left a few moments earlier but had been intercepted, entered followed by three men in tan raincoats, pistols in hand. One, speaking German-accented Italian, demanded to know how to reach the roof from the apartment. Gilda, hoping to warn Morandi, led the way but Morandi's ears were covered with a headset. She was shoved back down the stairs and made to join the others, who now stood silently against a wall, with their hands up. Shots rang out from the upstairs room, as German soldiers pushed into the apartment. No one knows exactly what happened up there, but Gilda asserts that none of the Cora group were armed. She believes one of the Germans must have put down his pistol to pick up the radio and that Morandi grabbed it and killed the man. A second German mortally wounded Morandi.

Bocci, Gilda and the others were piled into two cars and taken to Villa Triste for questioning. All of them were severely tortured, even though Bocci tried to assume full responsibility, hoping to spare the others. Only once did Gilda see her companions, when a guard let her talk briefly with Piccagli, by then so battered he was almost unrecognizable. For days Gilda was questioned, in between beatings: what had she studied; what languages did she speak; why wasn't she a Fascist; why had she "betrayed" her country; who was in this conspiracy with her; why had she allowed so many of her friends to be killed? Her interrogators were always Germans in uniform who spoke Italian. Frequently they shone a very bright light in her eyes for hours at a time. When the questioning was over she had to be led away because all she could see was flashing lights. (As a result of this, she is now legally blind.)

Finally, on June 17 Gilda Larocca was allowed a brief visit from her father and sister and a few days later she was sent to the concentration camp at Fossoli, still wearing the gray and white linen dress and blue coat that she had worn on June 7. Fossoli was a way station: the next stop would be a German camp or a factory, if one was lucky.

As soon as a busload of prisoners arrived at Fossoli they were registered and given a number. Gilda was number 2161. The numbers were printed on a colored cloth triangle to be attached to their clothing, the colors coded to various classifications. Red meant a political prisoner. After a cursory medical examination, the prisoners were assigned to barracks, crude structures of wood and cement with a hole in the floor for a toilet. Bedbugs crawled about night and day. Twice a day the women were given a bowl of liquid containing a little vegetable and sometimes a piece of potato, never meat, salt or fat of any kind. Once in a while, they received a piece of moldy bread made of rice flour. Among the women in Gilda's barracks was Orsola Biasutti, who earlier had been imprisoned with Andreina Morandi. She was a Party of Action member who spoke excellent English because her mother was American.

All the prisoners had to work: on account of her poor eye-

sight, Gilda washed pots and pans in the kitchen of the SS mess.
Kitchen work was torture in a more subtle form because of the
sight and smells of good food which prisoners were not allowed
to touch. Once Gilda succeeded in stealing a little salt, hiding it
in a twist of paper she poked into her brassiere. Another time she
stole a spoonful of sugar in the same way, but sweat dampened
the paper and the sugar dissolved on her skin.

Political prisoners were allowed to exercise together a half-
hour each evening, in a large yard facing the row of barracks.
There Gilda discovered Campolmi and Focacci, two other survivors of the raid on Radio Cora. One night, after the regular bed-
time head count, 72 men were separated from the rest, pushed
into trucks and driven away without explanation. Later it was
learned two had managed to escape, but the rest were machine-
gunned and buried a short distance from the camp. The massacre
was ordered by the Nazi High Command in Verona, in reprisal
for a partisan attack on a German troop train which had just left
Genoa.

Each morning there were daily departures of inmates for Germany. Gilda's turn came on July 28: her papers said she was
headed for the concentration camp at Brandenburg. Gilda and
Orsola were among a group that stayed overnight in an empty
school in Verona, from there to take a train for Germany. The
next day they were made to form a column three abreast, men
walking in front and women in the rear. They were escorted by
SS and Fascist guards carrying machine guns. Walking along the
streets of Verona to the railroad station, they saw that all shops
and doorways were closed, to block off a possible means of escape.
People on the sidewalks stopped to watch the long column go by.
As it passed through an especially crowded plaza some men in
the line tried to break away. Several guards chased the men and
in the momentary confusion Orsola, followed by Gilda and a
Yugoslav girl named Denka, made a quick dash towards the side-
walk. Bystanders hurriedly parted to let them through and because
they were dressed in their own clothes it was easy to assimilate
with the crowd, once they had torn off the red triangles.

The first problem was to get proper IDs before curfew, and then to look for shelter. Both Gilda and Orsola knew Verona quite well. They were aware that because the city was headquarters for the Fascists in the region, patrols would be especially vigilant about checking papers. Even as they discussed what to do, Orsola recognized two of their former guards heading their way laughing and talking, apparently on their way back from the railroad station. Someone had slipped a few lire into Gilda's hand when they ran from the column, so she pushed her companions towards the nearest café. Their former guards had the same idea and as quickly as possible the women headed for the bathroom where they stayed until the barmaid, apparently understanding the situation, let them know when the guards left.

Their next stop was the cathedral, where they hoped to get help from a priest. In fact, thanks to Don Angelo Accordini, they were directed to a nearby convent friendly to the Resistance. A nun led them to a small room which had three beds and running water. Gilda remembers that as soon as the nun left the room the three women bounced on the beds like children, and then ran to wash their faces with real soap. The convent was also a school, a cheerful and busy place. Gilda was able to phone her brother-in-law, who was an employee of the state railroad in Verona. He gave Orsola and Gilda a little money and a few ration stamps, so that they could eat in a restaurant. He also gave them train tickets to Milan and keys to an apartment he had there, but he could not locate false papers in such a short time.

On the train to Milan, Fascist railway police demanded their ID cards as they had expected. Gilda tearfully explained they were en route from Florence where they had been bombed out, that they had lost their luggage but luckily had put their train tickets in their pockets. There were so many refugees trying to leave the Florence area that the police accepted the explanation. In Milan the women were able to get official ID cards because a relative had accompanied them to the refugee office in city hall, and had vouched for their identity. They used assumed names: Orsola became Paola Bacci and Gilda simply changed her first name to Laura, Larocca being a fairly common last name.

For a few days Gilda worked as a typist in a patent office. She recalls two patents she had to file, one for an ink which would allow a lover to write messages on flower petals, and another for a design of a couch that could be converted into a coffin. Meanwhile, Orsola got in touch with the local Action Party which decided to send her to Bologna, where assistance was badly needed. Gilda agreed to go with her and for the rest of the war she worked as a *staffetta* in Bologna. The Action Party paid for her room and board with a family, and gave her a small monthly stipend which she would spend on such rarities as bread and salt. (Salt was so scarce that five pounds were offered as a bribe for anyone informing on a partisan.) Bologna was liberated on April 19, 1945 and on May 9 Gilda was finally able to return to Florence.

How Radio Cora was discovered and who betrayed the operation has never been explained. There are several theories, among them that a woman who lived in the building spied for her German lover, but none have been proven. Three members of Radio Cora perished almost immediately. Luigi Morandi died in a hospital before the Nazis could question him. Italo Piccagli was shot in the woods of nearby Cercina, together with the radio operators who had just arrived from Bari to join Cora, and other partisans, including a revered Resistance organizer who had no connection with the radio, Anna Maria Enriques Agnoletti. Enrico Bocci's body was never found, though it was known he had been so badly tortured he could not have survived. A memorial to Radio Cora has been placed in a small park across the street from 12 Piazza d'Azeglio.

Women like Gilda Larocca and Andreina Morandi were concerned mostly with their day-by-day work in the Resistance, which did not leave much time to think about the future. Yet, inevitably, their participation alongside men would open doors. In light of this, some women did begin actively planning for a different postwar role. In Piedmont, which before the war had been in the vanguard of an embryonic women's movement, a group of women representing the different political parties met in Turin early in

November 1943 to form an organization called "Gruppi di difesa della donna e per l'assistenza ai combattenti per la libertà" (Groups for the defense of women and for the aid of the freedom fighters). The organization was open "to all women of every social class and of all political and religious beliefs who want to take part in the task of freeing their country, *and fighting for their own emancipation.*" These last words added a new and significant objective.

The Gruppi di difesa immediately initiated an all-out recruitment campaign, reaching into factories, offices, schools and the countryside. They urged their members to agitate for milk and clothing for children, housing for the dispossessed and better pay. They taught how to sabotage industrial production and farm requisition programs, and in whatever way possible they gave comfort and aid to those being deported. Because the Gruppi were more politically oriented than former women's associations, they quickly recognized the importance of the Committees of National Liberation and involved themselves in the work of the regional and local committees. They became so valuable and effective that the national leadership of the committees—the Committee of National Liberation of Northern Italy—officially recognized the Gruppi as an affiliate in June 1944.

One of the five charter members of the Gruppi was Ada Gobetti, widow of the ardent anti-Fascist, Piero Gobetti. Ada was also a founding member of the Action Party chapter in Turin. She was an articulate, vibrant woman who was widely recognized as a dedicated anti-Fascist in her own right. Mussolini had rightly regarded Turin as a hotbed of subversive activity, and the Gobetti home at Via Fabro 6 was the center of much of this activity before and all through the war. Ada kept a diary of the war years, written in miniscule script in a number of pads the size of small address

OVERLEAF

Excerpts from Ada Gobetti's wartime diary which she wrote in English, in a form of shorthand. *Reprinted with permission of the Gobetti family.*

There is an alarm during
the night, but we don't
hear it. Wake at nine quite
rested. Stay at home working
After lunch go with Et. to Ba=
ths & the lake above.
Yeats on coming back,
about their house. go
on reading with P. at
home. Read De Stael

Et. goes to Turin. Hear
wonderful news. feel
almost frantic. lunch
early & go to Turin with P.
Find Et. gone with him to
Camptin, then to Gf.Gf. Go to
Cteark & proceed & buy two
rodes. go to bed early.

7 Martedì - s. Regina v.

Pick up predisposti before leaving for _Turin_ - Have a quiet morning - Go to Littleath to settle a/c - After lunch see Mario - Go to Littleath again. Come home & Typewrite MS. Franco. Catell the typewr. just in time - Arrive at _Meana_ quite right ? explain his theory

8 Mercoledì - Nativ. di M. V.

.... & running - Go to _Meana_ ... & redoing ... ... people particularly ... Go shopping ... Littleath hat so ugly. ... in the world, ... & others busy thr... of the ... After dinner see many people among whom Agostes ... comes to sleep at our house - We ... till half past two very tired & strangely calm books. She wrote in English, using seemingly disconnected words which were a shorthand no one else could decipher. (Eventually she rewrote her notes, now available as a published diary.)

When Mussolini was deposed on July 25, Ada, her second husband Ettore Marchesini, and Piero's eighteen-year-old son,

Paolo, were at their summer home in Meana, some twenty-five miles from Turin. They quickly went back to the city, where the next few weeks were spent greeting old friends returning from prison or exile. The happy interlude ended at four PM on September 10, as Ada watched a long line of cars drive by, filled with German officers. She had been standing on the corner of Via Cernaia and Corso Galileo Ferraris, distributing leaflets with her husband and son, when the Germans appeared. Without warning from the Fascist mayor of Turin, the city was quickly and efficiently occupied. Ada ran home to burn incriminating papers, especially lists of members of the Action Party and other political groups, while in the dining room the leaders of the Action Party held an emergency meeting.

It was the first of many surreptitious gatherings at Via Fabro which somehow the Nazis never suspected although Ada, her family and friends were among the better known political and intellectual leaders of Turin. Possibly the Germans overlooked Via Fabro activities because the family was careful to continue their daily routine as though nothing had changed. Ada was a teacher and never missed her classes, Ettore went to his office punctually, and Paolo attended the University as was expected of a boy his age.

In reality Ada had plunged into a hectic program of covert activities. She was an organizer. Before long she had established in the city a source of false identification papers, a network of safe homes for those who needed a refuge, and a crew to distribute clandestine newspapers and leaflets. She also helped establish a local Committee of National Liberation in the Val Susa region (where Meana was located) to coordinate the patriots of the countryside and link them with projects in Turin. Even Paolo's old nursemaid, who now owned a store in Susa, was enlisted in the network. One day, without advance notice, a group of twelve Susa peasants—men dressed in their Sunday / funeral black best— showed up at Via Fabro. They walked in groups of two or three, pretending to be tourists and stopping frequently to look at shops. Warned of the strange procession by a neighbor, Ettore hastily went out to usher the men into the house before they drew too much attention to themselves. Almost immediately one of them launched into a lengthy and tedious speech about their loyalty to the Resistance. They had come all this way simply to pay their respects.

Ada devoted her afternoons and evenings to the Resistance, leaving the mornings free for teaching. She frequently joined her son and his friends, either distributing leaflets or helping them plan sabotage which was now part of young patriots' daily routine. (In fact, it could be said at times she was a distinctly protective mother tagging along.) And always she was involved with the incessant comings and goings at Via Fabro, where as many as fifty visitors would show up in twenty-four hours. Personal visits were essential because it was foolhardy to say anything significant on the telephone, which was frequently tapped by the Fascists. Only once Ada forgot this precaution, as she made an appointment by phone for a British officer to meet several Committee of National Liberation members. After she hung up she sweated for hours, worrying that the call had been intercepted, which it had not. Usually, phone calls were made in prearranged codes, for example:

"Signora, I've found another dog like the one you showed me yesterday, a good watch dog." (Translation: Another British soldier is here.)

"Really—I'd like to see it. Mine isn't doing so well and I'd better send him to visit friends where it's warmer." (I.e., the British officer with her now is about to head South through enemy lines.)

"Good, let's meet tomorrow at the usual."

Ada also devoted time to the Gruppi which she had helped organize, although once this project was launched it developed its own momentum and did not require much of her time. Being a woman of action, she often took part in hazardous undertakings. One of the most daring exploits of this intrepid 43-year-old was a trip across the Alps to France in the dead of winter. Her son Paolo and several of his friends had already made the trip in October 1944 to work out some plans for cooperation between the Italian mountain partisans and the FFI—French Forces of the Interior (French Resistance). Turin is only some 25 miles from the French border, but the Alps form a significant barrier between the two countries.

In Grenoble FFI officials had reached an agreement with Paolo on several projects, but these also had to be approved by the Italian Committee of National Liberation. A return trip with the CLN answer was scheduled for early January, and Ada decided to join the group. She also wanted to meet with members of the French counterpart of the Gruppi, known as the UFF—Union Femmes Françaises. And, it should be added, she was eager to be with her son on the dangerous trip, rather than stay home and agonize about his safety. Their departure at sundown on December 30, 1944 was uneventful. It was not unusual for a party from Turin to spend several days skiing. The Germans knew the Torinese liked to hike or ski in the mountains, and they tolerated this harmless attempt at recreation, especially with a woman in the group. (Most of the mountain partisans had broken camp and descended to the plains by this time, so the Germans were not expecting to run across patriots hiding in the snowy peaks.)

There were six in the group; Ada, her husband and Paolo, and three other men. For over four hours they climbed, single file, over icy paths so slippery that steps had to be carved in the ice to make headway. At one point Paolo missed his footing and slid rapidly down an incline, stopping by pure luck just short of the edge of a precipice. They reached the Passa dell'Orso (an altitude of 2500 meters) at midnight, where they were met by two pro-Resistance Italian Alpine Army soldiers who escorted them the rest of the way. The descent was fairly simple by comparison, though Ada's hands nearly froze. By six AM they were on flat, snowy ground but not yet in France. As they approached the border post at Cle des Acles, German patrols spotted them and fired several volleys, hitting no one. French partisans on duty at the border checked identities and then gave them huge mugs of coffee, followed by a feast of sardines and bread. One member of the group, Pillo, was suffering from a severely frostbitten foot and regretfully parted from the rest, to go to a hospital.

In France Ada felt as though she was on a prewar holiday. Electricity, cars, no blackout and, because it was New Year's Eve, a bottle of cognac to celebrate before a sound sleep after a twenty-four-hour hike. The group spent over a month in France, exchanging information, making plans, and acquainting Ettore with a shortwave radio and code with which to maintain future communications. They also had to wait for a long snowstorm to end before they could attempt the return journey, which was to be made on skis. They decided on another route, to avoid a possible trap in the German-occupied area they would have to traverse.

It was a long and arduous trip made more difficult by a thin film of ice covering the snow, and by the heavy pack each carried. When they finally reached the top of the highest peak, they were confronted by a long, steep descent. The men went first, Ada last. She wrote that she was so frightened that when she reached the bottom, she fainted. The men were too exhausted to do more than wait for her to revive. But there was still a long way to go, and for three days and nights they travelled almost constantly, scarcely stopping for food and sleep. Their last planned way station, a small village on the Italian border, turned out to have been recently occupied by German troops. By this time they were all sick and literally incapable of moving another step. One by one they approached farms on the outskirts of the hamlet, and at last each found a resting place for the night. The next day—February 26, 1945—Ada and her family returned to Turin.

By this time the end of the war was in sight. Ada found that though sabotage and other covert activities continued, attention was now concentrated on plans for the imminent insurrection against the enemy occupiers. In recognition of her remarkable work in the Resistance, the Piedmont Committee of National Liberation had decided to name Ada vice-mayor of liberated Turin. Ada promptly set to work learning the details of the city government, having no intention of being merely an honorary appointee. Like virtually all members of the Resistance, she was determined that on arrival the Allies would find a smoothly functioning city, its adminstrators firmly in control.

On April 28, the day of liberation, Ada rode her old bicycle towards city hall. On the way she met a long line of cars heading in the same direction. The mayor, in the head car, promptly invited Ada to join him and they rode through the cheering crowds together, followed by a partisan escort. That same afternoon Ada began her official duties, first of all making sure the political prisoners had been freed and that the Gruppi had taken care of them. Then she went home to rejoin her family and to plan for the days ahead, when the Allies would arrive and the future would begin for a different Italy.

The new Constitution of the Republic of Italy, approved by the Constituent Assembly in 1947, promised equality for women, legally consolidating the social gains they had made during the war years. Forty years later, in 1987, women are successful in many fields rarely, if ever, open to them before. There is a woman in the Cabinet for the first time, and a woman member of the Communist party is president of the Chamber of Deputies, though women still trail far behind men in the number of government posts held. How much of this progress for women can be attributed solely to their role in the Resistance would be difficult to measure, but there is little doubt that their participation opened the door to a future of greater equality.

=7=
Fighting Back: The Jews of Italy

I wished to assault a commonplace still prevailing in Italy: a Jew is a mild person, a scholar (religious or profane), unwarlike, humiliated, who tolerated centuries of persecution without ever fighting back. It seemed to me a duty to pay homage to those Jews who, in desperate conditions, had found the courage and the skills to resist.

—PRIMO LEVI

BY THE END of the war some 3,000 Jews had joined the armed Resistance, almost ten percent of the Jews living in Italy. A fair amount of history is necessary to understand the place of Jews in Italian society when fascism began. At that time there were some 40,000 Jews in Italy, one-tenth of one percent of the population, then about 42 million.

Jews in large numbers did not exist in Italy until 70 A.D., when they were brought to Rome as slaves after Emperor Titus conquered Jerusalem. Recent research on Roman catacombs (the subterranean cemeteries in which were buried Jews, Christians and pagans alike) has revealed that some 100,000 of the million or so graves might be Jewish. By 100 A.D. there may have been as many as a dozen synagogues in Rome.

Across the centuries Jews from many countries—Spain, Portugal, France, Germany—sought refuge in Italy, settling mostly in Rome or in the central and northern regions, after a brief sojourn in Sicily and the South. The peak of this emigration was reached around 1500, when it is estimated some 120,000 Jews lived in Italy, mingling freely with other Italians. Their lives changed drastically in 1555, when Pope Paul IV decreed that Jews living in the Papal States must be segregated. Even before the Pope's decree Venice had begun to confine Jews to the ghetto, a word the Venetians contributed to the world's vocabulary. In time, most of the princes and dukes who ruled the territories north of Rome began to follow the Pope's example. As a result, ghettoes existed in Italy until the unification of the nation in 1861, when they were outlawed. The only exception was Rome, which was not wrested from Papal control until 1870.

After the unification, Jews were rapidly assimilated into the country's life as teachers, bankers, businessmen, lawyers and politicians. Rome elected a Jewish mayor in the early 1900s, Ernesto Nathan, who was also a respected friend of Pope Pius X. By the mid-1920s, just as fascism was gathering momentum, there were twenty-four Jews in the Senate and some eight percent of university professors were Jewish. Some religious intolerance of Judaism had continued, but it did not have the racist overtones that had developed in France and Germany. In spite of religious differences, between 1930 and 1937 over thirty percent of Jewish marriages were to non-Jews. Herbert Matthews, then Rome correspondent of the *New York Times,* commented: "There was no place in the world [like Italy] where the Jewish problem was so close to disappearing forever in complete assimilation."

This assimilation was counterbalanced to a certain extent by a Zionist movement, but most Italian Jews considered Italy their homeland. In an impassioned speech at a Jewish youth movement congress in Livorno in 1924, Nello Rosselli (later to become a Resistance leader) tried to explain why he was not a Zionist: "The integralist Jews find their peace or seek to find it in Zion. And we too, I too, must find my peace, the serenity of my life. It cannot be found except in the fountainheads of my individuality; in my consciousness as a Jew and as an Italian." This bifurcation was recognized by many, including Enzo Sereni, an ardent Zionist who did emigrate to Palestine. He returned to Italy to join the

Resistance and later died in a concentration camp.

Just as many other Italians were at first convinced that fascism would benefit the nation, so were a good number of Italian Jews. At least five Jews were among the group who worked with Mussolini in March 1919 to organize the "fasci di combattimento" which were to become the Fascist party. The hall in which the "fasci" first met was provided by the Milan Association of Merchants and Shopkeepers, many of whom were Jewish. Jewish landowners and businessmen helped finance the early Fascists because, like most of the middle class, they believed the new movement would be the salvation of the sharply divided nation. Over 200 Jews participated in the "March on Rome," and at least 700 were among the first Fascist party cardholders.

Mussolini personally, until he joined forces with Hitler, had not been especially anti-Semitic though he vacillated in his comments, depending on the objective of the moment. Some of his closest associates were Jewish, including Margherita Sarfatti, the mentor of his early years, and Angelica Balabanoff, the Russian Socialist who was his biographer and mistress. In 1919, when Mussolini was openly courting influential Jews, he wrote effusive articles in his newspaper *Popolo d'Italia:* "In Italy there is absolutely no difference between Jews and non-Jews, in every field from religion to politics, to the military or industry. . . . Italian Jews can find their new Zion here, in our land, which after all many of them have heroically defended with their lives." Later, in June 1922, again in *Popolo d'Italia* he held forth against right-wing Germans who did not recognize the value and contribution of German Jews, commenting on the "violent and exaggerated state" of the Germans. Mussolini made overtures to the Zionists, also, hosting a visit by Chaim Weizmann and suggesting that Italian firms be entrusted with the construction of the port at Haifa.

This rapprochement for a time controlled any generalized Jewish opposition to fascism, although dissent surfaced in subtle ways, as in a strong revival of interest in Jewish culture and traditions. Most Italians in the twenties were in the same state of generally passive acceptance. At the end of 1931, when an oath of allegiance was required from university professors, only three Jews were reported to have refused. But if the Jewish population as a whole did not feel threatened by fascism, a good number of individual Jews opposed the regime. They did so on ideological grounds and not because of discrimination against their religion. In fact, most Jews felt the Law of the Community passed in 1931 was a great achievement because it clearly established the rights of Jews to their religion, even though the Lateran Accords of 1929 with the Vatican had established Catholicism as the religion of State.

The Law of the Community recognized the Jewish community as a legal entity which could tax its people to provide funds needed for religious instruction and other benefits. The law also provided that members of the community were obligated to carry out its regulations unless they had formally declared they were abandoning the Jewish faith. One of the first results of the new law was the inauguration of Hebrew religious instruction in public schools and the printing of modified text books for Jewish children so that they would not be required to study Catholic dogma.

The climax of Mussolini's rapport with Judaism came in 1932, only six years before his complete about-face. That year Emil Ludwig's *Conversation with Mussolini* was published, in which Mussolini is quoted as condemning anti-Semitism as "stupidity" and as saying "Anti-Semitism does not exist in Italy. . . . Italian Jews have always been good citizens and as soldiers they have fought courageously." The Party followed Il Duce's lead, except for Giovanni Preziosi (a defrocked priest) and a few on the outer fringes of the Fascist hierarchy. Most Italian Jews, watching the gathering storm elsewhere and especially in Germany, considered themselves lucky.

After Hitler became chancellor in 1933, Mussolini on several occasions spoke disparagingly of the "junior Fascist's" racism, and he even advised the Führer to restrain himself on the grounds that world opinion would be against him and that international

Jewry would take economic revenge on Germany. This message was sent via the Italian ambassador to Berlin, Vittorio Cerruti, who delivered it in a personal audience with Hitler. Cerruti reported that Hitler interrupted him halfway through his remarks, declaring that the Nazi aim was to wipe out bolshevism and it was not his fault if German Marxists were Jewish. He added that America, too, would soon follow his example, to rid itself of the "Marxist peril."

But Hitler struck a responsive chord in some of Mussolini's colleagues, who feared the influx of German and East European Jewish refugees both because they might fuel the dormant fire of anti-fascism and because on a personal level they were economic and financial competitors. Anti-Semitic sentiments began to show up in segments of the Fascist press in 1933–34, and they were not suppressed by Mussolini. However, the major city newspapers, privately owned but under Fascist censorship since 1926, were able to continue publishing articles condemning racism. Several Jews still held prominent positions in the Fascist government, among them Aldo Finzi, an early undersecretary of the interior and member of the Fascist Grand Council, and Guido Jung, minister of finance. The Vatican newspapers criticized the anti-Christian nature of racist theory, though the Church was in an ambivalent position since it applauded Hitler's anti-communism.

For a time Mussolini tried to play the role of mediator on the "Jewish question." In September 1933 he intimated to the chief rabbi in Rome that he would try to persuade Hitler to permit Jews leaving Germany for Palestine to take along their money and belongings. Mussolini had his first meeting with Hitler in Venice, in June 1934. He was not impressed, and later described Hitler as "an imbecile and a rascal, a fanatic rascal and a frightening chatterbox." Apparently in Venice Hitler had reviewed most of *Mein Kampf* in a one-sided monologue. The Ethiopian war was to preoccupy Il Duce for the next few years, and his victory there brought Mussolini to the apex of his popularity among the Italian

Jews who volunteered (and were drafted) to fight in Africa. Others contributed considerable money to the war effort.

At the same time, Jews in the anti-Fascist movement were energetically and outspokenly voicing their opinions. In 1934 Carlo Levi, the well-known writer and painter, and several other prominent anti-Fascists in Turin were arrested and sent to prison or to semi-exile, under police surveillance. Levi was shipped off to a small town in Lucania, an experience he described in his famous novel, *Christ Stopped at Eboli*.

In June 1936 Mussolini appointed his son-in-law, Galeazzo Ciano, as minister of foreign affairs. Ciano favored closer relations with Hitler, and a few months later Mussolini made a triumphal journey to Berlin, where he assured Hitler of the growing ties between their two countries. Concurrently, the Fascist press stepped up its anti-Semitic attacks, and unlike previous attempts, this time Mussolini explicitly approved it, seconded by most of the Fascist hierarchy.

Stung by worldwide Jewish criticism of his war in Ethiopia and intervention in Spain, Mussolini now viewed the international Jewish community as his enemy. Among the Fascist inner circle, only Italo Balbo spoke up against the growing anti-Semitism. (Balbo later died in a mysterious plane accident in Africa.) Even the king of Italy, who until then had been rather indifferent to "the Jewish question," went along with Mussolini's turnabout. When Ribbentrop, Hitler's emissary, went to Rome in November 1937 to sign the Anti-Comintern pact on the part of Germany, Mussolini and Ciano assured him that a full-fledged propaganda campaign against the Jews was underway.

A distinction must be made between Hitler's and Mussolini's racism, without in any way absolving Mussolini. Extermination of the Jews was not Mussolini's goal, but he was determined to destroy Jewish involvement in Italian life, and if possible to deport every Jew from Italy. The press and radio campaign of 1937–38 was accompanied by other significant moves. The first official act was the publication on February 16, 1938 of a government

bulletin stating that international Jewry was unequivocally responsible for worldwide anti-Fascist opinion, and that therefore
the government would now monitor the activities of Jewish immigrants coming to Italy. A few months later Mussolini himself
crossed off the names of Italian Jews from a list of people slated
to attend international meetings. Dr. Italo Olivetti was among
those prevented from participating in a Technical Congress in
Berlin.

Then came the bombshell. At a conference in July under the
auspices of the Ministry of Culture a number of "scientists" offered
"proof" that there was a pure Italian race to which the Jews did
not belong. A manifesto, "The Defense of the Race," was published on July 14, 1938. The manifesto stated that Italian Jews
were a race apart, of non-European origin. Shortly after this
announcement a Bureau of Demography and Race (known for
years after as "Demorazza") was created, and its first official act
was to initiate a census of Jews in public office. Children of
immigrants were forbidden to attend public schools, and banks
were ordered to reveal the accounts and safe-deposit holdings of
all Jews. A further explanation of these actions was offered in
another document published on August 5, bearing the often-quoted
slogan "To discriminate does not mean to persecute." The intent
of its verbiage is clear: "The Fascist government does not have a
special plan to persecute Jews as such. It's another matter. . . .
The Jews in Italy number 44,000 . . . ; the proportion is one in
every thousand of the population. It is clear that from now on the
participation of Jews in national life must be regulated propor-
tionately."

The ambiguity of these statements would soon be dispelled
after a meeting of the Grand Council scheduled for October 6.
The king was aware of the preparations for the meeting, and
apparently his only recommendation was that patriotic Jews should
be rewarded in some way. The Vatican did not formally interfere
although it considered converted Jews to be Christians. *Civiltà
Cattolica,* the Jesuit newspaper, had for some time been publish-

ing articles accusing the "Masonic Jewish gang" of fostering anti-clericalism and communism. As it turned out, Mussolini ignored even the Vatican's stand on marriages with converted Jews, causing the Vatican officially—and ineffectually—to protest that the government had violated article 34 of the Treaty of 1929.

The Grand Council met at 10 PM on October 6 and continued the session until 2:45 AM. Only three members opposed the final results: Balbo, De Bono and Federozi. Balbo was the most vocal, arguing for recognition of Jewish war heroes (the king's point) and for the admission of Jewish children in public schools. The decisions taken at this meeting were announced in the Official Gazette on November 17 and became law on January 5, 1939. In a nutshell, the racial laws severely restricted (and in most cases eliminated) the rights of Jews to work, to own property, to teach or to study, and to enter into mixed marriages.

As these events unfolded, Mussolini was confronted with a new problem. The Fascist propaganda campaign which was supposed to have prepared the Italian people to go along with the anti-Semitic legislation had boomeranged. Many not only sympathized with the Jews, but began to have second thoughts about fascism. Catholic lay people, as well as many priests, were much more concerned than the Vatican hierarchy and were vocal about their concern.

As for the Jews themselves, many of them could not believe what was happening to them. In spite of the long press campaign, the July manifesto and other events, they seemed to be caught by surprise. Those who accepted the reality of the situation left the country if they could, or changed their names, taking whatever steps might protect them. At the same time, the Jewish leadership did not officially protest the October edicts. In fact, on October 12 there appeared the following statement: "The Council of the *Unione delle Comunita Israelitiche Italiane* (the Italian Jewish Community), meeting after the deliberation of the Fascist Grand Council, reaffirms strongly the complete dedication of Italian Jews to the Fascist nation, even though at this moment we are required to make heavy sacrifices.'' This statement reflected the sorrow and dismay of Italian Jews who regarded themselves as true Italians, and for whom Italy was their mother country. There were even some Jews who renounced their faith, in order to prove their loyalty to their motherland.

By the fall of 1939 Mussolini had other problems to occupy his attention. Anti-German sentiment in Italy was reaching new heights not only because of the Jews, but because of the realization that Nazi promises of peace were a total lie. When the Pact of Steel was signed in May of that year, Ciano had noted in his diary: ''Ribbentrop repeats Germany's interest in and intention to insure for itself a long period of peace, at least three years.'' But by August, Ciano's diary entry read: ''Starace [Chief of Staff of the Italian Militia] says that when Germany attacks Poland we must keep our eyes open to prevent public demonstrations against the Germans. A policy of neutrality will, on the other hand, be more popular and if it were necessary later, war with Germany would be every bit as popular.''

While Mussolini was preoccupied with foreign affairs, the Jewish community had somehow managed to adjust to the new regulations. Greatly helped by the generally sympathetic attitude of most people, Jews found or created new jobs in the private sector, having been ousted from public service. It was easy enough to change the name of a company to something generic and acceptable. Bank accounts could be put in the name of the new company and cash squirreled away in safe places. Since many of the Jewish enterprises made products essential to Italian industry and often to the war machine, these changes were not very carefully scrutinized. Those who could left the country: some 5,000 were able to emigrate between 1939 and 1943.

The non-Italian Jews who had arrived from Germany and other countries did not fare so well. For them camps were established in isolated regions, mostly in the far South. Italian Jews whose citizenship had been revoked for various reasons were also sent to these camps, which were actually loosely supervised settlements. By September 1940 fifteen of these camps were in existence. Life there was not cruel, but it was monotonous and there was the ever-present fear of what the future would bring. The facilities were usually crude, but internees were allowed a fair amount of freedom and they soon organized classes for the children and planted gardens to supplement their inadequate rations.

Mussolini's policies towards Italian Jews abroad took a different tack. Perhaps to prove he was not under Hitler's thumb, he refused to permit Hitler to deport Italian Jews in Germany to concentration camps in Poland, insisting that they be repatriated. Nor would the Italian government extradite to Berlin German Jews who had fled to Italy. The sections of France, Yugoslavia and Greece occupied by Italian troops became refugee centers for Jews in those countries, who knew they would be relatively safe under the protection of Italian armed forces. The Italian officers in charge insisted it was their right to establish policy in territory they controlled. At one point General Roethke of the SS in France complained: ''The Italian is and has been incomprehensible. Italian military authorities and Italian police protect the Jews in every way they can. The Italian zone of influence, especially on the Côte d'Azur, has become the Promised Land for Jews residing in France. In the last few months there has been a mass exodus of Jews from our zone to the Italian zone . . . facilitated by the terrain, help of the French and by false identity cards.''

It should be noted that Italian intransigence was not necessarily for humanitarian reasons: German demands were a threat to Italian military authority. When Ribbentrop himself insisted that Yugoslav Jews be taken to Trieste to be handed over to the Nazis there, Mussolini ostensibly agreed but then ordered his general to think up any excuse—perhaps lack of transportation facilities—to prevent carrying out the order.

After the fall of Mussolini on July 25, 1943 the situation for the Jews did not change. The interim Badoglio government left the racial laws in place, because, as Badoglio explained in his memoirs, ''It was not possible, at that time, to enact an open abrogation of the racial laws because it would have meant an open clash with the Germans. . . . I called in various Jewish leaders and explained that while for the moment I could not proceed to abolish the laws, they would in effect remain inoperative.'' The only relief actually granted the Jews was their release from internment camps, together with the release of political prisoners.

For a few weeks after the September 8 Armistice there was no move against the Jews except for the declaration by the new Fascist puppet government in the North that the Jews were now officially enemies of the Republican Fascist State, established under Mussolini by grace of Hitler. In Rome, which had been occupied by the Germans almost immediately, the Jews were not harassed until September 26, when the heads of the Jewish community were summoned to the German Embassy. There they were told by the regional chief of the SS that anyone with a drop of Jewish blood was considered an enemy. No exceptions would be made for conversion, abandonment of faith or any other reason. They were also ordered to hand over 50 kilos of gold (or the equivalent in dollars or sterling) within 36 hours or else 200 would be deported to Germany.

Well within the time limit the gold was found, made up mostly of jewelry collected from both Jews and non-Jews. (The Vatican had offered to lend the difference, if necessary, but there was even more gold than was required.) No sooner had the Nazis collected the gold, than on September 29 they invaded Jewish Community headquarters and seized the contents of a safe, over two million lire, as well as many important documents. In the following days SS men searched all the synagogues, removing anything of value including priceless books and religious objects. Finally, at dawn on October 16 German police surrounded the ghetto and removed every person living there. They also went to Jewish homes outside the ghetto: in all, over a thousand were arrested.

The official report of the raid, signed by SS chief Herbert

Kappler, cites active remonstrance by other Italians and complains that doubtless they managed to hide some Jews. Within days the thousand were shipped to Nazi extermination camps, principally Birkenau. One woman and 14 men survived from this group. Their homes and shops were looted and stripped of anything worthwhile.

Not all the Roman Jews had believed their lives would be saved by 50 kilos of gold. A tiny minority realized this was a trick, among them a young man named Bruno D'Ariccio. His first reaction was to fight back, not to surrender the gold which he regarded as temporary blackmail. He was convinced many Romans would come to the Jews' aid, but he was quickly silenced by the community elders.

As a young boy during the thirties, Bruno had worked in his father's stationery store. Anti-Fascist writers who stopped by for supplies often stayed and discussed their opinions. From them Bruno early developed a taste for rebellion. During the Spanish Civil War he secretly collected funds for the anti-Fascist International Brigade and he became friendly with an underground group in Reggio Emilia.

In Rome in the early forties Bruno and his friends would gather at the Bar Rosati to argue far into the night until, finally, suspicious police brought them in for questioning. The group then dissolved, except for Bruno and a few others who continued to meet secretly, changing locations frequently. During the spring and summer of 1943 Bruno managed to establish contact with Allied agents in Rome. When the September 8 Armistice was announced, his first thought was to secure a good supply of weapons. An opportunity came early in October, when the Germans decided to clear the *carabinieri*—Italian state police—out of their barracks, preparatory to deporting them to Germany. Bruno was familiar with the layout of the barracks, which was situated near a wooded area. He and his friends managed to sneak up to the rear of the building, overcome two German guards stationed there, and lock them in a small storeroom. While the rest of the Nazi guards were lining up *carabinieri* in the front courtyard, the young rebels got away with a large supply of guns and ammunition.

At the time Bruno lived with his parents and one of his brothers. Just as the October 16 roundup of the Jews was about to begin he received a warning phone call from one of his friends. He rushed to tell his married brother, but just as Bruno arrived at his street he saw his brother being led away at gunpoint, together with his wife and two small children. Bruno watched helplessly: for him to attack then would have meant certain death for all of them. He never saw the family again. Soon after, Bruno and another brother joined a Resistance group headed by General Montezemolo, one of the few Italian Army officers who had tried to defend Rome as the Germans entered on September 9.

The group's hideout was the Hospital of Santo Spirito. Evidently there was an informer in their midst, because on the night of November 13 a squad of German and Fascist police raced through the hospital and arrested many of the group, including another of Bruno's brothers, who was deported to Auschwitz and also was never heard from again. Bruno escaped because he had been out on an errand.

General Montezemolo decided to assign Bruno to planning strategy rather than active sabotage, but Bruno was too much of an activist to tolerate desk work for long. So his next assignment was to assume the identity of one Antonio Corsetti, a Fascist army lieutenant who for a while had been a prisoner of the British. For a month Bruno was drilled on Corsetti's life, background and habits and when he was considered letter perfect, he went to the new Fascist headquarters, declaring he had escaped from the British and was reporting for duty again.

Although Bruno had grown a mustache, changed his hair style and added eyeglasses, his disguise was by no means foolproof. His situation was made more dangerous by the fact that he had been on the Nazi wanted list since his brothers' arrests. However, for weeks he was able to give valuable information to Montezemolo, who in turn relayed it to Allied agents in Rome. During the May 3rd strike in Rome he was assigned by the SS to special duty. One of his duties was to find and arrest himself. At first he thought this was some kind of a black joke, and that he had been discovered, but it turned out to be a perfectly serious assignment. Shortly after, on June 4, Rome was liberated and D'Ariccio spent the rest of the war as a writer for the reestablished Rome newspapers.

Paolo Alatri was another young Roman Jew who refused to be optimistic about enemy intentions. As a boy he had been exposed to all the Fascist propaganda ploys, all the appeals to youth and patriotism. He did not begin to have doubts until high school, where he would join other students in lengthy discussions about art, literature and philosophy (which always had a political undercurrent). By 1937 Paolo was already involved in an underground group and that fall he was the driver of the auto taking a leading Communist, Giorgio Amendola, away from Rome just as the police were about to arrest him.

After the racial laws were passed in 1938, Paolo was excluded from public libraries so he began using the Vatican library, which was neutral ground, open to all. For a few years he wrote articles under a pseudonym, meanwhile joining the fledgling Action Party. When the Germans occupied Rome in September 1943 and then demanded their infamous 50 kilos of gold, the Alatri family contributed their share but that same day they deserted the apartment they had owned since 1925, and went into hiding under an assumed name. Paolo worked undercover for the Party of Action and "married" a Catholic woman (not in the civil sense since interracial marriages were forbidden). When she became pregnant early in 1944 they moved to her parents' apartment on Rome's Via Lombardia, just off Via Veneto. This was a brash move, since the Nazis had made their headquarters in the Hotel Flora and several other luxury hotels in the Via Veneto area.

While he lived with his in-laws, Paolo wrote a daily bulletin about underground activities which he mimeographed every morning, making some fifty copies he himself distributed. The first part of the bulletin was devoted to news from Radio London and other signals he could receive on his shortwave set. The second half was information of local interest and importance: news of upcoming roundups, of possible spies and their tactics, where black-market food could be bought, etc. The copies were left at the headquarters of the different political parties, where he would pick up leaflets to leave at central locations. He also helped raise money for the needy, and was a source of false identification papers. He himself carried papers describing him as Paolo Aniello, a refugee from the southern town of Avellino.

All this was done literally under the eyes of the Germans. It was a matter of knowing where to duck into a friendly courtyard if necessary, where there were convenient side streets and how to disappear into the intricate paths of the nearby Borghese Gardens, a large park just off the Via Veneto. The Nazis could not patrol every one of the alleys and side streets of Rome, nor did they want to, fearing ambushes. After Rome was liberated on June 4, Alatri, too, began a long career in journalism, becoming editor of the Action Party's *Italia Libera* and then of the newspaper *La Repubblica*. He also taught at the University of Palermo, and in 1963 was elected a Communist party deputy in Parliament.

The experience of Roman Jews was being repeated throughout Italy: for example, Venice had a similar ghetto raid in December 1943. The Republican Fascist government then sent its agents to scavenge whatever was left, especially in small localities the Nazis tended to ignore. In December the Fascists had announced that all Venetian Jews, even the *discriminati,* (those who had been allowed a little freedom) were to be sent to concentration camps. All their possessions were to be acquired by the State, which would distribute them to the "needy."

Desperate as the situation was for the Jews, it was not entirely hopeless. In Rome, for example, the underground groups had formed a Committee for National Liberation on September 9, the day after the Armistice was announced. One of the first actions of the CLN was to supply false IDs and ration cards to those Jews who had managed to escape the Nazi dragnets, or who had had the foresight not to wait for the raids to happen. Many families took in Jewish refugees and, in Rome alone, over 150 convents and monasteries offered hiding places. The Resistance helped in many other ingenious ways. Official orders to ship families to concentration camps were "lost"; advance notice was given to those whose homes were about to be searched; and in Turin a Dr. Domenico Coggiola established an "infectious ward" in his hospital, which he filled with Jews to keep them safe from the Nazis.

The Jews who fought back included some very young people. Adriano Vanzetti (Riccardo's younger brother) was only 14 when he began to work with the underground. His mother was Jewish and had tried to go to Switzerland in October 1943. When that plan failed, she managed to reach a French convent, where she remained until the end of the war. (His father, a professor at the University of Padua, continued to teach.) Adriano had become expert at deciphering codes while listening to Radio London and this talent was useful to a local Garibaldi Brigade which transmitted political and military information to the Allies in Bari, and coordinated parachute drops with them. In January 1945 Adriano was caught by the SS during a roundup and was taken to a prison in Genoa. As far as his family knew, he had disappeared. The prison was a way station for people scheduled for German labor camps. Because the starvation diet had made Adriano sick, he was detained until he would be strong enough to be sent to Germany. Meanwhile, he was put to work helping other sick people. The war ended before he was fully recovered. Genoa was liberated on Adriano's fifteenth birthday, although he never thought he would live to see it. In the last days of the occupation all the prisoners were brought into a large room, where a priest offered them communion and absolution. They were sure they were about to be killed, but events moved too fast even for a mass murder. The Nazi guards suddenly vanished, leaving them free.

Probably the youngest of the Jewish Resistance fighters was Franco Cesana, who died before his thirteenth birthday and was awarded the gold medal of honor posthumously. In 1938, when Franco was seven years old, he had to leave public school because of the racial laws. For a time he attended a special school for Jewish children, and then he was sent to the rabbinical school in Rome. Soon after the Armistice, Franco rejoined his mother and older brother, Lelio, (their father had died) in Bologna. In December 1943 they had to desert their home to escape arrest by the Nazis, and the family began a nomad existence which ended just before Christmas in the village of Serramozzoni.

Partisans were active in the nearby mountains, only a mile or so away, and within a few days Lelio had joined them. Franco continued to live with his mother but he became a courier for Lelio's unit, carrying messages and relaying information from Radio London. The unit did not have a radio, nor was there one in Serramozzoni: Franco had to walk miles to Casella Nuova, where someone owned the only radio in the vicinity.

Franco envied his brother and was determined to become a full-fledged partisan. But Lelio's unit commander thought Franco was too young for a fighting role. Late in April Franco decided to contact a Garibaldi unit in Gombola and left without telling his mother, who thought he was on one of his usual messenger routes. Franco was tall, articulate and self-confident, and apparently had no problem this time convincing the commander that he was old enough to fight. He wrote to his mother:

Dearest Mother,
    After I left I couldn't send news to you for reasons you can guess. Now I'll tell you the full story. I left not sure myself what I was going to do. I walked a long time, and finally stopped to sleep in a hayloft near Matteozzi. In the morning I continued walking toward Gombola. I was very hungry so I ate mulberries. I got there about 9 o'clock and managed to locate some patriots who showed me the way to partisan headquarters. I arrived there dead tired but I screwed up my courage and introduced myself and after a bit I was allowed to join Marcello's unit.
    Are you pleased? Because of my studies I've been assigned to a relatively safe post near Gombola. So you shouldn't worry about me because I'm living like a king. I'm very healthy; only sleep is a little precarious. So I'll end this letter. Be brave, the end is near. I think of you and send love.

Actually, Franco was also assigned to spy on the German soldiers stationed in town. He knew a little German and would try to eavesdrop on their conversations, as he counted their trucks and took note of the weapons they carried. Franco was given a horse to make longer trips possible, and occasionally he would stop by to see his mother. Eventually the Germans in Gombola became too numerous for safety, and Marcello decided to move headquarters to Pescarola. Franco and several others were sent to reconnoiter the new locality and on the way back, Franco visited his mother, promising to return for his thirteenth birthday. But the group was ambushed as they headed for camp and Franco was killed by machine-gun fire. His grieving commander made him a second lieutenant posthumously, probably one of the youngest officers in military history. Franco was buried in the Jewish cemetery in Bologna.

There are innumerable stories of Jews who, as Italians, wanted to join the fight against the enemy. The renowned psychiatrist, Bruno Bettelheim, has made the point that Italian Jews drew strength from the fact that they were surrounded by a generally friendly people. Many Jews elsewhere in Europe had hostile or indifferent neighbors, which added to their feeling of isolation. Italian Jews, because they felt supported, were reinforced in their will to live and fight back.

Although they did not live to join the armed Resistance of 1943–45, the Rosselli brothers, Carlo and Nello, are among the brightest stars in the annals of the Jewish resistance to fascism. Many who were close to the Rossellis went on to realize their dreams, including Riccardo Bauer and Ferruccio Parri (who eventually became the leader of the unified Resistance). The Rossellis were students at the University of Florence when the Fascist *squadristi* first made their appearance. They were part of a group called the "Circolo di Cultura," which clustered around the ardent and outspoken anti-Fascist, Prof. Gaetano Salvemini. They met regularly until New Year's Eve 1924, when *squadristi* invaded their meeting place, wrecked it and made a bonfire in the street of their books and furnishings. (Earlier that year Nello had made his passionate and patriotic address at the Jewish Youth Congress.) In defiance of the raid, in January 1925 the group published the first edition of the famous underground newspaper *Non Mollare!* which continued to appear until October, when all the contributors were arrested or forced into exile. The Rossellis managed to escape the dragnet and went into hiding in Milan for a time.

Carlo was the more aggressive of the two brothers, a natural leader, but Nello was no less involved. When in November 1926 it became apparent that Filippo Turati, the grand old man of Italian socialism, was a marked man, it was Carlo who helped organize his escape from Italy.

Turati's Milan house was under constant surveillance. The situation was further complicated by the fact that Turati had a heart condition and was also reluctant to leave Italy. When the opportunity finally came, he was spirited away through a back alley, where a car was waiting to get him out of Milan. For the next eleven days he was hidden in the country home of another old Socialist, Ettore Albini, while Carlo tried to devise a safe escape route, with Ferruccio Parri's help. They decided against Switzerland because Turati was too feeble to attempt a climb over the mountains, and trains were out of the question because they were too well guarded.

For five days the police guarded Turati's house, unaware that it was empty because it was not unusual for the old man to stay indoors for long periods. Once his absence was discovered, Mussolini himself gave the order to find Turati immediately. Tipped off that the Fascist police were about to question Albini, Carlo Rosselli first drove Turati to Ivrea, to the home of Camillo Olivetti (founder of the Olivetti Company), and then on to Turin, to stay with Prof. Giuseppe Levi. (Albini later spent nine months in jail for his role in the episode.)

At this stage, Rosselli and Parri were joined in the plot by Sandro Pertini (Italy's president from 1978 to 1985), then a young lawyer from the seaside town of Savona, and by Camillo Olivetti's son, Adriano. They all agreed the only escape route was France by sea. Pertini made the boat arrangements and Adriano drove Rosselli and Turati to a hotel in Savona, where they registered as father and son. The ocean liner *Augustus* was anchored in the harbor, and that evening—December 12—the group boarded a chartered boat allegedly to take a look at the liner. The local police accepted the explanation, since the ship was the pride of Italy and many had been going out to see her.

The group was, of course, headed out to sea. It was a cold, windy night with waves breaking constantly over the bow. After eighteen hours they reached Corsica, and the next day Turati left for Paris, accompanied by Pertini. Parri and Rosselli returned to Italy where they were immediately arrested, though they were not tried until the following September. By that time they had served most of the ten-month sentence they received, but the Fascist police managed to dredge up new charges against Carlo Rosselli, who was given an additional five years to be spent on the island of Lipari. In another boat rescue, this time engineered by Salvemini (then in exile in Paris), Rosselli and a group of friends escaped from Lipari in July 1929 on a forty-foot yacht, the *Dream V,* that had belonged to an Egyptian prince.

Soon after his arrival in Paris, Rosselli and other exiles began a new political movement called "Giustizia e Libertà" (GL—Justice and Liberty). The new organization was not intended to be a political party, though the *Giellisti* (as GL members were called) did aim to unify the non-Communist parties in a common assault on fascism. Their goal was the abolition of the monarchy and the establishment of a democratic republic.

The movement caught on quickly in Italy, and recruited members among exiles all over the world. The Turin branch, led by Leone Ginsberg, was the most active until the Fascists arrested almost the entire membership in 1935. When the Spanish Civil War broke out, GL organized the first Italian volunteers to help defend the republican government against General Franco. Carlo Rosselli was a commander of a unit in Catalonia until he developed severe phlebitis in his legs and had to return to Paris to recuperate. For the first six months of 1937 Rosselli did what he could for Spain from Paris. His broadcasts from France were an abomination to Mussolini, especially the frequently repeated slogan "Today in Spain, tomorrow in Italy." The broadcasts encouraged pro-Spanish republican agitation by Italian students at a time when Mussolini was sending both weapons and troops to help Franco.

When Nello Rosselli applied for a passport in June to visit his brother in France, it was granted with unusual speed considering that he, too, had spent some months in confinement and was held in suspicion by the Fascist police. On June 9, 1937 a few days after Nello's arrival, the brothers were ambushed as they drove along a lonely road in Bagnoles de L'Orme, in Normandy. Their badly beaten bodies were not found until two days later. The Italian press immediately denied that Fascists were in any way responsible for the murder, but public opinion both in Italy and abroad placed full blame on Mussolini. Not since Matteoti's death in 1924 had there been such an outcry: some 200,000 mourners followed the funeral cortege in Paris. An investigation conducted by Salvemini eventually disclosed that the crime was actually committed by Frenchmen hired by SIM, the military intelligence service, under direct orders of Foreign Minister Ciano. After the death of the Rossellis the GL movement virtually collapsed, until the remaining members eventually revived it in the form of a new political party, the Partito d' Azione (Action Party), founded in 1942.

In his persecution of the Jews, Mussolini lost for Italy some of the finest minds and talents of that time, among them Eugenio Curiel, a brilliant scholar of the early science of nuclear physics. Curiel had been convinced that intellectuals must also be political activists. For him this meant anti-fascism. Unlike Neapolitan writer Jaime Pintor who regarded his Resistance work as a duty, Curiel saw it as an ideal to be enthusiastically pursued. With typical thoroughness he studied Marx and became a member of the Communist party.

In 1938 he was dismissed from his university post because of the racial laws. He then went to Paris, ostensibly to accept a teaching assignment there but actually to work with Italian exiles in France. (Universities in both the United States and Switzerland had offered him teaching positions.) Curiel was not satisfied with what could be accomplished as an exile, and soon returned to Milan. He was arrested in June 1939 and sentenced to five years of confinement on the island of Ventotene, where he met many other members of the underground. In fact, so many political activists were sent there that Pintor referred to the island as the "Ventotene Government."

Curiel was freed, along with many others, in August 1943 during the 45 days of the Badoglio interim government. When he again returned to Milan, the Communist party asked him to be director of publications. In his articles in the newspaper *L'Unita,* Curiel stressed one of his favorite themes—that the Resistance was the first phase of a new, democratic Italy in which the present class system would disappear. He declared: "This is the final war that Italian peasants have regarded as a national war in which they are willing to participate voluntarily." Curiel also emphasized in his writings the need for cooperation between Catholics and the parties of the left. Most of all, he devoted his energies to rousing the young, to making them understand the importance of their role in the political life of a future Italy.

His enthusiasm was relentless and contagious. Yet it also left him vulnerable. On February 25, 1945 a Fascist squadron patrolling the Milan streets recognized him and shot him dead, without a warning. An old flower-woman was one of the few spectators of the savage scene. After the soldiers left, she walked over to the body and placed a few carnations on Curiel. Several days later a priest said Mass for him at the Church of San Carlo, a fitting ecumenical tribute to Curiel's efforts to unify the people of Italy.

If Mussolini was profligate in dispensing with Jewish intellectuals, he certainly recognized the value of selected Jewish industrialists, among them Camillo Olivetti. The company itself had been put in a special protected class, a pragmatic approach which even the Nazis adopted when their supply of typewriters ran dry. Camillo had been one of the "elder statesmen" of the Jewish community in Ivrea, headquarters of Olivetti S.p.A. The community dated back to the sixteenth century, when the first refugees arrived there from Spain. Camillo's strong moral and political beliefs were an important influence both in Ivrea and in his company. His social theories derived from the Socialist party which was founded in Italy at about the same time that Camillo started his first business. He also had been strongly influenced by several long trips to the United States. It was at the Chicago World's Fair in 1893 that he saw the typewriter which eventually started him on his own career.

In 1899 Camillo married Luisa Revel, a Valdesian Protestant and a woman with very definite ideas about the dignity of humanity. Their son, Adriano (who assisted in Turati's escape), was born in 1901. As a boy he was taught to ignore class distinctions: his playmates were peasants as well as children of the workers in his father's plant. After high school, he attended the nearby University of Turin, where he became great friends with Gino Levi and Piero Gobetti, youthful anti-Fascists from the earliest days of Mussolini's ascent to power. When Matteoti was murdered in 1924, Adriano helped organize a large public demonstration in Ivrea, earning for himself the scrutiny of the Fascist police and a dossier that listed him as "Olivetti Adriano di Camillo: Classifica–Sovversivo" (Classification–Subversive). It was shortly after this that Adriano drove the Socialist leader Turati on his escape from Italy, an exploit never discovered by the Fascist police.

In 1938, the year the racial laws were passed, Adriano became president of the Olivetti Company. Because he had been baptized, Adriano had been certified as Aryan and was allowed to travel on business in spite of Fascist suspicions about his past behavior. To protect them, some of Olivetti's Jewish employees were sent to safe plant locations abroad, especially in Latin America. Others, like Gino Levi whose mother also was "Aryan," changed their names. The fact that Adriano was permitted to move freely around Italy gave him the opportunity of making contact with anti-Fascists in many cities. Early in the war years Adriano became convinced that an Italian switch to the Allied side was a possibility. In June 1943 he arranged a meeting with the American diplomat Allen Dulles, in Switzerland, but nothing came of it. The next month Badoglio replaced Mussolini, and in doing so declared that "the war [against the Allies] continues." As a result, Adriano was denounced as a traitor for having dealt with the enemy and was imprisoned at Regina Coeli, in Rome. Efforts to release him succeeded only hours before the Nazis occupied Rome, after the Armistice was signed.

Ivrea, too, was occupied by the Germans soon after September 8, and it became clear that Camillo, although in semi-retirement, was in danger. Sick and disheartened, he went to live with some farmers he knew and trusted. He died in December. According to his wishes, Camillo was buried in the Jewish cemetery in nearby Biella. No one in the family attended the funeral because by that time they were scattered all over Italy and the world, and travel was almost impossible. But his faithful workers turned out in force, in spite of the danger of retribution for attending the funeral of a Jew. The Nazis had already begun their roundups and the funeral could have turned into a massacre, which the workers well knew. It was a miserable, rainy day and the mourners came mostly on foot, trudging for miles to pay their last respects.

All during the occupation the Olivetti factories continued operating because Germany needed the office equipment, although mandatory shipments were often skillfully sabotaged. The company and its 4,000 employees had been left in the charge of Gino Levi (he had assumed the name of Martinoli) and Giovanni Enriques, aided administratively by Giuseppe Pero. (Levi and Enriques were also members of the local Committee of National Liberation and so were in constant danger.) By their skillful management, they were able to outwit the Nazis. Books were padded to allow hiring an inordinate number of workers, thereby providing a living for a great many people. Because food was severely rationed, meals were provided at work and the cafeteria was opened to the town people also. The precision equipment at the plants was used at night to manufacture a stream of false identity cards and the Nazi passes that gave the holder the right to move about, especially important for the partisans.

Twenty-four Olivetti employees died fighting with Resistance forces. One, Willy Jervis, was given the gold medal of honor. Not one worker was deported to Germany because management had convinced the local Nazi commander that the men were more useful to the German war effort at work in Ivrea. When the Germans were about to retreat in the face of the Allied advance, they threatened to blow up the factories as they left. Enriques averted the disaster by bribing the officer in charge with the promise of a postwar executive position in one of Olivetti's foreign offices, a promise that was never kept.

By the time the Germans were defeated, some 8,000 Italian Jews had been deported to German concentration camps. Of these, just under 1,000 survived. About 9,000 Italian Jews succeeded in emigrating. A great deal of controversy still surrounds the role

An internal view of the German-installed crematory in Trieste, the only one in Italy.

of the Vatican during the Holocaust and specifically the neutral war stance of Pope Pius XII. The Vatican newspaper, *L'Osservatore Romano,* reported in October 1943 that the Pope recognized "no bounds of nationality, religion or race" in his desire to provide "universal and paternal succor." Many believe the Jews would have been helped if the Pope had taken an official stand against Hitler, especially since this might have split the loyalties of German and Fascist soldiers who were also Catholics. Others make the point, certainly debatable, that had Pius XII done so, Hitler might well have arrested him and taken over the Vatican, thereby making Catholics worldwide, as well as Jews, "enemies of the State." It is also argued that because of the Vatican's neutrality, its convents and other institutions remained a refuge not only for Jews, but for other hostages.

In any case, in remembering the Jewish contribution to the Resistance, one fact stands out: for a non-Jewish partisan who fell into enemy hands death was probable though there was a slim chance of imprisonment or exchange. For a Jewish partisan, death was certain.

=8=
The Catholic Clergy: The Loyal Opposition

THE NEUTRAL POSITION of the Vatican during World War II was not shared by many of the Italian clergy, nor by their parishioners. In the first place, Italian Catholics could not be considered as a bloc. Their opinions, especially their political opinions, then as now formed a spectrum from left to right. There were Catholic Communists and there were sincere Catholic Fascists, with the great majority falling somewhere in between.

The Vatican's neutral position was predicated on the fact that it was an international institution whose "constituents" lived all over the world. Therefore the Church had to, theoretically, maintain neutrality during conflicts among nations. Moreover, the Church was self-empowered to issue religious but not political directives. The Vatican's role in Italy at that time was further complicated by the fact that the Lateran Accords of 1929 had made Catholicism the religion of the Fascist state, a development that had been impossible during the anti-clerical governments that had ruled Italy since unification in 1861.

Mussolini had courted the Vatican assiduously because he believed the support of the Holy See would automatically mean the support of the masses. In 1924, only two years after Il Duce had come into power, he abolished Freemasonry (almost as evil in the eyes of the Church as the then fledgling Communist party). On another level, Mussolini pleased the Vatican by appointing chaplains to the Fascist militia, and allotting large sums to increase the clergy's salaries and rebuild churches.

Mussolini also succeeded in exiling Don Luigi Sturzo, founder (in 1919) of the Popular party. The then Pope, Pius XI, regarded the action quite favorably. Sturzo, a Sicilian priest, had based the Popular party platform on social reform. He had long worked with peasants and small landholders to improve their lives, helping to establish cooperatives and rural banks. These projects were greeted with enthusiasm by the clergy, who had been concerned about inroads being made by the "Godless" Socialist party. Benedict XV, Pius XI's predecessor, had regarded the Popularists with favor, and the party included millions of members from Catholic Action and Catholic trade unions. But the Popular party had given rural people a taste of political power, and Pius XI regarded this as an invasion of Vatican prerogatives. It is not surprising that he was gratified when the Popular party was outlawed in 1926, together with all other non-Fascist organizations.

The Concordat of the Lateran Accords, besides establishing Vatican City as the domain of the Pope, made religious education obligatory in both private and public schools and created a Catholic university in Milan. The Church was also given civil power over the marriage of Catholics. Catholic Action, an organization mainly for youth education, was legally permitted to exist on the condition that it either remain apolitical or openly support fascism. Pius XI expressed his satisfaction with Mussolini and the Concordat with these words: "Perhaps it needed a man such as Providence has sent us, a man devoid of the convictions of the liberal school. For the liberals, all laws, all rules, or rather misrules, were fetishes, the more intangible and venerable the more ugly and repulsive did they appear. We believe that, by means of the Concordats, we have given back God to Italy and Italy to God." Mussolini, however, did not exactly agree with this interpretation. In a speech to the Chamber of Deputies on May 13, 1929 he declared: "The Fascist state makes the fullest claim to all ethical character: it is Catholic, but above all it is Fascist, exclusively, essentially Fascist.'' So the question was raised: Which had first claim on individual conscience, the Church or fascism?

Pius XI's view of liberalism was by no means shared by all the clergy. Nevertheless it was the official Vatican line. Accordingly, it was preached in thousands of Sunday sermons. The Concordat had established that the clergy, from bishops on down, must swear allegiance to the king and the government, and that they must not take part in any action harming the State. After the Lateran Accords, relations between the Vatican and the State went along fairly smoothly until 1938, when the July proclamation on racial purity caused the Pope to mildly chide Mussolini. The racial purity laws, aimed at disowning and segregating all Italian Jews, again raised the question for many Catholics: Which had first claim on individual conscience, the Church or the State?

The death of Pius XI and the election in 1939 of Pius XII (the former Cardinal Pacelli) were followed in 1940 by Italy's entry into the World War. Although the Vatican maintained, as it would all through the war, its neutral stance there was a perceptible change in attitude. Besides opposing the racial laws on humanitarian grounds, the Vatican regarded the restrictions on Catholic–Jewish marriages as an infringement of the Lateran Accords, which had given the Pope control over Catholic marriages. Now that Italy was on a war footing with its Nazi ally, many priests, still forced to remain overtly silent, shared the anxieties of their parishioners about the new status with Nazi Germany. Yet, there were also clergy who approved of Mussolini's increasing involvement with Germany, especially some top men in the hierarchy like Cardinal Ildefonso Schuster, Archbishop of Milan. The Jesuits, who had been strongly anti-Semitic on religious grounds, now were quite careful to separate themselves from the Fascist/Nazi racial campaigns.

During this period, former members of the Popular party had begun to organize again as an underground group. On the day Mussolini fell, July 25, 1943, they announced the formation of a new party, Democrazia Cristiana (Christian Democrat—DC), with Alcide De Gasperi as its president. The DC stressed that it was not an official Catholic party, and that it was open to anyone. The new party rapidly gained members, especially among more conservative Catholics, who saw it as a bulwark against the increasingly strong leftist parties. It was also a party to which the clergy could relate.

The Vatican, meanwhile, refused to recognize de jure Mussolini's new puppet government, and Vatican City was an acknowledged sanctuary.The refusal of the Pope to recognize the RSI added to the resentment of the Nazis. In July 1944 the German Consul General in Milan complained to Cardinal Schuster, "I refer not only to the behavior of numerous priests, the rebellious conduct which reflects an attitude of open hostility on the part of certain clerical groups, but I refer also to the position taken by the hierarchy of the Church regarding the duty of Italian workers contributing to the German/Italian war effort."

The attitude of the clergy was especially important in rural areas, where a priest could influence whether or not a village would support the partisans with food and other supplies essential to the survival of the Resistance. As Richard Webster pointed out in *The Cross and the Fasces* ". . . . the real control of the Italian Catholic masses remained with the clergy. . . . The north Italian country priest often shaped or interpreted the attitudes of his parishioners." Often the church building itself and the priest's home would become storage depots for weapons, leaflets and other equipment as well as a meeting place for the partisans and later, for representatives of the Committees of National Liberation. Even the mausoleums in Catholic cemeteries were used as secure hiding places.

Priests frequently climbed steep mountain paths to visit the partisans, to bring them messages or to say Mass. Although the Vatican could not openly condone such behavior, there was indirect support. The archbishop of Piedmont in an Easter 1944 letter to the clergy quoted St. Thomas, "The use of power is God-given if it is carried out in accordance with the precepts and the norms of divine justice: it is not God-given if it is used to commit injustice.'' The Archbishop also repeated the words of Pope Leo XIII, ''In all cases where the laws of nature and the will of God are violated, it is equally iniquitous to obey as it is to command.'' The letter condemned ''terrorist attacks'' on ''local authorities'' because of the danger of reprisals on innocent people, but it carefully specified ''terrorist'' and not ''all attacks,'' thereby implying military action was permissible.

The Vatican's non-recognition of Mussolini's RSI gave the clergy the right to advise male parishioners not to give themselves up for service in the RSI army. When men were rounded up and forced to leave, priests were always present at their departure, comforting as best they could. The clergy also enjoyed outwitting the local police, many of whom were staunch Catholics. One priest, caught with a large number of guns, indignantly said he had robbed them from the partisans in payment for the money patriots had stolen from Sunday collections. He was let go.

Priests often acted as intermediaries for the partisans as well as the enemy. Occasionally farmers would complain about unfair demands by the partisans, which the priest would discuss with a partisan commander. The clergy were sometimes able to bargain with the Germans, to prevent homes from being looted and burned in reprisal for some real or imaginary offense by the villagers. Now and then a village would be subjected to days of a twenty-four-hour curfew, during which only the priest was permitted to move around. All by himself he would have to provide food, water and whatever else his parishioners required. At times even this was not permitted, and if a priest broke the curfew to give absolution to the dying, he was mercilessly beaten. Priests even offered themselves as hostages, to spare the populace.

As the war dragged on, the Germans felt increasingly helpless in the face of the clergy's intransigence. Heinrich Himmler, commander of the Nazi SS and of the Gestapo, had early recognized the value of priests both in terms of swaying public opinion and as sources of information. Believing they could be bribed, he had ordered storm troopers (the SS) ''to recruit numerous and faithful people among the Italian clergy . . . by handing out large sums of money." Himmler declared the expense would be nothing compared with "the usefulness of the information and the sabotage that the Italian priest might be capable of doing." Because most of the clergy refused to collaborate, in the Florence area alone 59 priests were tortured and killed. Yet not all were immune to bribery: one priest became quite rich gambling with his proceeds.

An especially diligent priest caught the attention, and the grudging admiration, of Field Marshal Albert Kesselring, Commander of the German Army in Italy. Don Giovanni Nardini lived in Rosignano, near Livorno. Because of the strategic importance of this area, Kesselring was there often. Don Nardini, who hid Jews and partisans in large numbers, did not hesitate to frequently visit German headquarters in an effort to get hostages released. Kesselring liked his stubborn boldness, telling his subordinates that "the pastor is to be considered the burgomaster of the village." Typically, Don Nardini's satchel was filled not only with holy oil and the cross, but with medicines, bandages and even stolen ration cards for those who lacked them.

Don Nardini's most memorable exploit was the destruction of a list of 400 villagers who were to be deported to work in Germany. Four Wehrmacht officers had gone to the priest's house to get his help with the deportation. Don Nardini poured glass after glass of wine and *grappa* (a vodka-like and very potent liquor) until the officers were so drunk they stumbled out, forgetting the list. Another time, when the Germans came to a nearby factory, again to recruit labor, Don Nardini explained that noxious fumes had made the workers tubercular. The Germans quickly left.

Almost every hamlet and big city diocese has a story to tell about the bravery and initiative of their priests during the Resistance. It must be understood that the clergy were in no way protected because of their religious status. The Nazis did not hesitate to arrest, torture and kill a priest if they thought he was guilty of anti-German activity.

Some priests responded to the situation by taking part in the militant Resistance, joining the predominantly Catholic or Catholic-led units. Among these was the Osoppo Brigade, which was organized mainly by two priests, Don Ascanio De Luca and Don Redento Bello (now a Monsignore). The Osoppo functioned in the Friuli region, a section of the Veneto bordered on the north by Austria and on the east by Yugoslavia. Here the Osoppo shared the battle against the Germans with the Communist-organized Garibaldi Brigades. The relationship between the two groups reflects the political situation in Italy then as now.

The Garibaldi units were the main strength of the Resistance: by the end of the war they numbered 575 brigades. It is estimated that some 42,000 Garibaldians died in the war and 18,000 were wounded. For their bravery 100 were awarded the gold medal and 250, the silver. A Garibaldi brigade was already operative in the Friuli region a few days after the September 1943 Armistice, when the Germans had overrun the area. The Garibaldi partisans were undoubtedly and wholeheartedly anti-Nazi, but many citizens of the Friuli region questioned their objectives because of the close ties between the Garibaldians and the Yugoslav Communist partisans.

Apart from ideological differences, the local people were vitally concerned about possible territorial ambitions of the Yugoslav Communists. As David Ellwood points out in his book *Italy: 1943–1945,* ''Of one reality the Allied command became more and more aware as Special Force missions reported back from the area in late 1944: that so severe were the risks of conflict between Italians and Slovenes (the local Slavic population around Trieste), and between Tito's forces with its PCI [Partito Comunista Italiano—Italian Communist party] brigades and the non-Communist brigades (notably the substantial 'Osoppo' division, largely Catholic or non-aligned), that it would be extremely difficult for any Allied force, army or AMG to impose its will on the area without being caught in the middle.'' The leadership of the Committee of National Liberation had frequently commanded both these factions to bury the hatchet and to fight together against the common enemy but such unity would be hard to achieve.

The birth of the Osoppo Brigade was due largely to the fact that early in September 1943 Don Ascanio De Luca had returned to his native Friuli on sick leave from his army duties. He had been a chaplain (with the rank of lieutenant) in the Italian Army Alpine Corps, and had served both in Greece and Albania. A tall, handsome 28 year old, he was resting at his parents' home in Treppo, near Udine, when news of the Armistice was broadcast.

Don Ascanio's first thought was of the previous occupation of Treppo during the First World War. Treppo was situated on the main road to Austria and so was especially vulnerable. Don Ascanio knew there was no time to spare if the local people were to defend themselves. Fortunately the commander of an Alpine Corps unit stationed nearby had served with Don Ascanio in Albania. The officer sent a message to the priest urging him to take advantage of the Corps' supply of weapons before the Nazis arrived. That night Don Ascanio, using a cart pulled by two horses, hauled away machine guns, rifles, pistols and hand grenades and hid them in the barns of trusted peasants. That same night the Nazis began to move towards Udine and by September 12 they had fully occupied the area.

In the first few days after the Armistice Don Ascanio had several visitors, young men who said they had escaped to the nearby mountains and were in need of clothes and food for themselves and their friends. The priest gave them supplies but he also decided to check out their stories. He bicycled to the house of another priest nearby, who told him that for some months Yugoslav partisans had been hiding in the area and that probably they had been joined by Italian Communists active in the Udine underground. Perhaps these were the visitors. Don Ascanio rode away, eyeglasses balanced low on his long, thin nose. As he thought over this information he stopped several times on his way home to invite a few friends to meet with him that night at what was to be the first of many sessions.

The upshot of the meetings was the formation of a new coalition of Resistance fighters which grew to 250 within a few weeks. Careful as the partisans were to get together in small groups, the

Germans soon became suspicious. One Sunday morning as he was saying Mass, Don Ascanio was approached by an altar boy who whispered that several cars driven by Fascist police were parked in front of the church. Don Ascanio whispered back that he would prolong the Mass while the boy ran for help. When the priest finally left the church, he was immediately stopped by a police officer who demanded that he go to Udine for questioning. As Don Ascanio played for time half a dozen men, each with one hand in his right pocket, formed a large semi-circle around the priest. Realizing they were outnumbered, the police then asked Don Ascanio if he would mind going to the local city hall to answer a few questions.

The group walked over to the Mayor's office where an officer in charge came right to the point. He said it was known Don Ascanio was in contact with the partisans hiding in the mountains. The Nazis wanted an estimate of the size of the "outlaw" group. "There must be about 4,000," answered the priest, exaggerating by several thousand. He was released with a warning to confine himself to preaching, but Don Ascanio felt it would be prudent to be transferred to a new parish. He was assigned to a church in Colugna, a village not far from Carlino, where another young priest, Don Redento Bello, was the pastor.

Like Don Ascanio, Don Bello had been a chaplain in Albania and Greece, but with the infantry. In Carlino he had organized about 300 patriots who operated as small units under his direction. Don Bello's men were involved in much the same activities as Don Ascanio's group: sabotage of German facilities and of the railroads leading to Austria, gathering information on German troop movements, and distributing anti-Fascist propaganda. They were also in contact with British special agents operating in the area.

Isolated groups like these began to be aware of each other by early 1944. Unlike the Garibaldi Brigades, which grew out of the Communist underground of the thirties and forties, the new groups, spontaneously formed, were not unified under one political banner. Citizens had joined together not for ideological reasons but to protect themselves and their towns against the invader. Among Don Ascanio's group was a man called Corrado Gallino, who had for some time been in touch with Don Bello. He introduced the two priests, and the upshot was the decision to organize the various groups into one strong partisan unit capable of military attacks on the Germans, as well as sabotage.

The deserted Ceconi Castle, in the village of Pielungo, was selected as headquarters. Pielungo was really a hamlet: just a few houses and the castle, nestled high on a hill. The castle was a yellow stucco structure with turrets and a tower, useful as a lookout. Small farms dotted the countryside below, far enough away so that their inhabitants would be oblivious to any activity on the hill.

The new brigade was named Osoppo in honor of a local village which had successfully rebelled against an Austrian invasion in 1848, and which had become a symbol of resistance to the people of Friuli. It was decided that each Osoppo partisan should wear a green kerchief around his neck, to distinguish them from the Garibaldians, who wore red ones.

By April 1944 the Osoppo was a fully organized fighting unit of ten battalions. But in May Don Ascanio's luck ran out. Two Fascist officers showed up at his house to tell him that his services as chaplain had been requested for a newly constituted RSI (Fascist) regiment based in Udine. Don Ascanio protested that he was still on sick leave and not well enough to serve. A week later he received a second order to report for duty, this time by mail. He ignored this order, too. But next day as he was cycling back to Cologna he was stopped by a little village girl who warned him that German soldiers were waiting for him at his house. Don Ascanio stayed away from Cologna for twenty-four hours and then returned. At dawn on the following Sunday, as he was preparing for the first Mass, a *staffetta* appeared at his door with instructions for him to go immediately to the cemetery: Fascist police were going to arrest him after Mass. At the cemetery the priest found the village butcher with his delivery wagon, waiting to take Don Ascanio to Pielungo.

Don Ascanio settled in at Castle headquarters, where he put his army experience to good use. In Albania he had become familiar with guerrilla tactics and he used this knowledge to help guide Osoppo strategy. He was able to persuade the men not to make massive attacks on German headquarters, pointing out that not only would Osoppo inevitably lose many men but also the Nazis would undoubtedly avenge themselves on innocent villagers. The better strategy was to keep up a barrage of sneak attacks on convoys as Nazi troops moved from one place to another, which would be much more destructive for the Germans than losing a few men at headquarters. After a quick attack, the Osoppo could easily disappear in the wooded or mountainous regions they knew so well, making pursuit difficult for the Germans who were unfamiliar with the territory.

Frequent and geographically spaced-out attacks also gave the impression of a much greater force of partisans than actually existed, compelling the Nazis to send reinforcements to the region. This was exactly what the Allies wanted, because German troops would have to be diverted from the Western front to Italy. Major Nicholson, head of one of the British missions in the Friuli, was especially appreciative of the efforts of Osoppo partisans. In a report to his commander he wrote, "I'm dwelling at length on the Osoppo because I think that at this critical time they represent a balanced force which will keep the civilian population calm because the civilians have a special regard for these men who are highly disciplined and have a sense of honor especially noticeable in a group which is almost regular army." Part of the discipline Nicholson admired was Don Ascanio's determination that his men should not kill unnecessarily. Besides being in keeping with Christian doctrine, this policy helped avoid Nazi reprisals, usually ten lives in payment for one dead German.

Nicholson was, of course, aware of the rivalry between the Osoppo and the Garibaldians. In writing of the latter, Nicholson commented: "The Communist party is the best organized political group in the Friuli region and though it does not have a very big local following it enjoys the support of the Yugoslav army."

In spite of their rivalry the two factions agreed on one important point: both must take orders from the Committee of National Liberation.

Osoppo's membership swelled during the summer of 1944. Socialists, Christian Democrats and unaffiliated partisans joined the organization. Typical of the new recruits was a young man named Danilo Missio, who came from Cividale, a suburb of Udine. He had finished high school in 1943 and had spent that summer vacationing near the Austrian border. He remembers the trainloads of Germans arriving in Italy during the 45 days of the Badoglio interim government. He also noticed that the Germans were building substantial heavy gun emplacements in the Friuli region. In the fall Missio enrolled at the University of Padua, which was a fairly short train ride from Udine. Allied bombing soon turned the trip into a day-long nightmare.

In the spring of 1944 the RSI called up men born in 1925 for service in the Fascist army. Missio evaded the conscription like many others, and went off to join the Osoppo. One of his former professors, now a partisan at the Castle in Pielungo, immediately put Missio to work. Because the young man was a tall, blue-eyed blond, almost German in appearance, he seemed to be able to move around quite freely once his false ID established him as older than the call-up age. One of his chores was to raise funds for Osoppo from the local population. Anyone carrying a large sum of money would be immediately suspect if he was searched at the frequent road blocks. Missio's solution was ingenious. He began wearing knickerbockers, which had copious trouser space providing an excellent hiding place for loose lire.

The local population was only one source of money: the Committee of National Liberation also allocated sums to the Osoppo as well as to the Garibaldians. Peasants had to be paid for the food they supplied, and married partisans needed money to support families who no longer could depend on their main wage earner. Don Bello and other priests, who generally did not have to help relatives, not only paid for their corn and rice but often gave peasants more than the going price to make up for those who could not afford to pay for supplies.

After a few months of fund-raising Missio asked for a more active role. He was assigned to the Guastatori unit, which specialized in railroad sabotage. The tracks leading in and out of Udine were closely guarded by the Germans. Sabotage had to be carried out at night, usually at a distance of about ten miles from the Udine station, which was located in the center of the city. The objective was to place an explosive under the flange of the rail so that it would go off on contact with the locomotive's wheels. This tactic made particular sense because replacement of locomotives was difficult, and also because the weight of the locomotive crashing across the tracks would cause extensive damage to the rails.

The impact usually derailed the entire string of cars, bursting them open. If the cars were loaded with prisoners heading for Germany, they might be able to escape with the help of partisans who were hidden nearby. If instead the train was made up of freight cars full of food and other supplies being taken away from Italy, the contents were "rescued" by the partisans. Train schedules were supplied by friendly railroad employees and by British intelligence, who wanted especially to disrupt German troop movements.

The Guastatori took elaborate precautions to avoid being discovered. Besides wearing dark clothing, they covered their shoes with socks to make walking about as soundproof as possible. Few words were spoken: a cough or a low whistle warned that a guard was approaching.

The men usually worked in teams of five. Two or three would carry the explosives, which were stuffed in plastic containers shaped like a salami. (Sometimes salami skins were actually used instead of plastic.) Another two, dressed as peasants or track workers, would act as lookouts. The worst danger were the flares used by German patrols if they suspected anything. Their brilliant flash could turn the darkest night into full daylight. Working on the rocky roadbeds was very tricky: displacing even a small stone could create considerable sound in the still night.

There were also spies to contend with. Missio recalls an elaborate plot to destroy the network of tracks at the Udine station. Missio and some 30 companions had coordinated the plan with British intelligence. The word was purposefully "leaked" to the Germans that Allied planes were expected to make a raid on a certain night. The Germans usually retreated to their bunkers during an air raid, leaving the coast clear for the Guastatori to lay explosives on most of the tracks approaching the station, in all directions. The explosives had been hidden by partisan railway employees in a small shack on the outskirts of the station, and two men were assigned to guard the hut. The rest of the men hid in a barn several miles away, waiting for the signal to converge on the station. A red flare on a nearby hill meant "go": green meant "stay put."

Not expecting to be in the barn more than a few hours, the men had little food and water on hand. Two days dragged by and finally at 2 AM of the third night, they saw the red signal. They crept across an open field towards the station, but as they approached the explosives shack they saw unexpected flashes of light. Suddenly there was much shouting in German as the two partisan guards ran from the shack, pursued by German soldiers. All the Guastatori managed to get away except one, the 18-year-old son of a railroad employee. The boy was seized and shot the next day. The Osoppo never discovered who had given away the plot, but it was concluded that it had to be an insider.

Although most Osoppo operations were successful, Don Ascanio at Pielungo headquarters was having new problems, not with the Fascists or the Nazis but with Garibaldi Brigade leaders. Early in July he had received a surprise visit from three Garibaldians, among them their leader Mario Lizzero. The two factions had been cooperating somewhat, but as Osoppo grew stronger so did the disagreements. The Garibaldi leaders suggested that a solution to the problem would be a complete unification of the two groups. Lizzero proposed that military decisions would be in Osoppo's hands, while the political command would be turned over to Garibaldi leaders. Don Ascanio quickly turned down this idea both for ideological reasons and because he suspected the PCI's ulterior motives might include territorial concessions to Yugoslav partisans. Other Osoppo leaders agreed with the priest, pointing out they might well lose most of their membership if the political leadership were Communist.

A few weeks later another meeting on unification was held at the Castle, this time attended also by Don Aldo Moretti, representing the Committee of National Liberation of Udine. Don Ascanio argued that even from a purely military point of view unification was unnecessary because the partisan war was not conventional warfare. It was better, he declared, to continue guerrilla tactics and operate in small, mobile units, rather than under a bureaucratic, military hierarchy. But Don Moretti reminded all of them that the leadership of the CNL had long ago stipulated that all groups must work together to fight the common enemy. The meeting ended with what seemed to be a concensus to cooperate on the military level. However, events of the next few days quickly changed this perception.

According to Don Ascanio, an Allied air drop had been expected on the night of July 19, 1944. At the recent meeting attended by Don Moretti, a system had been established of alternating guard duty between Osoppo and Garibaldi members. The most important lookout, from Pielungo's standpoint, was at Casiacco, a town which the Germans had to pass through if they were heading towards Pielungo. This lookout was especially important on July 19 because the pinpoint for the drop had been established near Pielungo. The supplies were to be shared by both sides. If the sentries saw anything unusual, they were supposed to telephone headquarters at the Castle.

The parachutes fell about midnight. Don Ascanio said he and several others were waiting in two trucks to carry away the supplies. They returned to the Castle about two AM, leaving the loaded trucks in the courtyard because the weapons were to be distributed later that morning. At four AM Don Ascanio was awakened by a boy on guard who said he heard a truck approaching. Clearly visible in the valley below was a line of German armored trucks.

Don Ascanio quickly woke up everybody, sent some of the men to hide in nearby woods and ordered others to drive the loaded trucks to a safe place. He remained behind to watch where the Germans were going.

At first they seemed to be taking a road away from Pielungo, but then they turned back, drove into the village itself and stopped, guns pointed at the Castle. When the Germans began firing, Don Ascanio ducked behind a cement wall. Besides himself and a few other partisans, the only people left in the Castle were nine German prisoners being held in the cellar for eventual exchange for partisans caught by the Nazis. Don Ascanio was about to head for the woods himself when he remembered both the prisoners and a briefcase he had left in his room containing some 300 original identification papers. (Each new recruit handed over his real ID in exchange for an assumed one.) Had the Germans found the papers, not only would they learn the real identity of many Osoppo members but their families would be in grave danger.

The priest raced back to the Castle, grabbed the briefcase, and then ran down to the cellar to free the prisoners, a decision that probably saved the village of Pielungo from drastic reprisals. While Don Ascanio and the others watched from the woods, trucks circled the Castle and set fire to it, bombing it for good measure. In a sense, the Osoppo had the last word because as the attackers left the ruins of the Castle a few hours later, they were ambushed by an Osoppo battalion. Some eighty German soldiers died in the attack.

The Garibaldi leadership accused Osoppo of abandoning the Castle and the parachuted supplies, a charge later proved not true because the loaded trucks were recovered safely. For their part, Osoppo blamed the Garibaldi lookouts for being negligent, at best. The Committee of National Liberation eventually absolved Don Ascanio of any fault in the episode. The CLN kept trying to resolve the feud between the two groups, even going so far as to have the Udine CLN consolidate the financial affairs of the opposing sides, but real unity was never achieved until the very end of the war.

With the Castle headquarters demolished, Don Ascanio left deskwork to become head of a battalion in November. As winter set in, most of the partisans would move to the plains, as they did in 1943–44, leaving only a few to guard mountain passes when weather permitted. Scattered as they were, military attacks in force were impossible but they still could carry on routine sabotage. Don Bello, Don Ascanio and other battalion commanders now met regularly with the CLN to plan for the spring uprising,

Don Ascanio De Luca (far right) with members of the Osoppo brigades, during the winter of 1945.

when it was hoped a united effort of partisans and civilians could rid the Friuli of the Germans once and for all. News from Radio London of the progress of the war on both the Western and Italian fronts made it seem probable that the Allies would reach the Udine area by March or April.

The other probability was that the Nazis, faced with defeat, would destroy whatever they could as they retreated. Precautions had to be taken not only to protect human lives but to save essen-

tial public works such as bridges, aqueducts and electrical installations. The Osoppo leaders were also deeply troubled by the
post-war prospects, fearing that the politicians in Rome were not
fully aware of the deep ties between the PCI and Yugoslavia,
although British intelligence offices in the area constantly assured
them the situation was well known to the Allies and to Rome.

Plans for the insurrection had to take into account a still formidable enemy. Early in 1945 German forces in the northern
Italian Adriatic region included 32,000 Wehrmacht troops, 11,000
military police, 277 Gestapo agents plus some 12,000 Italian Fascists and other collaborators. The Germans had also brought in
about 20,000 Cossacks who had settled in Carnia, near Udine.
They had been brought to Italy by the Nazis as a reward for their
efforts in Poland.

The joint Garibaldi–Osoppo units were theoretically outnumbered, but not if the thousands of patriots were taken into account
who belonged to neither group. They were ready to join the uprising with scythes and homemade bombs. Another important factor
weighing in the partisans' favor was the growing demoralization
of the German troops, as they realized Hitler was losing the war.
With the end almost in sight and the Allies about to enter the
region, the commanders of the Osoppo and Garibaldi units finally
agreed to a unified command and even to one man as its representative, Emilio Grassi, a former army officer. He appeared at
the first formal meeting of the joint command dressed half as a
Garibaldian and half as an Osoppo partisan.

By May 1 the joint attacks of Garibaldi–Osoppo units were
causing German soldiers to surrender in droves, or at best to fight
half-heartedly. The worst problem facing the partisans now was
defusing mines the Germans had hidden in facilities throughout
the region. At the new joint headquarters of the Osoppo–Garibaldi commanders two alternatives were being discussed: an all-
out attack on German headquarters in Udine, or an attempt to
bargain with its commander, Colonel Voight. The Germans were
holding eight partisans hostage, and this was made the excuse for
arranging a meeting at 9 PM on April 30 with Voight. After a

certain amount of hesitation, Voight finally agreed on an exchange of prisoners. He also agreed to cancel his orders to blow up the aqueduct, the gas and electric plants, a refrigeration facility and numerous warehouses. The quid pro quo was that the Germans be allowed to retreat unharmed during the night.

When dawn broke on May 1, Udine seemed a silent, deserted city. By 6 AM Don Ascanio and 200 of his men had arrived in the main piazza. As they raised the red, white, and green flag over the city hall, jubilant crowds poured into the square. Udine was once again under Italian control.

=9=
The Unification of the Resistance

T HE PARTISANS of the Italian Resistance have been described by Professor Delzell as being motivated by "a mixture of patriotic, ideological, idealistic reasons and self-interest." Many of the young men who went to the mountains in the early days after the September 8 Armistice were simply trying to save their skins. Simultaneously, longtime anti-Fascists at last saw the opportunity to build a new future for Italy. There were also intellectuals who had never contemplated political action before and did not relish it now, but felt it was inevitable. Jaime Pintor, a well-known Neapolitan writer, explained this last attitude in a letter written just before he died trying to cross enemy lines on a mission to Rome: "As for me, I assure you that the idea of becoming a partisan at this time amuses me very little: I have never appreciated as much as I do now the virtues of civilian life and I know I am an excellent translator and a good diplomat, but in all probability a mediocre partisan. Nevertheless it is the only choice and I recognize this."

How to integrate people with these varying motives into a force united against the enemy was the major problem confronting the Resistance. Even before the fall of Mussolini several anti-Fascist leaders had begun to try to coordinate their separate polit-

---

ical activities, recognizing that the Fascist government was undergoing a fatal crisis. Groups known as the Committee of Opposition, The National Front, and the Interparty Committee held frequent meetings to try to establish a cohesive network. These groups often consisted of just a few people, usually found in the large cities: Rome, Florence, Milan, Turin. In Bologna, an especially important effort was made to create a regional committee of anti-Fascists. By the end of 1942 there had been a significant reawakening of political party activity, albeit clandestine. Besides the more established Socialist and Communist parties, several new ones had appeared: the Action Party (which included many members of the former Justice and Liberty movement), the Christian Democrats (successors to the Popular party), the Liberal party, and a southern group called the Democracy of Labor.

Following the March 1943 strikes in Turin and other cities, the Minister of the Interior echoed the concerns of many Fascists when he wrote in a memorandum to Mussolini that "the clandestine parties seem to have gained a certain influence on the population." However, there were mitigating forces within these parties which kept them in line, from a Fascist point of view. The moderates and conservatives of the opposition, though anti-Fascist, were still suspicious and fearful of the leftists, especially the Communists. They were particularly concerned about the role Communists might play in postwar Italy. These considerations in no small way prevented unification against fascism, and the bickering continued until the fall of Mussolini on July 25. Forced by this event to end their procrastination, the conservatives began to work with the leftists. They realized further delay would hamper both the Resistance and their own postwar political ambitions.

During the 45-day lull between the fall of Mussolini and the September 8 Armistice, the opposition groups began to operate more cohesively, although the ban on political parties was still in existence. In Rome the anti-Fascist United Freedom Front had been created in April under the leadership of the ex-Socialist Ivanoe Bonomi (who served as prime minister from July 1921 to February 1922). This organization put pressure on the interim prime minister, Field Marshal Pietro Badoglio, to revoke Fascist laws and institutions. From Milan the Committee of Opposition sent its spokesman, Giorgio Amendola (a Communist in exile from 1937 to April 1943, who returned to become a leader of the underground), to Rome with the following demands: the restoration of civil and political rights, the release of political prisoners, and the formation of a government representing all the anti-Fascist parties.

Badoglio ignored most of these demands, reflecting the wait-and-see attitude of the population in general. However, agitation by the committees did succeed in August in gaining the release of most political prisoners, some of them just days before the Nazis occupied the country. The Resistance committees had been aware of the growing influx of German troops in the North, especially after the August 6 meeting at Tarvisio of Hitler's representatives, Ribbentrop and Dolman, with a Badoglio delegation headed by Guariglia, the Minister of Foreign Affairs. Ribbentrop expressed Hitler's displeasure with the continued lack of cooperation on Badoglio's part, and he made pointed remarks about suspicious deals with the Allies. Guariglia assured the Nazi contingent of Badoglio's loyalty, vehemently denying contacts with the Allies.

Neither side believed the other and in fact, as was later revealed, by July 27 the German High Command had already drawn up plans for "Operation Alarico" according to which Mussolini would be freed, Rome would be occupied, the Italian Navy would be seized, the Italian Army would be eliminated, and the Wehrmacht together with SS troops would establish key positions throughout Italy.

Immediately after the Tarvisio meeting, German soldiers began pouring through the Brenner Pass, a silent invasion that convinced the committees of the North that it was time for decisive action. On September 1 Bonomi again confronted Badoglio, insisting that he respond to a now widespread demand to negotiate with the Allies for peace. Neither Bonomi nor the committees were aware that Badoglio had been dealing covertly with the Allies all this time. On September 2 the Central Committee of the United

Freedom Front in Rome prepared a memorandum to be delivered
to Badoglio openly denouncing the German alliance. The Committee also appealed to local organizations to mobilize the people
and the armed forces for battle.

Badoglio set the document aside, waiting for his negotiations
with the Allies to come to a conclusion. The frustrated Central
Committee, meeting on September 8 in Bonomi's home, heard
about the Armistice from an excited phone call by a friend in the
Ministry of Culture. Badoglio had made the following announcement in a radio broadcast: "Recognizing the impossibility of continuing the war in face of the overwhelming strength of the enemy,
and in order to save the nation from further and even greater
disasters, the Italian Government has asked General Eisenhower,
commander-in-chief of the Allied forces, for an armistice. This
request has been acceded to. In consequence all hostilities by the
Italian armed forces against the British and American forces must
now cease. They will, however, repel attacks from whatever quarter
they may come."

During that night the king, Badoglio and assorted generals
and ministers fled Rome, leaving the capital with no one officially in charge. In his memoirs Badoglio assumes responsibility
for the decision to leave Rome. He wrote that soon after his radio
address, he and the royal family went straight to the Ministry of
War, where troops were stationed to protect the group from a
probable attack by the Nazis. At 4 AM the Chief of Army Staff,
General Roatta, awakened Badoglio to inform him that the Italian
defense was being completely overwhelmed by the Germans.
Roatta advised an immediate departure by the one route still open,
the Via Tiburtina and Porta San Lorenzo.

Badoglio asserts that his reason for deciding to leave was not
to save their lives, but to reach the South in order to keep the
Armistice in force. He feared that if the government remained in
Rome and was captured by the Germans, a Fascist government
would be substituted which would repudiate the Armistice.

Rome fell rapidly to the Germans. The only real defense was
at Porta San Paolo where Italian troops and several thousand poorly

armed civilians tried to hold off a massive charge by German armored detachments and parachute contingents. Deserted by their commander-in-chief and by most of the Army officers in Rome, the few who attempted to make a stand soon had to give up the uneven fight.

The leaders of the United Freedom Front met in an emergency session. They changed the organization's name to the Committee of National Liberation (CLN), elected Bonomi its president and issued the following statement: "In this moment when the Nazis attempt to return their Fascist ally to Rome and to Italy, the anti-Fascist parties are joining together in a Committee of National Liberation to call Italians to resist and to fight and to win again for Italy the place it deserves among free nations." A similar decision was made by the anti-Fascists in Milan and Turin. The newly formed Milan CLN also issued a rallying call: "We are all mobilized for a common cause. Whoever has the means should give to those who suffer. Let us not allow anyone to be deported to a foreign land. We will not work for the German enemy: we will not let ourselves be forced into its armed force."

They were bold words, but the unity called for would not happen overnight. The Germans were rapidly crushing any opposition. In Rome the chaos of the first few weeks of Nazi occupation (when the "open city" policy was in force) was followed on September 23 by the imposition of martial law. The Nazis had moved quickly and efficiently to take control of strategic facilities throughout northern Italy. Direct communication had become difficult, if not dangerous, and travel was sharply curtailed.

Badoglio and the king did not officially declare war on Germany until October 13. This news, as well as the news that a new government had been formed in Brindisi with Allied approval, did not reach many Italians in the occupied North for weeks. The new Badoglio government's declaration of war on Germany was followed by the Allies granting it co-belligerency status. Meanwhile Hitler had rescued Mussolini and on September 29 had established him as head of a new government of German-occupied Italy, which Il Duce called the Italian Social Republic

(Repubblica Sociale Italiana—RSI). Italians referred derisively to the neo-Fascist "republic" as *"la repubblichina"* or the "little republic" and to its members as *"i repubblicchini"* or "little republicans." The *repubblichini* were essentially tools of the Nazis. They were used as spies and as a police force, especially in rounding up able-bodied men for forced labor or military service either in Italy or Germany.

The roundups forced more and more men to escape to the mountains or to otherwise go underground, usually joining the partisans. But the men were poorly armed. Ferruccio Parri, a leader of the Milan CLN, began to devote his considerable abilities to the problem of acquiring weaponry. Parri had been a staff officer in the infantry during World War I and had distinguished himself for bravery and skill in warfare. As one of the founding members of the Action Party in 1942, he had early recognized the need for an armed as well as a political Resistance. Even before the Armistice, Parri had proposed a plan to organize an armed resistance force to deal with the Germans. In autumn of 1943, when it became obvious that the partisans' own efforts would never break the weapons supply deadlock, Parri became determined to get help from the Allies. For this purpose he made his first trip to Allied headquarters in Switzerland, in November 1943.

It was largely thanks to Parri that the Allies began to realize the Italian Resistance consisted of more than isolated patriot groups adept at sabotage. Parri knew it was vital for the future of the Resistance that the Allies recognize the fact that the Italian people, not just the partisans, were uniting to oust the enemy. The partisans were, in a sense, the peoples' army.

The problem for the Allies, and for Churchill especially, was that the CLNs were perceived as a growing political force, not just as a means of unifying the Resistance. Representing all the political parties, the CLNs had begun to voice postwar aims that did not necessarily jibe with Allied postwar planning for the Mediterranean area. For the CLNs, the war was indeed a war of liberation not only from Germany but also from fascism and from the past. The anti-monarchical stand of the CLNs did not sit well with Churchill, let alone the Italian king.

In its September proclamation the Rome CLN had clearly signalled its thoughts on the future:

"The CLN, confronted by Mussolini's attempt to revive fascism under the guise of a so-called republican state, confronted by the horror of civil war, must reaffirm its determined and active opposition. . . . Confronted also by the situation created by the king and Badoglio and their formation of a new government with the agreement of the United Nations, the CLN maintains that the war of liberation—the first and main aim of the national insurrection—demands the sincere spiritual unity of the country and that this is not possible under the aegis of the government created by the King and Badoglio: it is necessary to promote the establishment of a government which represents the political forces which have consistently fought against the Fascist dictatorship and which since September 1939 have joined together against the Nazi war.

The CLN declares such a government should:

1) assume all the constitutional powers of the State, avoiding, however, any attitude which would compromise agreement among nations or prejudice future decisions by the people;

2) carry out the war of liberation at the side of the United Nations;

3) convene the people, at the end of hostilities, to decide on the future form of government.

The CLNs multiplied throughout central and northern Italy, although coordination of their activities was extremely difficult due to the breakdown in communication facilities. The PCI prodded the other parties to push for the extension of this new form of self-government: it called for the establishment of CLN units not only in cities and villages, but also in factories and farmers' cooperatives, no matter how small.

The rural CLNs found a receptive audience in the peasant population. Fascism, essentially a middle- and upper-class movement, had never struck a very responsive chord among most peasants (who were not, in general, politically oriented). Constantly increasing government requisitions of crops to support Fascist wars had diminished their already meager incomes. In addition, their sons were taken away to fight in military campaigns in Ethiopia, Albania, and Greece, campaigns which had little significance for the average peasant in spite of Mussolini's best propaganda efforts.

The CLNs were especially well established in towns in Piedmont, Lombardy, Liguria, Tuscany and the Veneto. They were unable to function wherever German troops were bivouaced because those villages were administered by the *repubblichini* under the watchful eye of a Nazi commander. However, the Germans could not occupy every town and village, so the network of CLN self-government spread, replacing previous Fascist hierarchies. Mayors and other local officials who had been Fascists in name only were sometimes retained.

As the regional CLNs became better organized, they turned more of their attention to the needs of the partisans, often helping in their sabotage projects. Soon local patriots began to form their own SAP (Squads for Patriotic Action) units under the direction of the CLNs. The work of these units was tied into partisan strategy, and slowly a cohesive network began to emerge.

By November 1943 the Milan CLN, led by Parri and Luigi Longo (a major figure in the Communist party), had emerged as the strongest of these organizations. Accordingly, it assumed overall leadership as the Committee of National Liberation of alt' Italia (Upper Italy)—the CLNAI. The Rome CLN, the only other possible source of national leadership, was hampered by several factors: the city was general headquarters for the Nazis; the neutral Vatican was a strong presence; the lack of large industries meant a lack of vigorous trade unions, essential for strike activity. Also the 72-year-old Bonomi, who headed the Rome CLN, was not an energetic spokesman for a new order.

After Parri's rather unsuccessful trip to Switzerland early in November 1943, the CLNs of the North decided, in a sense, that God helps those who help themselves, and that it would be wise to meet with the CLNs of the liberated South to work out a unified program for all Italy. (The Allied armies were stalled below Rome, near Cassino, and it was doubtful that much military progress would be made towards liberating Rome until the spring offensive.) Representatives of the northern CLNs attended a meeting held in Naples on November 24, 1943. There it was decided to schedule a large conference (also in Naples) which would include both northern CLNs and anti-Fascist exiles.

At this time, the Allied Military Government (AMG) was in control of Naples. AMG was uneasy about the proposal for a conference, which would be the first open meeting of Italian political parties in twenty years. At first AMG stalled by declaring Naples was unsafe for such a convocation because, being under Allied control, it was officially a war zone. After loud protests by the CLNs, AMG agreed to permit a congress to be held in Bari, which was Badoglio government territory.

The date for the Bari Congress was finally set for January 28, 1944. However, the Allies stipulated that no public demonstrations should take place, that the number attending would be strictly limited to participants except for selected journalists, and that broadcasts of the proceedings and discussions would be prohibited. Again the CLNs protested at the restrictions and towards the middle of the week-long meetings the number of participants was raised to 800, and of journalists to 50. In his memoirs Badoglio referred briefly to the Congress: ''Many speeches were made, the proceedings were both lively and inconclusive, while abuse of every kind was hurled at the King, the Crown Prince, and the Government.''

The main achievement of the Congress was verbal agreement that the king should abdicate in favor of his son, who would receive the title of lieutenant-general. The leftists had wanted abolition of the monarchy, but they finally accepted the decision to postpone discussion of the future form of government until after the war. It was obvious that the Badoglio regime was to continue at least for a time as the official government of the South. Churchill's comment on the Congress hardly endeared him to the CLNs: ''The present regime is the lawful Government of Italy

[and] . . . will obey our directions far more than any other that we may laboriously constitute. On the other hand it has more power over the Fleet, Army officials, etc. than anything else which can be set up out of the worn-out debris of political parties, none of whom have the slightest title by election or prescription.''

The CLN Executive Committee of Naples promptly called for a 10-minute strike to protest Churchill's words, but the strike was forbidden by AMG; however, it did allow a public meeting, thanks to the more liberal viewpoint of General Henry M. Wilson, who had in November succeeded General Eisenhower as Supreme Allied Commander in the Mediterranean. Wilson did not totally agree with Churchill's opinion of Britain's former enemy, and early on advised both Churchill and Roosevelt to take a more positive approach towards Italy. Wilson's attitude was shared by Adlai Stevenson, who reported to Roosevelt after a fact-finding mission to Italy in January 1944: ''It is the observation of this mission that the government of the King and Badoglio receives scant respect or support from the people. The present not very happy political situation will constitute a formidable obstacle to the orderly and effective realization of our objectives and economic operations.'' Cordell Hull, Roosevelt's Secretary of State, echoed these impressions in his memoirs: ''I myself was not at all sympathetic to the idea of keeping King Victor Emmanuel on the throne. He had, to all intents and purposes, gone along with Mussolini. . . . As for Badogolio, he was the apprentice of a king with whom we had no sympathy. . . . I felt that, as soon as feasible, the people of Italy, represented by the parties in opposition to Fascism, should be permitted to express their choice of the form and personnel of the government they wanted. . . . I found that the President was fully of the same opinion.''

Among the many problems to be faced by the CLNAI leadership was a tendency towards defeatism (referred to as *''attesismo''* i.e., a wait-and-see attitude) stirred up primarily by conservatives in the CLNs. They claimed they were acting for humanitarian reasons, that is, to prevent brutal Nazi reprisals in response to Resistance activities. But the *attesisti* had other motives as well. They had little interest in revolutionary objectives, hoping at best for a return to the pre-Fascist status quo.

The CLN leadership, in dealing with *attesismo,* was careful to deal also with the question of revolutionary change. Mindful of how Mussolini had used the "war against Bolshevism" as an excuse to install fascism, the CLNAI outlined clearly its policy towards the Communist party: "The Government of the North reaffirms the pact of mutual support and democratic unity into which all parties have entered, and declares that any person who may attempt to undermine this unit shall be considered as an enemy of the country."

Although there was sometimes very bitter controversy among the parties, there was usually good cooperation in major efforts. The Communist party (PCI) was credited with much of the success of the CLN-organized general strikes of March 1944 which took place simultaneously in Turin, Milan, Genoa, Florence and Bologna as well as in smaller cities. In Turin, work at the huge Fiat Mirafiori plant came to a complete standstill. The *New York Times* commented at the time: "As a mass demonstration nothing has occurred in occupied Europe to compare in scale with the revolt of workers in Italy. It is the climax of a campaign of sabotage, local strikes and guerrilla warfare that has received less publicity than resistance movements elsewhere because northern Italy has been more cut off from the outside world. But it is an impressive proof that the Italians, unarmed as they are and under a double bondage, will fight with reckless courage when they have a cause to fight for." Hundreds of thousands of workers were involved. In Milan the trolley operators joined in, bringing public transportation to a standstill. In retaliation the Nazis declared a state of siege, shipped at least 2,000 strikers to concentration camps, and ordered factory owners not to pay the strikers.

Shortly after the wave of strikes, the Badoglio government made a dramatic announcement: the USSR had asked to resume diplomatic relations with Italy. According to Badoglio, he had been approached by Andrei Vishinsky, Soviet delegate to the Allied Control Commission (ACC). Badoglio claimed that immediately after their conversation, he had reported the request to General Joyce (head of the ACC) as required. The ACC version was that Badoglio acted unilaterally and against the rules, which stipulated that all conversations with other nations should be carried out through ACC. In any event, the recognition by the USSR was allowed to stand except that the diplomats exchanged would be known as "representatives" rather than "ambassadors."

In the wake of this event, at the end of March, the national council of the PCI met in Naples under the presidency of Palmiro Togliatti, the leader of the Italian Communists who had just returned from eighteen years of exile in Moscow. Togliatti startled everyone by calling for a nationally unified government, even if this meant serving under Badoglio and the king. Such unity was essential, Togliatti declared, in order to achieve the main objective: to crush the Nazis and the Fascists. Until that point, the CLNs, because of their anti-monarchial stand, had resisted participating in the Badoglio government. Largely as a result of Togliatti's proposal, a second Badoglio government was soon created with all parties represented. Togliatti himself became a minister without portfolio. The most important policies of the new government were: all-out prosecution of the war; postponement until peacetime of the question of the future nature of the State; and the creation of a Consultative Council with which the CLNs would collaborate. Both the CLN of Rome and the CLNAI in Milan, preoccupied with tremendous problems of their own, approved the new regime although with reservations.

The winter of 1943–1944 had been a bleak, frightening time for the people of occupied Italy. Forced requisitions by the Germans had caused already scarce food stocks to dwindle. Because Italy lacked imports of any kind, its own agricultural produce had to supply city people, peasants, partisans and the occupying German armies. In addition, the Germans were shipping food back to their homeland, where scarcities were also being felt. Much of the Italian population was left in a state of constant hunger.

Resentment of the pressure put on the farmers by the Germans was beginning to politicize even the most apolitical rural populations. The clergy also played an important part in the political awakening of the peasants, because of the active support given to the Resistance by many local priests. As a result, peasants who ordinarily had paid little attention to local, much less national, affairs, began to get involved in regional CLNs. Many farm workers regarded them as the most effective buffers against Germans and Fascists alike. Even the Communist party, in disfavor because it was staunchly opposed by the Church, had lost its ugly image in the light of what Don Sturzo (founder of the former Popular party) once referred to as "the communism of the belly." However, there were still, and there would always be, many peasants who feared Nazi reprisals much more than they appreciated partisan activities.

With the advent of spring, the situation improved greatly for the armed Resistance, just as it had for the political side. The partisans were able to return to the mountains better armed, better organized and in much greater numbers. More frequent parachute drops by the Allies, though deficient in heavy weapons, helped enormously. In Milan, the CLNAI's military command was now functioning smoothly. It had been divided into several sections, with the most important, Operations, headed by Parri and Longo.

Rome was liberated on June 4, 1944, bringing to an end the King's reign and the second Badoglio government when it ran into serious opposition from the Rome CLN. After the Cabinet resigned in accordance with parliamentary practice, Badoglio met with the ministers in order to form a new government. At that meeting it was decided that the new head of government should not be a military man, and Ivanoe Bonomi was selected to replace Badoglio. Churchill immediately demanded the return of Badoglio to office and the suspension of the new government which he described as made up of an "extremely untrustworthy band of non-elected comebacks." Roosevelt did not agree with Churchill and, after a certain amount of compromise, the Bonomi government remained in place. One of Bonomi's first actions was to appoint General Raffaele Cadorna "military counselor" to the CLNAI. General Cadorna was a highly respected career officer, and one of the few who had tried to defend Rome against the Nazis.

The summer months of 1944 proved to be a period of sustained success for the Resistance as the Germans began their long retreat. Unification accelerated in the newly liberated areas where the local CLNs helped restore order under the direction of the CLNAI. Regional and provincial CLNs were urged to communicate to the leadership "the needs and will of the people." Yet, after twenty years of dictatorship, many simple democratic procedures literally had to be relearned. Since voting equipment was not available, decisions were often made by show of hands. But the principle of self-government did begin to take hold, and the extent of this progress would later be seen during the liberation of Florence in August.

The strength of the CLNAI was put to a severe test in November by the disconcerting radio appeal of General Alexander asking the partisans to cut back their activities until the Allied offensive resumed after the winter months. Later Parri was to say, chari-

Allied troops enter Rome on June 4, 1944.

tably, that Alexander's request was not treachery (which many partisans thought at the time), but a misunderstanding or a miscalculation of what the Nazi reaction would be. The eminent historian of the Italian Resistance, Prof. Charles Delzell, referred to the Alexander statement as the "much maligned and often misinterpreted proclamation." Whether it was a matter of intention or of inappropriate wording, Alexander a few days later did issue a second message trying to mitigate the first, and in spite of bad weather some attempts were made to send supplies to the partisans by plane.

Shortly after the Alexander episode, four members of the CLNAI (including Parri) met with General Wilson to try to clarify the status of the CLNAI. Wilson said he would urge the Allied Commission to convince the Bonomi government that it should recognize the CLNAI as the legitimate government of the occupied North. Little could be done at the moment in this respect because the government was undergoing a Cabinet crisis. However, an agreement was reached on December 7 between the Allies and the CLNAI, which gave the latter some of the recognition it wanted, subject to the following stipulations:

1. The CLNAI must include representatives of all the anti-Fascist parties.

2. The Allies must approve the members of the military command of the CLNAI, known as the CM/CVL (Military Command/Corps of Volunteers for Liberty), which would take general orders from the Allies.

3. CLNAI must hand over reins of government of a newly liberated area as soon as AMG (Allied Military Government) arrived on the scene.

4. The Allies would supply 160 million lire monthly towards the expenses of CLNAI and all other anti-Fascist units, to be distributed on a specified basis, with Piedmont getting the lion's share. The document was accompanied by a letter from General Wilson in which he wrote: "I hope that when the present crisis in the Italian government is resolved, early considerations may be given to the recognition of the CLNAI as the agent of the Government in enemy occupied Italy."

A few weeks later, with his government crisis resolved, Bonomi also signed an accord with the CLNAI which stated: "The Italian government delegates the CLNAI to represent it in the struggle which the patriots have launched against the Fascists and the Germans in that part of Italy not yet liberated." The gap had finally been bridged between the occupied North and the liberated South, at least in official terms.

Though politically the situation had improved, militarily the Resistance—like the Allied forces—was once again stymied by the weather. During the winter months of 1944–1945 the partisans again left the mountains and scattered to various locations on the plains. The military command of the CLNAI, now under the leadership of Allied-approved General Cadorna, had planned the descent to the plains long before Alexander made his announcement. The purpose was not just to avoid winter in the mountains, but also to prepare for the eventual insurrections which would liberate the major cities of the North still occupied by the Nazi/Fascists. Regional military commanders were instructed to divide their territory into zones, which in turn would break down into smaller units, all under one central command. The directives stressed that there must be the closest possible cooperation between all partisan formations and that the entire population should be encouraged to participate in the insurrection.

The conditions stipulated in the agreement between General Wilson and the CLNAI clearly indicated Allied anxiety. The Allies were still very concerned about maintaining ultimate authority over the CLNAI and over the northern regions as they became liberated. In fairness, it should be remembered that Italy was a former enemy. Also, the Allies were still uncertain about the residual strength and influence of fascism. The CLNAI was equally concerned that the Italians should liberate themselves, because the Resistance leaders knew it was essential that the world recognize that the Italians themselves had fought and won against the Nazis *and* the Fascists.

Bonomi tried to reassure the Allies, declaring that the CLNAI "remains in a subordinate position and does not have the least character of a de facto government." Much of the CLNAI Military Command's planning was plain common sense and coincided with the Allies' own strategy. Regional partisan commanders were given instruction for protecting power stations, aqueducts and other facilities subject to destruction by the retreating Germans. A specific method of defense was outlined for the most vulnerable structures in the cities, as differentiated from the less vulnerable installations in the plains and high in the mountains. Factory owners were also told how to safeguard their plants.

By the end of January 1945 insurrection plans were well in place. Although many towns and cities had been liberated by then, travelling was still hazardous and the Resistance necessarily had to operate covertly in the major, still-occupied cities of the North. Yet the CLNAI was now organized enough to function effectively in areas with large concentrations of German troops. In fact, even the arrest of Parri and several other leaders did not slow down partisan activity. Parri had been caught by the Nazis on December 31 as he was returning to Milan from his meeting with General Wilson, and he remained in jail for nine weeks. He was finally released in March through the efforts of Allen Dulles, Roosevelt's Special Envoy in Switzerland. (Since February Dulles had been meeting secretly with several German officers who wanted to negotiate a separate peace.) Dulles had told Nazi General Wolff that he would not continue the discussions unless Parri was freed.

As the war drew to a close, the CLNAI stepped up its insurrection plans. On March 29 at a meeting attended by a representative of the Allies, a "Committee for the Insurrection" was appointed. On April 10 the PCI issued the following directive with the approval of the CLNAI, which soon announced a series of similar directives:

Procedure. Partisan formations will attack and eliminate Nazi-Fascist headquarters and effect the liberation of cities, towns and villages. Gappists and Sappists will break up roadblocks and wipe out Nazi-Fascist command posts. The appropriate organizations will proclaim a general strike whose character must be clearly and unmistakably defined, i.e., it must be made plain from the first that this strike is not a mere popular demonstration of anger, but that it is the culmination of the people's long campaign for freedom and the expression of their unshakeable determination.

Disintegration of the enemy. The enemy will be faced with the following alternatives: 'Surrender or Die.'''

The Struggle against attesismo. The Gordian knot of attesismo must be cut without delay. On no account whatsoever must our comrades in military or civil organizations accept any proposal or advice or consider any plan designed to limit, prevent or obstruct the national uprising. . . . A combination of firmness, tact and skill must be employed in all discussions with Allied Military Missions which have elected to be the mouthpiece of the attesisti, and are therefore inclined to attach too little importance to our urgent requests for the arms and ammunition needed to ensure the success of the insurrection. . . . In the circumstances, we must be prepared to face the fact that the Allies may decide, for one reason or another, to withhold their support, instead of making the contribution for which we have asked.

The official CLNAI directive for the insurrections was signed by representatives of each party, among them Parri for the Action Party, Longo for the Communists, Pertini for the Socialists and De Gasperi for the Christian Democrats. The stage was now set for the final act of the Resistance.

=10=
The Insurrections

"WAR IN A MUSEUM"

IN SEPTEMBER 1943 the Neapolitans had fought the enemy bravely and spontaneously, literally with sticks and stones and overturned trolleys. A year later the situation was fundamentally different. As the Germans retreated in northern Italy they faced a relatively well-organized, if not always well-armed, Resistance. Although the major northern cities would not be liberated until the very end of the war (April 1945), the partisans had first begun to realize their dream of a new Italy during the bitter fight to liberate Florence in August 1944. "War in a museum," the battle of Florence has been called, and the wonder is that any of its treasures survived. This was the first well-organized insurrection, and as such became a symbol for the rest of the country.

Florence was important to the Germans' route from Rome back to Germany, and the Germans were determined either to hold or destroy the city. When the Allies finally reached it, instead of the chaos of Naples and the resignation of Rome, they found a functioning government. The Florentines' achievement was glowingly described in a report submitted by the OSS Research and Analysis Branch a few months after the liberation.

When the Allied armies arrived in Florence they encountered, for the first time in a major Italian city, a nearly complete administrative organization established by determined and purposeful anti-Fascist forces. A provisional system, worked out to the last detail, already was functioning as an unchallenged de facto authority under the auspices of the Tuscan Committee of National Liberation, which regards itself as the legitimate representative of the Italian Government and aspires to Allied recognition as such.

The duration and intensity of the underground struggle in northern Italy have produced highly developed resistance organizations with a considerably more independent outlook than in the South. For eleven months prior to the liberation of Florence, the CTLN (Tuscan Committee of National Liberation), which includes all five of the Tuscan anti-Fascist parties, directed the clandestine press, organized strikes and sabotage, and functioned as the high command of partisan military activity in the region. . . . While the Germans were still in Florence the mayor and city council took possession of the municipal offices, and they were dealing with the public when AMG [Allied Military Government] officials arrived.

As the report points out, the CTLN had taken charge, and provided Florence with strong leadership from the earliest days of the German occupation. Soon after the Armistice of September 8, 1943 was announced, representatives of the CTLN pleaded with the commander of the Italian Army's city garrison to give them weapons to fight off the invader, but he refused. Though civilian patriots were stymied, as they had been in Rome, a futile attempt was made by the Bersaglieri (a crack Italian army unit) to hold back the Germans at the Futa Pass. On the morning of September 11 columns of tanks and armored cars rumbled into the city. Florence was occupied, and it was obvious that the Germans planned to make the city headquarters for a long and determined stand against the Allies.

North of Florence the Nazis had established a formidable line of defense, the so-called Gothic Line, extending from Massa/Carrara in the West across the Apennine mountains to Pesaro,

ON THE FACING PAGE
The Ponte Vecchio on the right and the Duomo in the background, photographed as the battle for Florence raged.

on the Adriatic Sea. The German High Command believed this was the best position in Italy, and perhaps in Europe, from which to defend the Reich. In fact by September 1, even before the Armistice was announced, units of the SS Panzer Corps had established themselves in main passes to the Apennines.

During the eleven months of the occupation of Florence, Gappists and Sappists harassed and sabotaged the enemy almost daily. Local Fascists and their organizations were a favorite target. In reprisal the *repubblichini* established in Florence alone a special police force known as the Banda Carità, so named for its chief, Mario Carità. To this day the word *carità* (which literally means charity) is synonymous in Florence with cold brutality. Carità began his career in 1922, at the age of 15, as one of a group of *squadristi* accused of assassinating anti-Fascists in Milan. In Florence he became known for sadistic behavior which was feared even more than torture by the SS.

Although the organized patriots were actively subversive, many Florentines tried to insulate themselves, obeying the German rules except for listening to Radio London. Florence was not an industrial city, and it lacked the core of PCI-trained workers who in Milan and Turin successfully undercut their enemy bosses. However, the city was also the home of a vital group of intellectuals who had long cherished the tradition of free thought and action. The Rosselli brothers, Gaetano Salvemini, Enzo Enriques Agnoletti, Piero Calamandrei and Carlo Ragghianti are only a few of a long list.

Anti-Fascist sentiment was also strong in the Tuscan countryside. The peasants for miles beyond the city had long resented fascism, identifying it with the bourgeois owner-class that, in effect, owned them. As crop requisitions for Mussolini's military adventures had increased, so had the spirit of rebellion. The Fascists tried to split the peasants from the more politically-conscious city dwellers, largely by trying to convince farmers that urban requirements were responsible for food shortages. But at the same time the CTLN was making inroads on the traditional apolitical attitude of the peasants. From the first days of the

Armistice Tuscan peasants had willingly sheltered disbanded Italian soldiers, Allied prisoners-of-war and Jewish and political refugees. Now they began to be responsive to the larger objectives of the CTLN.

Florentines who did not actively participate in the underground showed their solidarity in other ways. Faith in the CTLN was amply demonstrated in April 1944 when a fund drive was launched to support its work. Until then most expenses had been fairly well covered by contributions from different sources, but intensified action by the partisans in the surrounding hills had increased the demand for weaponry. The CTLN decided the only answer was a direct appeal to the general public for financial aid, a difficult task in an occupied city. Bonds were offered ranging from as little as 50 lire to 5,000 lire, with a goal of 5 million to be raised. Collection was entrusted to the political parties and to the local branches of the CTLN. The fund drive was a test of both faith and courage, since anyone caught contributing would have been in serious danger. Within a few days the issues were sold out and the demand was so great that another 5 million was quickly raised. (A month later the PCI organized its own ''fund drive.'' A team of Gappists disguised as Fascist soldiers invaded the railway headquarters and carried off a safe containing millions of lire.)

Cooperation between the PCI and the other political parties, especially the strong Florentine Party of Action (PdA), was the official rule of the day, but at times the relationship became a bit strained. In spite of indisputable party difference and a certain amount of sparring, the CTLN developed into a well-coordinated organization whose moral and actual authority was recognized and accepted by partisans, peasants and city dwellers of all political leanings. As early as January 1944 the CTLN proclaimed itself the provisional government of the city, pledging to take over the reins as soon as circumstances permitted.

The PdA and the PCI, the two most influential parties in Florence at that time, devoted part of their energies to putting across their own ideological premises. The PdA's newspaper, *La Lib-*

ertà, was highly polemical though it also contained straight reporting on the progress of the war. Various PdA leaders wrote and distributed leaflets such as "The Reconstruction of the State" (Emilio Lussu); "Liberty" (Carlo Ragghianti); "Program Directives" (Tristano Codignola) and an anonymous "The Peasant Revolution." Leaflets were also distributed with contents of a more practical nature, containing specific instruction on how citizens could help in harassing the enemy. Covertly printing these materials was difficult enough, but distribution was even more dangerous.

For a considerable period a young student, Enzo Ronconi, was in charge of a stockpile of PdA leaflets kept in an apartment on Via Carlucci. The twenty-year-old Ronconi had been brought up in a conservative household, hardly one that could be called anti-Fascist. Ronconi's political awakening began with the passage of the racial laws in 1938. A teenager at that time, he witnessed the persecution of several close friends. When he began attending the University of Florence in 1942 he joined in discussion sessions on politics which made a great impression on him. After the September 8 Armistice he had bitter arguments with his father, joined the PdA and ultimately left the family fold.

Provided with false documents, Ronconi began a nomad existence, changing hideouts frequently while he carried out any tasks the underground assigned to him. He stole weapons left unguarded by the Fascist police; he learned to make the three-pronged nails used to flatten tires of German trucks; he gathered information for Radio Cora and ran errands for the group; he carried supplies to partisans in the hills. But the assignment that lasted the longest, and was the most successful thanks to his ingenuity, was the distribution of leaflets and press materials. Leaflets and newspapers were a major force in constructing and maintaining the network of patriots which would eventually act in unison during the mass insurrection.

But organization and cohesion were useless unless the patriots had the weapons to carry out their uprising. The winter months of 1943–1944 had depleted the already low stocks of guns and ammunition. Replacing them became a major objective. The only Allied air drop in Tuscany in February had been a complete disaster. The air drop had been arranged for the night of February 14. An unexpected snowstorm hit the area that evening. As the nineteen heavily loaded parachutes floated down, one by one they sank deeply into the fresh snow. The people assigned to recover the canisters floundered for hours trying to find them. When they actually did, they knew they had an excellent haul: 51 Sten machine guns, grenades, lots of ammunition, incendiary bombs, explosives and also some food and clothing.

Getting the supplies back to Florence was almost as difficult as retrieving them. The group had a car and a charcoal hauler's wagon, pulled by two horses. They somehow managed to avoid the inevitable roadblocks. By morning everything had been stored at 14 Via Guicciardini near the Ponte Vecchio and at an apartment in the Viale dei Mille, which also contained a newly acquired printing press. And then luck ran out. On February 20 Carità's men, tipped off by an SS officer who had managed to infiltrate the PdA, stormed the two hideouts, which contained much of the underground's stockpile of weapons, as well as the new haul. A subsequent roundup of suspects for a time devastated the leadership of the Florentine Resistance. Those who were not captured were forced to suspend activities to avoid further arrests. As a result, the Resistance was seriously hampered for the rest of the winter.

In April and May of 1944 the Resistance had begun to recoup its losses. The CTLN fund drive had helped immensely and the news of the liberation of Rome on June 4 was a great boost to morale. While the capture, on June 7, of Radio Cora and its members was a great loss, much more important was the fact that the Allies were advancing northward at last. The CTLN hastened to complete planning for an insurrection before the Allies could enter the city. A united Military Command was established under Col. Nello Niccoli, a highly respected officer of the former Italian army.

At the same time, the CTLN had to contend with equivoca-

tors *(attesiti)* among the Florentines who opposed an armed uprising, favoring instead reaching an agreement with the Nazis to
declare Florence an open city. The objectives of the equivocators
were not all humane. Many were middle-class businessmen who
hoped to protect their establishments from destruction.

There were also attempts made by the *repubblichini* to trade
their anti-Fascist prisoners in return for a guarantee of safe conduct out of the city when the Allies arrived. The CTLN opposed
all such deals, except for the exchange of a few prisoners on a
one-for-one basis. The equivocators then decided to enlist the aid
of Florentine Cardinal Elia Della Costa. Cardinal Costa proceeded to bypass the CTLN by personally approaching the Nazis
to try to work out some kind of compromise which would keep
the city from becoming a battleground. Elaborate precautions had
already been taken to remove and hide many art treasures, but
priceless buildings were impossible to protect. As these negotiations went on, the *repubblichini* were largely passive, making
only feeble attempts to keep their Nazi patrons from stealing works
of art from the Uffizzi and other galleries. The cardinal's overtures—largely ignored by the CTLN—ultimately failed to achieve
the results he desired.

While the equivocators maneuvered, the CTLN put the finish-
ing touches on the organization which would take over control of
the city when the Nazis were ousted. An interim mayor was
selected, and two vice-mayors, one from the PCI and one from
the Christian Democratic party. The presidency of the CTLN, it
was decided, would go to the PdA. The right-wing Liberal party
was given the presidency of the Consiglio Provinciale dell' Econ-
omia, and other positions were distributed among the Socialists
and the other parties. The CTLN was convinced that unless Florence liberated itself and immediately had a new government firmly
in place, Italy would continue to be regarded essentially as an
occupied country by the Allies and not as a true partner (full
Allied status being out of the question at that point).

Even as the CTLN consolidated its plans, the Germans had
begun issuing a series of ominous orders. On June 10 the gas

supply, for cooking and other purposes, was abruptly terminated. On June 14 the populace was ordered to save water because it might be shut off momentarily. At the same time telephone service was severely curtailed, to be used by civilians only in medical emergencies. Thanks to good weather, fruit and vegetables were in fair supply but meat was unavailable except on the black market, and then at exorbitant prices. German soldiers increased their stealing and looting from the stores officially designated as supply centers for the Florentines.

As both sides stepped up their activity, the scene changed abruptly. About July 7 Mario Carità suddenly left town followed in a few days by many other members of the Fascist hierarchy. They left in charge of the bureaucracy a few functionaries who were not especially close to Mussolini's Salo regime. These minor officials promptly negotiated with the CTLN, which equally promptly replaced them with its own men. This was a vital first step in taking over the city government. Alessandro Pavolini, secretary of the neo-Fascist party, who had made the elegant Hotel Excelsior his headquarters, abandoned *his* post on July 13. And on the 23rd the Fascist head of the Tuscan region also deserted, accompanied by the remaining top Fascists.

Before they all left, a last issue of the Fascist newspaper appeared with a banner headline "Arrivederci" (until we meet again). The issue was largely devoted to an article trying to disassociate the Fascists from the most vindictive of the Nazi leaders. It recommended that the Florentines comport themselves with dignity when the Allies arrived, and warned the populace not to attack any remaining Fascists, on pain of retribution.

Of the old Fascist guard, only the sharpshooters organized by Pavolini were left behind, apparently under orders of the Nazis. At the same time the German soldiers stationed in Florence were replaced by a large force of highly trained Nazi paratroopers and commandos under the command of Colonel Fuchs. The colonel had brought with him a good number of armored cars and several Tiger tanks. It was clear that the Nazis were preparing for street-by-street battle. As the other German troops retreated they took with them every wheeled vehicle in sight: ambulances, hearses, fire engines and even the motorized three wheelers used by street cleaners. They stole whatever they could move, even hospital beds and lenses from doctors' microscopes.

At this point the Allied armies were only some ten miles from Florence. Colonel Fuchs was totally preoccupied with military strategy and had abandoned all pretense of handling city government matters. This left it to the CTLN to try to maintain some kind of civic order while it also prepared for military action. The partisans in the surrounding hills were fairly well armed, but the civilian population still lacked weapons, never having fully recovered from the Via Guicciardini fiasco. Two major partisan units were lined up just outside Florence to help in the uprising: the PCI Arno Division led by "Potente" and made up of four brigades totalling 1,600 men, and the 1,000-man Rosselli Brigade, belonging to the PdA.

The Arno Division included the Sinigaglia Brigade which was, in a sense, an international brigade. It was named in honor of Alessandro Sinigaglia, son of Santina White, a black woman from Missouri. White had been a maid in the Florentine home of an American family, and she had married an Italian Jewish shopkeeper. Their son, Alessandro, an ardent Communist, had fought in Spain and had later been imprisoned on the island of Ventotene until the fall of Mussolini. He had been killed leading a Gappist attack in Florence. The Sinigaglia Brigade included many foreigners, most of whom were escaped Allied prisoners-of-war. Among them were two young Americans known simply as "Edo" and "Victor." They had been captured during the Anzio landing but had managed to jump from the train taking them to Germany, as it wound through a wooded area. Victor spoke some Italian, and after two days of wandering they met some partisans and decided to join them. Months later they found themselves part of the Brigade which would play a vital role in the liberation of Florence.

The strategic problem on the eve of the insurrection was how to coordinate the partisans waiting outside Florence with the patriots inside the city. The two main partisan units would not be able to join the uprising until the patriots of the city had broken down German defenses enough to permit large-scale entry of the partisans. To carry out the insurrection the CTLN had divided the city into four sections. Each of the parties had undertaken to organize its members in each section and to give them specific combat assignments. Centers had been established for first aid, weapons and food. An estimated 3,000 men and women made up the organized patriot units of the four regions, but all they had to fight with were some 900 shotguns, about 1,000 pistols and 1,000 grenades, and perhaps 50 automatic rifles. And ammunition to last less than an hour.

The plan was to attack and wipe out Fuch's forces as they worked their way through the city. Fuchs had repeatedly claimed he would declare Florence an open city but, even as he spoke, large red arrows and colored stripes appeared on the walls of certain streets. These were correctly interpreted by the CTLN to be a code for a surprise attack plan. The Nazi-controlled newspaper, *La Nazione,* warned the population that civilians who fired on German soldiers would be disobeying "international law" and would be shot. The article also promised once again that Florence would be considered an open city. The warning had no effect. If a German soldier happened to walk alone down a street he would likely be killed, and to avoid reprisal the body was either hidden or stripped of its uniform and thrown in the Arno. If a *repubblichino* was caught and did not resist, he would be taken prisoner.

On the afternoon of July 29 Nazi wall posters announced that, because it was expected that Allied forces would attempt to cross the bridges to enter the center of Florence, a wide area surrounding the bridges would have to be evacuated. The actual order to evacuate was given the next day. At the same time electrical power and water supplies were shut down.

About 150,000 people were affected by the evacuation order: they were given only a few hours to leave and to find new lodgings. With no trucks or even horse carts available, those who were able-bodied hauled a few belongings on their backs. A lucky handful found wheelbarrows which were used mainly to move the sick and the infirm elderly. A wealthy merchant, Gaetano Casoni, noted in his diary how he accompanied the archbishop on July 30 in a last vain attempt to get concessions from the Nazis, in this case to postpone the deadline for evacuation to give people more time to find lodgings and to salvage a few more possessions. On their way to see Colonel Fuchs, Casoni and the archbishop watched Allied planes fly over the city dropping leaflets signed by General Alexander. The leaflets contained directions for helping Allied soldiers to enter the city:

. . . Stop the enemy from exploding mines probably placed under bridges and major public buildings. . . .

Protect the railway station and all means of public transportation. . . .

Hide your food reserves from the enemy. . . .

Take note of mine emplacements and notify the Allies immediately, when they arrive. . . .

Leave open major streets and squares so Allied vehicles can pass through.

Casoni wrote that Fuchs received the delegation "with cold courtesy." The colonel declared that the Germans still adhered to the open city policy, but that they were taking precautions because the Allies—and he quoted the Alexander leaflets just dropped—obviously intended to fight their way through Florence. The archbishop in reply pointed out that Alexander's leaflet had come the day *after* the order to evacuate, a point which Fuchs ignored. Instead, Fuchs reminded the archbishop that the Germans had left the bridges intact after Rome was declared an open city, and that they were rewarded by the Allies using the bridges to trap 10,000 German troops.

The archbishop then asked for safe conduct to travel to Allied headquarters to personally tell them of Fuch's open city policy, but this request was brushed aside with the answer that only the German High command could grant such permission. The cardinal's final request was that two hospitals in the bridge area be

allowed to remain open, and to this Fuchs responded with a simple "No," repeated three times.

Casoni went on to tell how friends living in the proscribed
bridge area had to find shelter in his place of business. Eighteen
in all set up housekeeping in the waiting room, the mailroom and
various offices. Among his guests were Maya and Gerardo Kraft,
owners of the Hotel Excelsior and several other establishments
situated close to the river. The Krafts' daughter was a nun, Sister
Fantoni. Nuns were among the few people allowed to move around
freely, and she became an invaluable source of information to the
virtually imprisoned group.

As the situation in the city came to a climax, a few partisans
succeeded (unknown to the Germans) in taking over local police
headquarters by holding the police chief's wife and daughter hostage. The terrified chief went about town pretending he was still
in charge, petrified of revenge on his family. This feat secured
for the patriots all the ammunition stored in the police barracks.
But the evacuation of the bridge area had created new and serious
problems in terms of the insurrection plans. Besides negating
General Alexander's request that bridge access be protected, it
cut off the partisan units scheduled to support the city patriots.
Equally disastrous, of the 3,000 urban patriots organized to conduct the uprising, 800 lived on the side of the river away from
the city center, and they had part of the precious weapons and
ammunition supply.

Even as Commander Niccoli worked frantically to revise the
insurrection plans, at 2 PM on August 3 a Nazi order brought the
city to a complete standstill. From that moment no one was permitted to leave his house. All windows and doors, including those
of shops, were to be kept closed and anyone even appearing at a
window would be shot on sight. The Florentines were now
imprisoned without water, electricity or gas. Only doctors, nurses
and the clergy were allowed to move about. In short order many
of these "professionals" going about their business were actually
patriots in disguise. By now it was obvious the bridges were in
danger but all attempts to cut the clearly visible dynamite wiring

were unsuccessful. At 10 PM on Thursday, August 3, the explosions began and continued until 5 AM.

The night the bridges were destroyed had been a fine, clear evening. Casoni and his guests had been sitting on the sheltered terrace of his office building, cooking dinner on a small charcoal brazier. He wrote in his diary that the physical jolt and the noise was like that of a terrible earthquake, followed by immense clouds of smoke and dust filling the sky. From the roof of their five-story building, Casoni and Kraft were able to get a glimpse of the destruction. So violent were the explosions that flying stones and mortar reached well into the interior of the city.

Of the six bridges over the Arno, five were destroyed: only the Ponte Vecchio, allegedly Hitler's favorite, remained. Later that morning advance units of the Allied forces reached the left bank of the river. On the other side, in spite of German patrols and the debris scattered through the streets near the river, a few patriots were making their way around the city, carrying CTLN orders. The most audacious of these, perhaps, was Enrico Fischer, a member of the PdA and a commander in the third section of the city. Early on the morning of August 5 Fischer had managed to reach the Palazzo Vecchio, which was Colonel Fuch's headquarters. Thanks to a friendly civilian guard who was not a patriot but was willing to help, Fischer slipped inside the Palazzo and made his way to the adjoining Uffizzi Gallery. From there he quickly reached the secret corridor above the Ponte Vecchio which had been built by the Medici nobles to enable them to cross the river to the Pitti Palace without being seen by the people on the streets.

The old wooden beams of the bridge had been seriously weakened by the nearby blasts. Both ends had been mined and were under the surveillance of Fascist sharpshooters. But Fischer was able to scramble through the passage unseen. Once on the other side he presented his documents to the Allied officer in charge. Both agreed the passageway was structurally too weak and vulnerable for regular use, so it was decided to run a telephone line along it which would enable the CTLN to communi-

The ruins of Borgo San Jacopo, destroyed by German mines, as seen from the Ponte Vecchio, the only bridge over the Arno River to remain standing.

cate with the partisans and the Allied officers until temporary bridges could be built across the river. The center city end of the phone was located in the Palazzo Vecchio, almost under the noses of the German command. CTLN headquarters on Via Condotti were fairly nearby, as was Colonel Niccoli's office in the Piazza Strozzino. Niccoli used the secret passageway to pay a brief visit to the advance Allied officers, but otherwise he remained in the city.

Conditions in the city grew worse by the hour. Lack of water was the worst problem but food had become very scarce, too. The stench of garbage in the hot August streets was almost unbearable, but even worse was the sight of many unburied bodies and the rats running over everything. Women had been forced to disobey Nazi orders to stay indoors, making desperate forays in search of an old well that might still produce water. On August 6, Fuchs finally permitted women and children to search for food and water at certain hours. Men were still not allowed on the streets. Supplies were running short for the Germans, too, and Niccoli was sure that in a matter of days the Nazis would make their move. He ordered all patriots to be on the alert for the signal telling them to attack—the ringing of the great bell in the Palazzo Vecchio nicknamed "Martinella."

On the 10th, Casoni decided to visit his friend the archbishop, led there by Sister Fantoni who had covered Casoni with bandages so that he would look like a desperately ill old man seeking consolation from his priest. Casoni wrote in his diary: "The streets seem more deserted than usual, while from every side we could hear cannon which seemed closer today. I was told the usual sad news: always rapes, looting, wounding and killing. . . . The only happy news was that things were much better on the other side of the Arno. The Allies were distributing badly needed food (white bread, condensed milk, canned meat) and medicines. But above all it gave me great pleasure to learn that life there was very orderly: the CTLN has quickly taken over control of that part of the city, and has organized daily life with great ability and energy. So much so that when the Allies arrived . . . they found a civilized city whose citizens, overcoming all odds, had respected and exercised the principle of self-government.'' Apparently Casoni, too, was unaware that the Medici passageway had been used, because he wrote that news—and even a package from the Vatican to the archbishop—was being delivered by means of a secret tunnel *under* the river.

Colonel Niccoli had been coordinating some of his insurrection plans with Maj. Charles MacIntosh, who was in charge of the advance Allied group in Florence. The Allied Command was not enthusiastic about an open revolt or about the continuing patriot attacks on the Germans. Nor did Allied headquarters relish the important part being played by the CTLN and by the partisan brigades, who by now had been infiltrating the city through various routes. Partisan warfare was effectively decimating and demoralizing German troops, although some Florentines still hoped that the Germans would retreat in orderly fashion if left alone, as Fuchs promised.

In her memoirs Maria Luigia Guaita described how the Germans tried to keep control:

Every now and then there appeared a German patrol or a small bivouac, there were a few everywhere, usually formed by soldiers who were armed, or who had their submachine guns near at hand; in the daytime they were often indifferent to everything, as by now they were too tired and discouraged. During the night, instead, they did nothing else but fire here and there without reason, blindly, perhaps to make us keep still, quiet, to keep the city calm and dead, perhaps to give themselves courage.

The patriots suffered heavily also. On August 8, a group of partisans and Allied officers meeting in Piazza San Spirito had been shelled. Among those badly wounded was Potente, commander of the Arno Division. As he was carried off, dying, he urged his comrades to fight on: ''I die happy, take this red shirt off me and wave it over Florence when it is free.''

At 5 AM on the morning of August 11, Maria Luigia Guaita was awakened by a loud banging on her door. She was told to

A group of patriots in Florence organize to rout Fascist snipers hiding in the roof tops.

Florentine patriots searching out
Fascist snipers during the battle
to free Florence.

hurry to Niccoli for orders. Niccoli in turn asked her to run directly to the Palazzo Vecchio, where only a civilian guard was on duty. The message she gave him was simple: ''The Martinella must be tolled immediately and the Tricolor must be raised over the Palazzo.'' During the night the Germans had abandoned the center of the city.

As Guaita ran back towards CTLN headquarters she could hear the bell, previously silent for four years. People poured out onto the streets and windows were flung open as bells of many churches soon joined the Martinella. Even as jubilant citizens hugged each other, sniper shots began to fill the air. A problem for the next few days would be to again keep the people indoors until the street fighting ended and the sharpshooters were brought down.

The funeral cortege of "Potente," beloved leader of the Florentine Garibaldi Division. Potente was killed during the fighting to liberate Florence.

The Germans were still in control of many parts of the city, and of Fiesole and other hill towns from which their cannon could blast Florence. In the city they had now secured a position that extended from the Arno to the Cascine Park, along the Mugnone to Piazza delle Cure and from there, along the Florence–Rome railway line. The partisans in the second and fourth zones were

Florentines precariously crossed the Arno on makeshift bridges after the city was liberated.

separated from the center of the city, which had been effectively cut in half. Meanwhile in the center section more men were joining the advance unit of the partisan Arno Division, crossing the Arno along the Santa Rosa fish weir together with officers of the British Eighth Army. At the Mugnone, the Rosselli Brigade took on Nazi paratroopers supported by a Tiger tank. Elsewhere patriots were trying to pick off sharpshooters strategically located on rooftops.

The CTLN lost no time in issuing directives to the populace on how they could help the patriots. Those who had been turned out of their homes along the river were urged not to return until mines and sharpshooters had been cleared away. Citizens who had joined the patriot squads were given a choice of returning to their homes and helping to put the city in order or of participating in the street fighting. Many chose the former: there was a great deal of work to be done and water had begun to flow again, helping the clean-up process. The interim mayor had settled in at the Palazzo Vecchio hours after it was vacated by the Germans. His priorities were to restore public transportation, electricity and the telephone system.

For the first two days of the insurrection the partisans were doing well, but they had suffered heavy casualties and were running out of ammunition. After the initial success, they were facing an enemy which not only had regained the initiative, but was fighting back with superior weapons. Early on the morning of the 13th, Allied infantry began crossing the Arno to join the partisans. With this new support the tide changed again, but not before the Germans had managed to come back as far as Via Cavour, a few blocks from the Duomo (the cathedral), Giotto's belltower and other magnificent treasures. A few Germans even reached the Hotel Excelsior, where Major MacIntosh and other officers were now bivouaced and to which the Krafts had returned on the 14th.

Allied Military Government officials arrived on the 15th and on the 16th the provisional government established by the CTLN came to an end. A communiqué from AMG clearly stated that it would work closely with CTLN representatives in recognition of their "splendid work" and of the fact that the CTLN was obviously trusted by the citizenry. This was a reversal of a previous AMG announcement which had been vigorously opposed by the CTLN. The earlier communiqué stated that certain members of the local aristocracy would be put in charge of city affairs, and that even the mayor would be replaced. That decision was greatly resented by CTLN not because the aristocracy was necessarily connected with fascism but because many members of the aristocracy had not taken part in either the earlier fight against fascism, or in the insurrection, and thus did not represent the will of the people.

For the last two weeks of August Allied forces and partisans fought side by side, forcing the Germans to retreat once again. A temporary bridge had been built by Allied engineers on the site of the fifteenth century Ponte Santa Trinità, and troops, cars and truckloads of food and medical supplies streamed into the city. Although retreating, the Germans kept up a ceaseless bombardment of the inner city, all promises of "open city" completely forgotten. Casoni in his diary describes the anguish he felt when on Friday, August 18, bombs damaged the Santa Croce Church and the Uffizzi Gallery. He wondered if the Duomo could survive the day. And in fact on August 21 a bomb exploded on the pavement between the Baptistry and the Duomo. On the 23rd, a projectile hit the north façade of the cathedral and another broke off a small section of the Giotto tower. The fragments were quickly gathered and brought to Prof. Giovanni Poggi, who was in charge of salvage and restoration. By August 27 the German cannon no longer could hit the center of the city, and by August 31 the battle for Florence was over. Two hundred and five partisans died in the battle and four hundred were wounded.

On September 7, 1944 a ceremony to honor the patriots was held in the courtyard of the Fortezza da Basso, which was jammed with partisans, their families watching from the sidelines. A fourteen-year old boy who had fought with the Sinigaglia Brigade had been chosen trumpeter for the occasion. At his signal the men came to attention to welcome the arrival of Allied General Hume, who would review the troops. The Italian Tricolor flew beside the American flag, and nearby was the flag of the Arno Division, topped by the red shirt of its fallen leader, Potente.

A few words should be added about the salvaging of the incomparable art treasures of Florence. Most of the paintings and sculptures had been hidden early on in villas throughout the Tuscan countryside. Yet the Germans had discovered a great many and had sent truckloads to Germany, including works by Botticelli, Caravaggio, Fra Lippo Lippi, Lorenzetti, Pollaiuolo, Raphael, Titian, Verrocchio, Donatello, Michelangelo—and the foreign masters, Van Dyck, Rubens, Velàzquez. The list could go on and on. For many Florentines even more distressing than the thought of losing these treasures to the Germans was the knowledge that many were being grievously mishandled.

Cesare Fasola, an official of the Monuments and Fine Arts Service of Florence, tried to keep track of the condition of the still hidden treasures. On one visit to a storage villa he discovered a near disaster because the villa had become a residence for German troops. In his report Fasola wrote: "The rooms containing our collections had been literally turned upside down. . . . Almost all of them [the paintings] had been removed from their places, but it was not easy to find out at once if any had been carried off. . . . The packing cases had all been opened, the pictures taken out and flung about. Some had been piled in a dark corner." Fasola knew masterpieces by Cimabue and Giotto had been hidden there. "The custodian has watched over them with zealous care, doing his best even in the most critical moments. When he made his nightly round of the paintings, most of them of a religious character, he was in the habit of exclaiming 'Little Saints, help us!.' "

Many of the treasures were gone from Italy by mid-July at Himmler's orders, "to save them from the American troops." In one instance of Teutonic efficiency, a receipt was left for 58 chests of paintings. The happy ending, of course, is that today most of the art is back in Florence or, at least, has been found.

Montalcino, July 1944.
Above, **partisans receiving instructions after taking control of the town from the German and Fascist troops.**
Left, **a local partisan poses with his wife and family after helping the Allies rout the German invaders.**
Photos: Office of War Information Archives

THE FINAL ACT: THE NORTHERN INSURRECTIONS

The Allies began their final offensive in Italy in early April. As the war drew to a close, the major cities of the North prepared for insurrection as did many towns and villages which had been forced to play host to the Germans. The pattern was to be very like the chain of events in Florence: armed uprising of urban patriots and civilians organized by the local Committee of National Liberation aided by the partisans, followed by the departure (and sometimes the capture) of German troops, and the establishment of CLN-controlled local government, all before the arrival of the Allies.

Allied forces broke through the Gothic line in mid-April. They faced 27 German divisions augmented by five divisions made up of Italian soldiers representing Mussolini's puppet government. The Allies had 23 divisions and, although outnumbered, they had superior artillery and the invaluable help of the Resistance. Even before the breakthrough partisans fighting Germans on the outskirts of Modena were able to block all the main roads, cutting off the German retreat there and capturing many men and much materiel. Bologna was freed by the Resis-tance on April 19 and Modena on April 21, together with many surrounding towns and villages. The following are very brief accounts of events as memorable as the liberation of Florence, each of which could fill a separate volume.

GENOA

Of the large Northern industrial cities, Genoa was the first to revolt. The city itself had been occupied by some 10,000 German and Fascist soldiers. More troops were stationed in nearby towns, manning heavy calibre cannon trained on the city. Inside Genoa were about 3,000 patriots armed mainly with pistols, hand grenades and homemade bombs. They were backed up by some 4,500 partisans operating in the neighboring hills and plains.

Early in April, Gappists had disabled the 30,000-ton ship *Aquila*

Top, **Bologna, April 26, 1945. Italian patriots bring machinery out of hiding after the liberation of Bologna Italian partisans and Allied troops.**
Bottom, **alongside a captured German Mark IV tank. Private Ralph Gomez of Los Angeles, California, talks with two partisans who fought with the Allies to free the town of Rosignano.** *Office of War Information Archives.*

(formerly the transatlantic liner *Roma*), thereby foiling a German plot to sink the ship and block the entrance to the harbor. The Germans had hoped to destroy, at the same time, most of the docks and other harbor facilities, to paralyze one of Italy's major ports. But for over a year harbor workers had been frustrating German plans to wreck the harbor by disarming mines as fast as they were planted.

As the patriots stepped up their sabotage the German commander, General von Meinhold, made the usual proposal: if his troops were allowed to leave safely, he would declare Genoa an open city. The local CLN ignored this "guarantee." It did not want to facilitate a retreat which not only would allow the Germans to join other German troops in the Veneto region, but would also mean undoubted destruction of towns and power facilities on the way.

On the morning of April 23, the first German convoy left and that evening the CLN held an emergency meeting. Twenty-five political prisoners had been taken away with that convoy. It was time for Gappists, Sappists and other patriots to strike in force before more harm was done. The first move was a surprise attack on Fascist headquarters, where the patriots netted a good supply of weapons. The *repubblichini* did not resist, allowing themselves to be disarmed. Some even joined the rebels and proceeded to fight their former allies.

Next, the patriots cut the telephone wires and water and electricity supplying the German garrisons, while railway workers sabotaged the tracks to prevent German troop movements by rail. General von Meinhold reacted by threatening to order the encircling German troops to bombard the city if the patriot attacks did not stop immediately. The patriots answered that at the first bomb they would kill 1,000 of the German soldiers already taken prisoner. On the morning of the 25th an all-out attack on the German garrisons was so successful that von Meinhold had to take refuge in the archbishop's residence, from which he agreed to surrender. At 7:30 that evening the general signed a document of unconditional surrender which was accepted and signed by Remo Scoppini, president of the Genoa CLN, on behalf of the patriots. In a mass surrender some 9,000 Germans handed over their weapons, tanks and armored cars. But the city was not safe yet: a German demolition squad still controlled and threatened to blow up the port. Supported by a Fascist unit, they held out until the 27th, when they finally gave up.

MILAN

In Milan, the CLNAI had received a directive from Allied headquarters requesting that members of the armed resistance mainly devote their energies to protecting power plants and industrial installations. The ostensible goal was to preserve facilities so that the postwar recovery would be less difficult. The Allied armies, the directive made clear, would take care of the Germans. To the Resistance the true significance of the order was obvious: the Allies did not want the Italians to claim victory over the Germans because of the political implications this would raise at the peace table. The day after news of the successful Genoa uprising reached the CLNAI, a statement was issued declaring that all of northern Italy was now in a state of insurrection.

By afternoon of April 25, the citizens of Milan were out in force: workers at the Pirelli and Breda plants subdued the Germans in charge and took over the plants, as did workers in smaller factories. Police headquarters, the radio station and other public buildings fell to the insurgents that night. In her memoirs, Daria Banfi, who together with her husband had been a longtime member of the Resistance, recalls her amazement on the morning of the 25th at receiving a telephone call and being able to speak freely. For twenty years no one had dared talk openly on the phone about anything political.

At dawn on the 26th columns of German trucks began driving away. As agreed beforehand, the patriots permitted the demoralized Germans to leave without being attacked provided they did no damage. If the Nazis had any second thoughts about a counterattack, these were dispelled by the arrival that day of substantial partisan forces, pouring in from the hills around Milan. On the 27th the city was almost back to normal, stores were opened, trolleys began running and municipal authorities installed by the CLNAI had begun their work.

TURIN

Turin had previewed its insurrection with an effective general strike on April 18, 1945. General Schlemmer, the Nazi commander there, operated from strongly fortified headquarters in the center of the city, backstopped by some 35,000 troops located on the outskirts of the urban area. When the Turin CLN learned that Allied units would soon reach the city, a coded order was released establishing that the revolt should begin at 1 PM on April 26. The message read: "Aldo says 26 for one Stop enemy in final crisis Stop actuate plan E27 Stop examine all vehicles and hold suspicious people Stop commanders of zones involved should take all precautions to assure clear path for Allied forces on the Genoa–Turin and Piacenza–Turin routes Stop."

While workers were to take over the Fiat and other plants, SAP squads helped by mountain partisans were supposed to attack and chase out remaining Nazi/Fascist troops. But at 7 PM on April 25, the partisans received another order, contradicting the first message and telling them to wait for further instruction. The second message turned out to be falsified, the work of an enemy agent who was quickly caught and arrested. But the situation had been further complicated by the receipt of a similar restraining order from the head of the British military mission, which did delay the arrival of some partisan units.

In the general confusion of contradictory orders, apparently no one had advised the industrial workers of a delay in the insurrection deadline and for a good many hours the workers, together with SAP and GAP forces, bore the brunt of the battle, holding their own in spite of Tiger tanks racing through the city streets shooting at random. The Turin CLN military command was issuing directions from its headquarters in the Lancia auto works.

General Schlemmer was alternately offering compromises and threatening to make the city "another Warsaw." On the night of the 27th Schlemmer and his men broke through a barricade at the bridge spanning the Dora River and escaped to the highway to Chivasso, heading for Val d' Aosta and the Swiss border. He never made it: on May 3 the general and his troops surrendered to the pursuing Allies.

THE VENETO

Venice was next to liberate itself on April 28. Although there, too, the patriots were miserably armed they saved the bridges and the port and even captured 3,000 prisoners before the Allies arrived the next day. Nearby Vicenza, Treviso and Belluno followed in short order: Udine, on May 1, was among the last cities to liberate itself. In fact, fighting continued until May 7 throughout the whole Friuli region, with the partisan forces of the Osoppo and the Garibaldi brigades fighting side by side. By May 8, when World War II in Europe officially came to an end, all Italy was free.

=11=
An End and
a Beginning

"JUSTICE FOR THE ITALIAN PEOPLE"

FIVE GUNSHOTS in a garden near a lake ended Benito Mussolini's life at 4:10 PM on Saturday, April 28, 1945. This was the man who once commanded an empire, who had heard hoards of people thundering "Duce! Duce! Duce!" whenever he graced them with his presence.

The events leading up to the execution of Il Duce began on April 16, as the CLNAI was making final plans for the insurrection of the still German-occupied North. That day Mussolini announced at a meeting of his ministers in Salò that he was returning to Milan. Several days later he left Lake Garda in a convoy of five cars and a truck loaded with luggage, escorted by German SS guards. The convoy proceeded directly to the prefecture in the town of Corso Monforte, where the Duce had decided to rest before going on to Milan.

On his arrival, several hundred still loyal followers gathered under the balcony of the Prefecture, hoping to hear a few words of encouragement from their leader. For a few moments Mussolini stood there, pale-faced, staring at the crowd. Then he raised his hand in a brief Roman salute and turned away without saying a word. It was his last public appearance.

Well aware that the Germans were being defeated, Mussolini

spent the next few days alternately doing nothing and dreaming up impossible schemes. He sent a message to Sandro Pertini, a leader of the Socialist Party, suggesting that the Socialists take over the puppet government of Salò. Then the former dictator proposed that the Socialist and the Action parties together might absorb the RSI. Failing to receive a response to either proposal, he held a series of meetings with the remnants of the Fascist hierarchy who still surrounded him, to review alternative plans ranging from seeking refuge in Switzerland to making a last, grand stand against the Allies. Then, in one more about-face, Mussolini abruptly sent word to the CLNAI in Milan, through his friend Cardinal Schuster, Archbishop of Milan, that if he would be given a safe-conduct to Valtellina (near the Swiss border) he would surrender to the Allies there. This last idea was anathema to the CLNAI, which intended to claim Il Duce as its prize prisoner.

During these days of twisting and turning, Mussolini could easily have saved himself. A plane stood ready at the Brescia airport, secretly prepared to fly to Spain where arrangements had been made to harbor Mussolini. And in fact the plane took off safely on April 22, with a number of Germans and Fascists as well as the family of Claretta Petacci, the Duce's mistress. She herself refused to go, preferring to remain with her lover.

So disoriented was Mussolini at this time that even as he discarded plan after plan, he busied himself with trivial governmental affairs. His Minister of Education noted in his diary that on April 22 at 11 AM he was called to an audience with his chief to deal with "urgent matters." The urgent matters turned out to be the scheduling of a radio announcement regarding projected improvements for the University of Trieste. During all this time, Mussolini seemed to be totally unaware of the maneuvering by SS General Karl Wolff to arrange a surrender of German troops in Italy to the Allies.

In an interview after the war ended, SS Colonel Eugen Dollman explained that Wolff did not dare let Mussolini know what was going on because the German command in Italy was negotiating on its own, unknown to Hitler and the German High Command. By then, Dollman said, Mussolini was so ill and confused that he probably would have divulged the surrender plans to Claretta who would no doubt tell her brother Marcello (who had also remained in Italy, hoping to connive with the Nazis) and the news would have been sent on to Germany. If Hitler had found out, he would have destroyed Wolff and Dollman as well as the plot. Nor was Mussolini aware that on the morning of April 25th the CLNAI leadership had approved a decree which in effect condemned to death Mussolini and the top Fascist hierarchy: lesser officials were to receive a life sentence.

During that meeting the CLNAI had also announced that all occupied Italy was now officially in a state of insurrection, and that the CLNAI had therefore assumed full military and civil powers. Military tribunals would be established to deal with captured Germans and Fascists, who would be considered prisoners of war. The CLNAI further decreed: "The death sentence will be passed on all members of the Fascist government and the Fascist hierarchy guilty of having contributed to the suppression of the people's freedom by denying them their constitutional rights, guilty of having led to the creation of a tyrannical regime, and guilty of having compromised, betrayed and plunged Italy into a disastrous war. In cases where only second-degree guilt is established, the sentence will be reduced to a term of imprisonment, the length of which will be determined by the circumstances." The decree also stated that the laws of the puppet Fascist government were null and void.

As the CLNAI meeting was coming to an end, Marozza, the Christian Democrat representative, received a phone call from Archbishop Schuster's deputy who said that Mussolini was prepared to surrender to the CLNAI and that he had requested a meeting that day in the cardinal's palace. Actually, Mussolini hoped to bargain with the CLNAI, which had already clearly stated its terms: unconditional surrender. Mussolini arrived at the Palace at about 3 PM on the 25th and spent an hour talking with Cardinal Schuster while they waited for the delegation from the CLNAI. While the two conversed, Mussolini's retinue, including his Minister of Defense, Marshal Rodolfo Graziani, waited in another room. In a postwar interview, Pino Romualdi, a member of the puppet government, said that neither he nor the Fascist party secretary, Alessandro Pavolini, had been informed of the meeting, probably because Mussolini knew they would advise against it.

Cardinal Schuster in his memoirs described Mussolini as being very depressed and said he offered his guest a biscuit and a liqueur, to try to relax him. The Cardinal recalled that after a few desultory remarks, Mussolini outlined a plan to retreat to Valtellina with "3,000 of the most faithful." Schuster said he suggested 300 might be a more realistic number, which Mussolini did not quite accept though he agreed 3,000 might be too high. Finally the CLNAI contingent arrived, consisting of the CLNAI's Military Commander General Cadorna, and representatives of half of the six parties: the Party of Action, the Christian Democratic party and the Liberal party.

During the confrontation, the CLNAI lost no time in establishing the fact that only unconditional surrender was acceptable and that no compromise was possible. Cadorna pointed out that the Germans, too, would have to accept such terms from the Allies in Italy. Mussolini claimed to be taken totally by surprise by this information about German negotiations for peace. He declared loudly that he had been betrayed, that it could not be possible, but Schuster confirmed that General Wolff had reached an understanding with the Allies. The Germans had agreed not to destroy factories and other facilities, nor to take hostages, in exchange for a guarantee that they would be treated as prisoners of war in accordance with international law. Wolff also had agreed to disarm Fascist troops.

In a rage, Mussolini asked the cardinal for an hour to think things over and said he would return with his answer by 7 PM. As he and his followers went quickly down the steps of the Palace, Sandro Pertini was racing up them. For a brief moment and for the first time in 23 years, these longtime enemies met face to face. Then Mussolini turned and left without a word.

Pertini had been working on insurrection plans when a *staffetta* brought him the news of the meeting between Mussolini and some members of the CLNAI. He jumped into a friend's "Topolino," the miniature Fiat two-seater, and rushed to join them. His greatest fear, Pertini said later, was that the CLNAI representatives were unaware of the presence of Allied agents in the Palace. He was afraid that if the agents had realized Mussolini was there, they might have seized him for the Allies, thus denying the Resistance one of its major victories. The capture and judgment of Mussolini was as important, symbolically, to the Resistance as was the liberation of cities in advance of the Allies. Both events meant that Italy was at last in control of its own destiny, and that Italians themselves had earned their freedom.

While the delegation waited for Mussolini to return, Pertini reaffirmed the CLNAI decision to treat the Fascist hierarchy as war criminals. "But my children," exclaimed the archbishop, "then there will be bloodshed!" This was too much for Sereni, the Communist party member who had also belatedly joined the group. "We are not your children," he retorted, reminding Schuster of his many sermons condemning partisan activities, preached on Sundays from the pulpit of the Duomo of Milan. As they spoke Don Bicchierai, one of the cardinal's aides, entered the room and whispered in his ear: "Mussolini has left Milan." Immediately after hearing this news, the CLNAI took over the empty prefecture, formerly Mussolini's Milan headquarters. Riccardo Lombardi (Party of Action) was installed as prefect and Antonio Greppi (Socialist) as mayor.

There are several versions of Mussolini's last days, but most sources agree on the broad outline. He lost no time in leaving Milan. By nightfall of the 25th he and his party had arrived at Como and, after a futile attempt to cross the Swiss border, they regrouped at the local prefecture for a late supper and yet another review of the options open to them. His wife Rachele and their two younger children, Anna Maria and Romano, were at a villa nearby but Mussolini did not join them. Instead, before dawn the next morning he moved on to Menaggio, breaking an appointment to meet Romualdi and other Fascists at 8 AM in Como. Trailing behind Il Duce was the faithful Claretta and her brother. (Graziani split with the group at Menaggio, and was later captured by an American Army captain, Emilio Daddario.)

At Menaggio, Mussolini discovered a German anti-aircraft unit still stationed there. The commander of the unit had just decided to pull up stakes and head for Alto Adige, on the Austrian border. For Il Duce, after all his own indecision, it was a relief to encounter someone who knew what he was going to do. He decided to throw in his lot with the Germans. Early on the 27th the convoy left Menaggio, with Mussolini and Pavolini riding in an armored car at the head of the column. Mussolini supposedly carried with him a leather case full of documents to use in his defense at a war trial, among them some letters allegedly written by Churchill after the two nations were at war. Pavolini was said to have in his custody several suitcases full of jewels, Swiss money and British sterling. (None of these cases was ever found.) After a bit, Mussolini decided to disguise himself as a German soldier, and moved to a truck at the rear of the column.

There were 38 cars and trucks in the convoy. The itinerary was to take them along the left bank of Lake Como north to Merano, and on to Austria and Germany. But the citizens of Menaggio had become aware of unusual activity at the local Fascist headquarters and had already notified the 52nd Garibaldi Brigade located in the vicinity. The partisans quickly prepared a road block to stop the convoy near Dongo and there the column came to an abrupt halt. Although the Germans were well armed, their objective was to get away rather than to fight. They were also openly fearful of the partisans, believing themselves to be outnumbered by the Italians. After some discussion, the brigade commander agreed to let the Germans continue provided they give up any Fascists in the convoy. As the search got underway, one of the partisans—Giuseppe Negri—noticed a soldier lying in the corner of one of the trucks. According to his companions, he was sleeping off a night of drinking.

Apparently out of pure curiosity Negri lifted the cap covering the "drunk's" face and immediately recognized Il Duce. Pretending he had noticed nothing, Negri quickly left the scene and raced to report his find to the brigade leaders. He soon returned with three other partisans and led Mussolini away at gunpoint. Il Duce was taken to the city hall, where he found a frightened Claretta Petacci, who had been discovered earlier. After a few hours, both were escorted to a nearby barracks. Finally, at 1 AM on the 28th, his head wrapped in bandages to prevent recognition, he was bundled into a car, together with Petacci. They were driven to a small farmhouse in Giulino de Mezzegra, which belonged to Gaetano De Maria, an old peasant friendly to the partisans. De Maria was told shelter was needed for a wounded German and his wife.

Meanwhile the news of Mussolini's capture had reached CLNAI headquarters in Milan. A meeting was quickly convened, the situation having become especially urgent because it was known the American Captain Daddario was in the Dongo area and might seize Mussolini as he had Graziani. The Dongo CLN had suggested that Il Duce be transferred to Milan, but this plan was vetoed as being both too time-consuming and too vulnerable to pursuit by Daddario. Pertini remembers the discussion: "Cadorna," he recalls saying to the general, "We can't lose time. We must hold onto Mussolini ourselves. And if justice must be done, it should be up to us, not to the Allies. Let's send someone to Dongo with authority to execute Mussolini." The CLNAI chose Walter Audisio (alias Colonel Valerio) and Aldo Lampredi, both Communists and highly regarded members of the CVL (Corps of Volunteers of Liberty), the military arm of the CLNAI. Audisio was put in charge.

Walter Audisio had been active in the labor movement since the early twenties and had long been an anti-Fascist. He had spent many years in prison, and had fought with the International Brigade during the Spanish Civil War. He had a reputation for bold action, and was not intimidated by an assignment which might have shaken a less confident man. Audisio's memoirs, published two years after his death in 1973, describe in detail the Duce's last hours. In accordance with the terms of the CLNAI decree of April 25, Audisio, upon his arrival in the Dongo area, called together the leaders of the local partisan units and asked them to function as a military tribunal to judge Mussolini's fate. The tribunal condemned to death Mussolini and 16 of the 52 Fascists accompanying him, and ordered that the sentence be carried out immediately.

Audisio had selected a small, walled garden in a secluded orchard as the site for Mussolini's execution. On his way to get Il Duce he decided to tell him he was going to be liberated, to make things easier. His companions ridiculed the notion, pointing out the former dictator was not stupid and would never accept such an explanation. When they arrived at the farmhouse they found Mussolini standing by a window and Petacci lying, fully clothed, on a bed. On seeing the men Mussolini was immediately suspicious, but he soon willingly accepted Audisio's story. Full of bravado, he marched towards the car which would take him to "freedom." According to Audisio, for a brief moment he resembled the former dictator, as he grandly promised Audisio an empire. Petacci stumbled along behind them, her high heels catching on the rocky path.

During the short ride Mussolini asked about his followers and was told they, too, were being "liberated." Then there was silence. When they reached the orchard, Audisio ordered the driver to stop while he checked the road for passersby. On returning to the car he saw that Mussolini was ashen-faced, aware at last that something was wrong. Petacci had not been included in the list to be executed but she was allowed to accompany Mussolini. The couple was escorted into the garden, where Mussolini was asked to stand against the wall. Audisio insists that he told Petacci to move away, unless she, too, wanted to be shot. He then quickly pronounced the sentence: "By order of the general command of the CVL I have been entrusted to render justice for the Italian people." Mussolini did not seem to hear, let alone understand,

Top, the farmhouse room in which Mussolini and Claretta Petacci, his mistress, spent their last hours.
Bottom, gate to the small garden in which Mussolini was executed by the partisans.

the words. He stared in a daze at the gun pointed at him, mumbling "But, but—Colonel." Petacci put her arm around his shoulders. At 4:10 PM both were dead.

That same afternoon the other condemned Fascists were shot in the main piazza of Dongo. At 6:30 PM all the bodies were loaded in a truck, to be carried to Piazzale Loreto in Milan. Twice the truck was stopped by Allied soldiers who, satisfied that partisans were driving, waved them on their way without checking the cargo. Piazzale Loreto was selected as the final stop for the bodies because it was there, on August 10, 1944 that fifteen patriots had been killed by the Fascist "black shirts." Now the scales were balanced. The subsequent macabre hanging by the heels of Mussolini and Petacci was an episode that many Italians regarded as shameful. Others, like spectators at beheadings during the French Revolution, revelled at the sight. The CLNAI soon ordered the cadavers to be removed and brought to a mortuary, but not before they had been reviled and even ravaged by thousands. Mussolini eventually was buried in his family vault at Predappio.

THE DREAMS REALIZED?

Fascist Foreign Minister Ciano wrote in his diary on January 29, 1940: "The Duce is irritated by the internal situation. The people grumble. . . . He ranted about the possibility of an uprising: 'when the instincts in a people are stationary and without ideas, only the use of force can save them. . . . Have you ever seen a lamb become a wolf? The Italian race is a race of sheep. Eighteen years are not enough to change them. It takes 180 years and maybe 180 centuries.' "

Today united Italy is a democratic republic and one of the world's most successful economies, with an active voice in international affairs. The achievement of much of Giuseppe Mazzini's dream of 150 years ago had belied Mussolini's prophecy. How much did the Resistance contribute to the realization of Mazzini's wish for a unified, republican Italy, and what happened to the dreams of the Resistance leaders?

With the end of hostilities in May 1945, it was time for Bonomi to resign as provisional prime minister of the wartime Cabinet. A delegation from the CLNAI went to Rome to join in the debate over the selection of a new premier. After much discussion it was decided that Ferruccio Parri, the Action Party leader, was the most suitable candidate. He had emerged as an honored hero of the Resistance and was known and admired for his dedication and honesty. Also, as a professor of economics, it was hoped he could provide leadership in the effort to reconstruct the country's war-torn economy. On June 20 Parri became prime minister in the first anti-Fascist government of postwar Italy, with Crown Prince Umberto II as the nation's lieutenant-general. Parri's Cabinet included representatives of the six major political parties. Many of them had not participated in the armed Resistance but had other political and administrative qualifications.

For six months Parri grappled with the hopes and fears of his countrymen. The partisans had saved many industrial plants in the North (only some ten percent of the factories were destroyed), but the nation's infrastructure was in ruins. Railroads had been badly damaged and two-thirds of the bridges had been demolished. In addition, agricultural production had been cut in half. In Parri's first broadcast, he introduced himself as "Professor Ferruccio Parri, President of the Council of Ministers," and admonished the war-weary people: "Enough murders and reprisals: let us roll up our sleeves." Unauthorized attacks on former Fascists were creating an atmosphere of terrorism, which added to the fears formed by unemployment, inflation and hunger. (Some reports say as many as 20,000 ex-Fascists were killed.) The Communist leader Togliatti, in his role as Minister of Justice, relieved some of the tension by declaring a general amnesty for minor Fascist political prisoners, who had been imprisoned by virtue of a membership which some of them had regarded mainly as a prerequisite for employment.

The CLN's role in government had ended in the North with the June 1 installation of the Allied Military Government, although CLN-selected prefects were allowed to remain in place in Milan and several other cities. But problems were developing in the provisional Italian government. Parri, who had been an excellent military leader, turned out to be an ineffective political leader. Neither he nor many of his appointees had governmental experience. Also, his Action Party had a very small mass following, outside of a group of dedicated intellectuals, leaving him with little real political clout. For all his fine qualities, Parri could not cope with the tremendous problems confronting him. These problems included inflation and the black market; demands for land reform; settlement of regional differences; dealing with Fascist holdovers; and most important, preparing for the forthcoming elections. The right-wing Liberal party, taking advantage of his predicament, withdrew from the Cabinet on November 21, 1945, precipitating a government crisis and the formation of a new Cabinet in December under Alcide de Gasperi, head of the center-right Christian Democratic Party.

For many former members of the Resistance the coming into power of the Christian Democrats symbolized a return to the status quo before fascism, and an end to revolutionary hopes. To others the new regime signalled a return to stability and an end to fear of the unknown, of radical changes which could bring disaster as easily as progress. Industrialists and the Vatican realized their futures were at stake, and each group in its own way vigorously beat the drums for a "return to normalcy." De Gasperi had a strange political bedfellow in Togliatti, who went along with the Christian Democrats in an effort to transform the image of the Communist party as bent on change through revolution.

De Gasperi's first objective was to replace the monarchy with a republican form of government. To this end he called for a referendum on the monarchy in June 1946, and for the election of a Constituent Assembly which would draw up a new constitution to supplant the one in existence since 1848. For the monarchists, the establishment of a republic was a jump into the dark. For the anti-monarchists, the new republic would be a purging of the immediate past, and a definitive blow to fascism and to the possibility of its return. Fortunately for the republicans, King Victor

Emmanuel III had taken many steps guaranteed to topple the institution of royalty, culminating with his flight from Rome after the Armistice of September 8, 1943.

To help their cause, the monarchists had finally persuaded the king to abdicate before the referendum, and he reluctantly did so on May 9, 1946 going into exile in Egypt. His son, Umberto II, reigned as king until June 12, when the Republic was officially recognized as a result of the referendum in which Italians voted 12 million to 10 million in favor of the republic, with 90 percent of eligible voters casting their ballots. Umberto II left for Portugal with his family on June 13.

The June 2 voting for a Constituent Assembly gave the Christian Democrats 207 seats (35 percent), 115 to the Socialists (20.7 percent) and 104 to the Communists (18.9 percent). Women and many rural citizens voted for the first time, and were openly pressured by the Vatican and clergy to vote for the Christian Democrats. Enrico de Nicola, the Neapolitan jurist, was elected provisional president, partly to placate the pro-monarchist South.

Whatever other postwar goals the Resistance leaders may have failed to achieve, there are few who would argue that defeating the monarchy was not a Resistance victory. The unification of 1861 had been anchored on the institution of the monarchy, which represented long-held traditions of authority and stability of social classes. By contrast, working together in the Resistance and in local and regional CLNs had given many Italians their first experience of self-government and of participation in national affairs. The 90 percent turnout in the June 2 elections was an extraordinary affirmation of the new faith in the democratic process, although the monarchy *did* win well over 40 percent of the vote.

On the international scene, the break between East and West was becoming ominous. In February 1946 Stalin had declared it was impossible to coexist with capitalism, and in March Churchill made the famous speech at Fulton, Missouri, in which he observed that from the Baltic to the Adriatic "an iron curtain has descended across the Continent." Almost a year later Bernard Baruch, speaking in South Carolina, said: "Let us not be deceived—today we are in the midst of a cold war.'' De Gasperi, who had visited the U.S. in January 1947 and who had been given an inkling of American economic aid possibly forthcoming, was astute enough to absorb the significance of these statements and of the Truman Doctrine, which had been announced in March 1947. The latter gave financial aid to the pro-Western Greek and Turkish governments so that they could fight against Communist insurgents in their nations.

In a radio address on April 28, 1947, De Gasperi reviewed the situation in Italy, declaring that a crisis in government was at hand because the old wartime coalition of political parties had been unable to cope with postwar problems and had, instead, become frayed by internal dissension. In May the Council of Ministers convened, and the upshot was the end of the participation of the Communist party in the government, the last time Communists would be included in an Italian government. For some, this was a bitter pill to swallow. As David Ellwood has remarked in his book on Allied-Italian relations during the Resistance period, ''For years afterwards it was to seem to all those parts of the Italian political spectrum left of center that an unparalleled opportunity for radical change had been lost in 1945, and that this loss was somehow connected with the presence of the British and the Americans.'' It is perhaps fairer to say that the scenario was *reinforced* by the British and the Americans. At any rate, expulsion of the Communists from the government began the polarization of Italian politics between left and right, establishing the Communists as a numerically powerful and vocal opposition.

By the end of 1947 the Constituent Assembly had drawn up a new constitution and approved it 453 to 62. One of its crucial provisions, from the Christian Democrat point of view, was Article 7 which retained the Lateran Accords of 1929. Although this meant Catholicism would continue as the state religion, freedom of conscience and equality of all religions were also guaranteed by Articles 8 and 19. Among other provisions:

1. The President, as head of State, would be elected by a joint

session of both houses of Parliament for a 7-year term. Although a position of honor, the powers of the president were limited.

2. Italy was divided into 19 regions, and in recognition of regional differences a certain amount of administrative autonomy was granted to each region.

3. Legislation by decree had to be approved by Parliament within 60 days, or it would be nullified.

4. A Supreme Constitutional Court was to be established (and was in 1956).

5. Senators would be elected, not appointed.

The influence of the left was evident in clauses granting citizens the right to a living wage, free health care and free education, as well as some clauses that proved to be, as Delzell commented, "little more than pious expressions." Among these was a statement to the effect that workers were to share in profits and management.

How much the Italy of today owes to the Resistance is to some degree a matter of opinion, and perhaps even of prejudice. One of the foremost authorities on modern Italy, the British historian Denis Mack Smith, in writing of the postwar transformation of Italy, observed: "Possibly the partisans suffered greater casualties than the regular armies in this campaign: certainly their achievements were a big factor in restoring Italian morale and self-confidence. Some of the very best elements in the country were prominent in the Resistance, and it provided a fine training in social consciousness as well as a new kind of idealistic patriotism. No one who lived through such an experience could forget it; never before had so many citizens participated so actively in national life. From many sources . . . the impression emerges that this liberating war against Mussolini and Hitler penetrated far more deeply into peoples' consciences than the nineteenth-century Risorgimento had ever done."

Max Salvadori, who worked with the Resistance, in his history of the period concluded, "The Resistance had saved the soul of the nation, but it was a divided soul." If the nation was left divided, that is part of the democratic process. However, in 1985, during the 40th anniversary of World War II, the memory of the Resistance was celebrated across the country, regardless of political affiliation.

Throughout the postwar years the Resistance has been the theme of books, art, and many great movies in Italy, beginning with Rossellini's *Open City* in 1945, and including Bertolucci's *1900* and the Taviani brothers' recent *The Night of the Shooting Stars. The Four Days of Naples,* first released in 1962, is now available in video cassettes which, according to one Neapolitan taxi driver, are owned and proudly replayed by many a Neapolitan household today. Among the many fine memoirs and novels written about the period are the books by Vittorini, Calvino, Fenoglio, Zangrandi, and the tremendously moving series by Primo Levi. The Resistance has also been made an integral part of history textbooks, and the subject continues to be discussed in political commentaries on radio and TV.

A widely read and reviewed book of 1986 was Ennio Di Nolfo's *Le Paure e le Speranze degli Italiani* (The Fears and the Hopes of the Italians), which deals with the Resistance and the postwar years. Di Nolfo wrote: "The Resistance was a catharsis which cancelled the past and permitted hope for a new society. . . . Hope did not belong to only one political group or to one class . . . the idea of hope belonged to all, it was a way of thinking that crisscrossed the fabric of Italian society, independent of political affiliations. For this reason the Resistance was a significant unifying force. It removed from the country the climate of death, decadence and crisis in which it had lived for years, and put in motion positive forces of transition, the bases of a movement which would gradually give birth to a new nation with new institutions."

Bibliography

THE FOLLOWING LIST is a very partial selection of the many books and documents which have been written about the Italian Resistance during World War II. Excellent and much more comprehensive bibliographies are available in *Italy, A Modern History* by Denis Mack Smith, and in the footnotes to source materials found in Charles Delzell's *Mussolini's Enemies*. Specialized bibliographical compilations can also be found in the libraries of the Resistance Research Centers in Italy.

Arfe, G. *Storia del socialismo Italiano, 1892–1926*. Turin: Einaudi, 1965.

Ascarelli, A. *Le fosse Ardeatine*. Rome: Palombi, 1945.

Audisio, Walter. *In nome del popolo Italiano*. Milan: Teti, 1975.

Babini, A.F. *Giovecca*. Giovecca: Comitato Antifascista, 1980.

Badoglio, Pietro. *Italia nella guerra mondiale*. Milan: Mondadori, 1946.

Barbagallo, Corrado. *Napoli contro il terrore nazista*. Naples: Maone, 1944.

Barbieri, Lucia. *Enrico Bocci*. Florence: G. Barbera, 1969.

Barzini, Luigi. *The Italians*. New York: Atheneum, 1964.

Battaglia, Roberto. *Storia della Resistenza Italiana*. Turin: Einaudi, 1953.

Battaglia, Roberto. *The Story of the Italian Resistance*. Transl. and ed. by P. D. Cummins. London: Oldhams, 1957.

Bertoldi, Silvio. *I tedeschi in Italia*. Milan: Rizzoli, 1964.

Bianco, D. Livio. *Guerra partigiana*. Turin: Einaudi, 1954.

Bisiach, G. *Pertini Racconta*. Milan: Mondadori, 1983.

Boldrini, A. *Enciclopedia della Resistenza*. Milan: Teti, 1980.

Borgese, G.A. *Goliath: The March of Fascism*. London: Gollancz, 1938.

Brome, Vincent. *The International Brigades*. New York: Wm. Morrison, 1966.

Brown, Anthony C. *The Last Hero*. New York: Random House, 1982.

Caizzi, Bruno. *Gli Olivetti*. Turin: UTET, 1962.

Calamandrei, Pietro. *Uomini e citta della Resistenza*. Bari: Laterza, 1955.

Calvino, Italo. *The Path to the Nest of Spiders*. New York: Ecco Press, 1976.

Cammett, J.M. *Antonio Gramsci and the Origins of Italian Communism*. Stanford: Stanford University Press, 1967.

Candelaro, G. *Storia dell' Italia moderna.* Milan: Feltrinelli, 1970.

Cargnelutti, F. *Preti patrioti.* Udine: Arti Grafiche Friulane, 1965.

Casella, L. *The European War of Liberation.* Florence: LaNuova Europa, 1983.

Casoni, G. *Diario fiorentino.* Florence: Societa Leonardo da Vinci, 1956.

Castagnino, P. *Immagini e avvenimenti della Resistenza in Liguria.* Genoa: Silvio Basile, 1979.

Catalano, F. *Storia del C.L.N.A.I.* Bari: Laterza, 1956.

Centro Studi Piero Gobetti. *Piero Gobetti e il suo tempo.* Turin, 1976.

Cervi, Alcide. *I miei sette figli.* Rome: Rivusti, 1955.

Churchill, Winston. *The Second World War.* London: Cassell, 1950–52.

Ciano, Galeazzo. *Diaries 1939–43.* New York: Doubleday, 1946.

Corpo Volontari della Liberta. *La Resistenza Italiana.* Milan: Ufficio Stralcio, 1947.

Croce, Benedetto. *Per la nuova vita dell' Italia.* Bari: Laterza, 1944.

De Felice, Renzo. *Storia degli ebrei Italiani sotto il fascismo.* Milan: Mondadori, 1977.

De Jaco, Aldo. *Le quattro giornate di Napoli.* Rome: Riuniti, 1975.

Dellavalle, C. *Guerra e resistenza nella Val Sangone.* Comunita Montana Val Sangone, 1985.

Delzell, Charles F. *Mussolini's Enemies.* Princeton: Princeton University Press, 1961.

Di Nolfo, Ennio *Le paure e le speranze degli Italiani.* Milan: Mondadori, 1986.

Donati, G. *Ebrei in Italia.* Milan: Centro di documentazione ebraica, 1980.

Ellwood, David W. *Italy 1943–1945.* New York: Holmes & Meier, 1985.

Enciclopedia dell' antifascismo e della Resistenza. Milan: La Pietra, 1971.

Falzone, V. *La costituzione della Repubblica Italiana.* Rome: Colombo, 1948.

Fermi, Laura. *Mussolini.* Chicago: University of Chicago Press, 1961.

Finer, H. *Mussolini's Italy.* New York: Holt, 1935.

Forcella, Enzo. *La Resistenza Italiana.* Milan: Mondadori, 1975.

Formiggini, G. *Stella d'Italia, Stella di David.* Milan: Mursia, 1970.

Francovich, Carlo. *La Resistenza a Firenze.* Florence: La Nuova Italia, 1965.

Gervasutti, Sergio. *La stagione della Osoppo.* Venice: La Nuova Base, 1976.

Gobetti, Ada. *Diario partigiano.* Turin: Einaudi, 1956.

Gobetti, Paolo. *Le prime bande.* Turin: ANCR, 1983.

Gortoni, M. *Il martirio della Carnia.* Tolmezzo: Grafico Carnia, 1966.

Gramsci, A. *Lettere dal carcere.* Turin: Einaudi, 1947.

Gracci, A. *Brigata Sinigaglia.* Milan: Feltrinelli, 1976.

Guaita, Maria L. *Storie di un anno grande.* Florence: La Nuova Italia, 1975.

Hentze, Margot. *Pre-Fascist Italy: The Rise and Fall of the Parliamentary Regime.* London: Allen and Unwin, 1939.

Hood, Stuart. *Pebbles from my Skull.* London: Hutchinson, 1963.

Hughes, H. Stuart. *America and Italy.* Cambridge: Harvard University Press, 1953.

Hughes, H. Stuart. *Prisoners of Hope.* Cambridge: Harvard University Press, 1983.

Keene, Frances. *Neither Liberty nor Bread.* New York: Harper and Row, 1940.

Lambiase, S. and Nazzaro, G.B. *Napoli 1940–1945.* Milan: Longanesi, 1978.

Larocca, Gilda. *La "Radio Cora" di Piazza d'Azeglio.* Florence: Giuntina, 1985.

Levi, Primo. *The Periodic Table.* New York: Schocken Books, 1984.

Lewis, Norman. *Naples '44.* New York: Pantheon, 1978.

Libenzi, E. *Ragazzi della Resistenza.* Milan: Mursia, 1971.

Lombardi, G. *Montezemolo, Quaderni del Museo Storico,* Rome, 1972.

Longo, Luigi. *Un popolo alla macchia.* Milan: Mondadori, 1947.

Mack Smith, Denis. *Italy, A Modern History.* Ann Arbor: University of Michigan Press, 1969.

MacIntosh, Charles. *From Cloak to Dagger.* London: Kinder, 1982.

Malaguzzi, Daria Banfi. *A Milano nella Resistenza.* Milan: Riuniti, 1960.

Malvezzi, P. and Pirelli, G. *Lettere di condannati a morte della Resistenza Italiana.* Turin: Einaudi, 1952.

Matthews, Herbert. *The Fruits of Fascism.* New York: Harcourt, Brace, 1943.

Maugeri, Franco. *From the Ashes of Disgrace.* New York: Reynal Hitchcock, 1948.

Michelozzi, Andreina M. *Le foglie volano.* Florence: La Nuova Europa, 1984.

Montanelli, I. and Cervi M. *L'Italia della guerra civile,* Milan: Rizzoli, 1984.

Mussolini, Benito. *My Autobiography.* Transl. by R.W. Child. New York: Scribner's, 1928.

Newby, Eric. *When the snow comes, they will take you away.* New York: Washington Square Press, 1971.

Ochetto, Valerio. *Adriano Olivetti.* Milan: Mondadori, 1985.

Origo, Iris. *War in Val D'Orcia.* Boston: Godine, 1984.

Origo, Iris. *A Need to Testify.* New York: Harcourt, Brace, 1984.

Pansa, G. *Storia e documenti del primo Comitato Militare, del C.L.N. regionale Piemontese.* City of Turin, 1965.

Parri, Ferruccio. *Scritti 1915–1975.* Milan: Feltrinelli, 1976.

Perona, G. *Torino fra Atene e Varsavia.* Turin: Centro Studi Piero Gobetti, 1975.

Quazza, Guido. *La Resistenza italiana: appunti e documenti.* Turin: Giappichelli, 1966.

Saitta, A. *Dal fascismo alla Resistenza.* Florence: La Nuova Italia, 1961.

Salvadori, Massimo. *Storia della Resistenza.* Venice: Pozza, 1956.

Salvemini, Gaetano. *Under the Axe of Fascism.* New York: Viking Press, 1936.

Schiano, P. *La Resistenza nel napoletano.* Naples: Foggia-Bari CESP, 1965.

Sensoni, V. and Ceccarini, V. *Marzabotto.* Milan: Teti, 1981.

Tannenbaum, Edward. *The Fascist Experience.* New York: Basic Books, 1972.

Tannenbaum, Edward and Noether, Emiliano P. *Modern Italy.* New York: New York University Press, 1974.

Tarsia, A. *Napoli negli anni di guerra.* Naples: Napoli Istituto della Stampa, 1954.

Taviani, P.E. *La guerra partigiana in Italia.* Rome: Civitas, 1983.

Tompkins, Peter. *Italy Betrayed.* New York: Simon and Schuster, 1966.

Vigano, Renata. *Donne della Resistenza.* Bologna: S.T.E.B., 1955.

Vittorini, Elio. *Men and Not Men.* Marlboro, VT: Marlboro Press, 1985.

Webster, Richard A. *The Cross and the Fasces.* Stanford: Stanford University Press, 1960.

Zangrandi, R. *Il lungo viaggio attraverso il fascismo.* Milan: Feltrinelli, 1962.

Zingali, G. *Liberalismo e fascismo nel mezzogiorno d'Italia, 1860–1932.* Milan: Treves, 1933.

Index